Churchill's Children

Churchill's Children

The Evacuee Experience in Wartime Britain

JOHN WELSHMAN

OXFORD
UNIVERSITY PRESS

OXFORD
UNIVERSITY PRESS

Great Clarendon Street, Oxford OX2 6DP

Oxford University Press is a department of the University of Oxford.
It furthers the University's objective of excellence in research, scholarship,
and education by publishing worldwide in

Oxford New York

Auckland Cape Town Dar es Salaam Hong Kong Karachi
Kuala Lumpur Madrid Melbourne Mexico City Nairobi
New Delhi Shanghai Taipei Toronto

With offices in

Argentina Austria Brazil Chile Czech Republic France Greece
Guatemala Hungary Italy Japan Poland Portugal Singapore
South Korea Switzerland Thailand Turkey Ukraine Vietnam

Oxford is a registered trade mark of Oxford University Press
in the UK and in certain other countries

Published in the United States
by Oxford University Press Inc., New York

British Library Cataloguing in Publication Data

Data available

Library of Congress Cataloging in Publication Data

Data available

Typeset by SPI Publisher Services, Pondicherry, India
Printed in Great Britain
on acid-free paper by
Clays Ltd, St Ives Plc

ISBN 978-0-19-957441-4

1 3 5 7 9 10 8 6 4 2

Acknowledgements

As ever, numerous people helped with both the research for this book and the production process. I am particularly indebted to those former evacuees whose stories I have drawn upon and who were generous in responding to my requests for additional information and personal photographs: Edna Ackrill, Mary-Rose Benton, Maggie Cade, Carl Coates, David Hodge, Dave Pinchon, George Prager, and Frank Walsh.

I am grateful to Richard Overy for his encouragement in supporting the idea of a book-length study of evacuation, and for commenting on the original synopsis. Susan Hess invited me to be the External Examiner for her 2006 Exeter PhD thesis, on evacuation to Devon, as did Sue Wheatcroft on her 2009 Leicester PhD thesis, on the experiences of 'handicapped' children during the war. John Stewart did all the archival work for our joint article on evacuation in Scotland. John Macnicol inspired much of my early work on evacuation, Maggie Pelling supervised it, and the Economic and Social Research Council funded it. I would also like to thank: Paul Addison, Sue Ashworth, Gill Betts, David Cooper, Elizabeth Darling, Fiona Haslam, Nigel Ingham, Ronnie Johnston, Maggie Mort, Colin Pooley, Ellenor Swinbank, Jean Turnbull, and Mike Winstanley.

I am grateful to the editors of the following local newspapers, who published my requests for evacuee stories: the *Belfast Telegraph*, the *Birmingham Mail*, the *Birmingham Post*, the *Bradford Telegraph and Argus*, the *Ealing Times*, the *Edinburgh Evening News*, the *Hampshire*

Chronicle, the *Hampstead and Highgate Gazette*, the *Harrow Times*, the *Lancashire Evening Post*, the *Lancaster Guardian*, the *Manchester Evening News*, the *Portsmouth News*, the *Sheffield Star*, the *Southampton Daily Echo*, the *Sunday Post*, and the *Sunderland Echo*.

I am particularly grateful to those who took the time to respond to my letters and articles: Joyce Adams, Edith Allan, Marie Allen, Robert Anchor, B. Anderson, Mrs J. M. Ashworth, Alan Aveyard, Marjorie Aveyard, Norman Backhouse, Betty Baker, Mrs E. Baker, Lilian Bailey, Norman Bailey, Edna Ball, Joan Banton, Mavis Barfield, Mr R. Barlow, Audrey Barnett, Joyce Bean, Harry Beckett, Betty van Beek, Jean Bell, Betty Bennett, James Benton, Joan Bishop, William Blanche, Eric Bland, Robert Blow, Brian Boland, Josephine Boland, Mary Bold, Jean Bradshaw, Leonard Bragg, Raymond Brennan, Rick Brent, Patricia Broadley, Jack Brown, Sidney Brown, Vera Bruty, Robert Bryant, Nora Burnett, Peggy Burns, Alan Cairns, Nancy Cantle, Betty Carey, Alicia Carr, John Carrington, Margaret Carter, Ivan Caulfield, Margaret Causer, Jean Chase-Long, Mr J. G. Cheverton, Mary Childs, Pam Chipperton, Eileen Clancy, Peter Clarke, V. M. Clements, Mrs N. Cleverly, Frank Clutterbuck, Michael Cody, Myra Cohen, Mary Conboy, Paul Connolly, Ron Connolly, Eva Cooke, Betty Corrie, Joe Cromer, Barrie Cross, Gillian Cusick, Robert Darragh, George Davidson, Kath Davies, Phyllis Davies, José Dexter, Dorothy Dobson, Mary Dodd, Mr B. P. Donaghy, Sheila Donnelly, Elsie Downey, Margaret Duncan, David Durant, Beatrice Edwards, Thomas Edwards, Norman Ellis, Stella Emmanuel, John Evans, Dorothy Farrell, Michael Franckeiss, Pat Galvin, Joan Gay, Sheila Gibson, Tom Ginn, Ann Glavin, Margaret Goater, Evelyn Graham, Gracie Gray, David Green, Nigel Green, Dan Greenwood, Patricia Greenwood, Beryl Grimes, Olwen Grimshaw, Andrew Groat, Albert Grover, Pamela Grubb, Winifred Haley, Mrs D. Hall, Jean

Hamilton, Isabella Harker, Audrey Harrison, Edward Harrison, Freda Harrison, Shirley Harrison, Joan Hartland, Jim Haslam, Mary Haslam, Betty Hatch, Joyce Hattersley, Jean Havelock, Bill Hawkins, Mrs P. J. Hayes, Margaret Henderson, Mary Henderson, Bill Henry, Genevieve Hibbs, Mrs N. Hill, Edwin Hills, Hazel Hobbs, Celia Hodkin, Norah Holder, Geoff Hollebon, Alan Hollinshead, Jean Hollinshead, Barbara Hopton, Joan Horspool, Doreen Howarth, George Howell, Lilian Hunt, Audrey Ibbotson, Eric Isaac, Beryl James, Alan Jarvis, Mrs P. Jarvis, George Jeffery, Nina Jennings, Sylvia Jennings, Joan Jobling, David Johnson, Mrs M. E. Johnson, Eric Jones, Maurice Jones, Patricia Jones, Sylvia Jones, Mrs J. Kelly, Peter Kelly, Doreen Kemp, Alan Kerry, Mrs R. M. Kirton, Rosie Knowles, Vicky Koerner, David Krause, Patricia Lamb, Joan Lee, Fred Leeming, May Leonard, Eileen Lewis, Robert Lewis, Gerrie Ley, Marie Ling, Barbara Lloyd, Jimmy Lockett, Derek Long, Ruby Lucas, Donald McClean, Sam McConnell, Agnes McCrory, Timothy McCullen, Isabel McEwing, Tony McGuinness, Bob McKenzie, Doreen McSherry, Georgina McWhirter, Margaret Malpus, Jessica Marshall, Jean Martin, Ken Martin, Rita Martin, Mrs M. R. Matthews, Rene Mead, Violet Merry, Vera Miller, Eunice Milliken, Joan Mills, Ray Mole, Freda Molyneux, Evelyn Moore, Syd Morley, Roger Morris, Joan Mortimer, Derek Mozley, Don Murdoch, Gerald Myers, Joyce Nally, Jean Newbould, Mary Newman, Stella Noakes, Patricia North, R. Norton, Dorothy O'Beirne, Michael O'Reilly, Cyril Orr, Christopher Oxborrow, Myra Paddock, Dave Parish, Dorothy J. Parker, Marion Parker, Joseph Patterson, Leo Payne, Norman Payne, Joan Pepper, John Phillips, Joyce Phillips, Violet Pickets, Doreen Pilkington, Joan Pinder, Frances Pinn, Gwen Pitchford, Gerald Poole, John Porter, George Powis, Shirley Le Prevost, Ron Price, Jean Rand, Brenda Randall, Mr D. Randall, Allan H. Ratcliffe, Joyce

Redfern, Jaqueline Reid, Betty Rees, Isabelle Remmer, Morris Richards, Roy Riley, Pauline Robinson, Audrey Roome, John Rowthorn, Leslie Ruddock, Joyce Russell, Jim Rustidg, Mrs D. Sanders, Robert Saunders, Mrs J. Savage, Eric Schofield, Eric R. Sephton, Brian Shackleton, Rosamund Shackleton, Aubrey Shaw, Beryl Shaw, Pat Sheridan, Brenda Sherwood, Margaret Shimbles, Jill Simmonds, Mrs M. Simpson, R. W. Slade, Mrs I. Slingsby, Matthew Smaldon, C. H. Smales, Ken Smallwood, Joan Smith, Lilian Smith, Winifred Smith, Raymond Smyrl, Eric Sotto, Dennis Southwell, Bryan Spinney, Mrs F. Starling, Ron Steele, Roy Stevens, June Stewart, Sheila Stocks, Shirley Stopford, Ernie Stout, Beryl Street, Sylvia Street, Margaret Sullivan, Mrs N. Sullivan, Pat Sumner, Evelyn Sutton, Anne Swatton, Margaret Swift, Brenda Swinton, Mary Szpitter, Ruby Tagg, Pat Talbot, Marg Taylor, Mrs M. H. Taylor, Ron Teears, Irene Theabould, Alan Thorpe, Jean Townshend, Mary Trouth, T. Tuer, Helene Turner, Joan Turner, Mr K. H. Twine, John Virgo, James Wallace, Maggie Watson, Thelma Watson, Marjorie Welsh, Ronald Welsh, John West, Mr E. J. Wignall, Jean Wilkins, Patricia Wilkins, Alan Williams, Betty Williams, Eileen Williams, Eric Williams, June Williams, Tony Willmott, Margaret Wilson, Mr D. G. Wood, Pat Wood, Roy Wood, May Wright, Mrs M. Woodvine, Donald Wroe, Mrs M. A. Wroe, Peter Young, and Walter Young. I am only sorry that, given my focus on a small number of children and adults, I was not able to use more of the material they kindly sent me.

The staff of the National Archives at Kew have been unfailingly helpful. Articles exploring aspects of this story have been published in the *Centre for North West Regional Studies Newsletter*, the *Historical Journal*, the *Journal of Scottish Historical Studies*, and *Twentieth Century British History*. Papers on evacuation have been given at the Universities of Glasgow Caledonian, Lancaster, Leicester, and Oxford.

I am grateful to all those who came to listen, and for their comments. Corinna Peniston-Bird and Mathew Thomson kindly read the complete manuscript, and made many helpful comments on it, while Becky Johnes did much valuable proof-reading and checking of names and dates at a late stage. I would like to thank my anonymous readers at Oxford University Press, and my editors and picture researchers, especially Matthew Cotton, Luciana O'Flaherty, Jeff New, Deborah Protheroe, Zoe Spilberg, and Claire Thompson. Finally and most importantly I am grateful to my family, Rose, Thomas, and Juliet: we have had the evacuees billeted with us for many years.

Contents

List of Plates

List of Abbreviations

ARP	Air Raid Precautions
BAT	British American Tobacco
LCC	London County Council
LEA	Local Education Authority
MOH	Medical Officer of Health
NA	National Archives, Kew, London
RAF	Royal Air Force
RIBA	Royal Institute of British Architects
SMO	School Medical Officer
UAB	Unemployment Assistance Board
WVS	Women's Voluntary Service for Civil Defence

Introduction: A Child's War

In a sense, the starting-point for this book is my own childhood. When I was a child in the 1960s we went most Saturdays to the house in which my mother had grown up. It was about an hour's drive away from where we lived, outside a town called Banbridge, in Northern Ireland, and was also in the heart of the County Down countryside, a quarter of a mile from a place called Six Road Ends. Roads radiated from there to Donaghadee, Groomsport, Bangor, Conlig, and the one that led up past the house, to Newtownards, a larger town three miles away. The house was called 'Crosshill', because of the steepness of the hill that began to the right of the front gate, and the fact that, historically, horse-drawn carts had had to criss-cross up it, if heavily laden. At that time, when we went there, there were still pigs, bantam hens in a shed, and a hen-house. One of the first things we did when we arrived was to go and look at the pig, in its sty. At the other end of the house was a large yard and workshop.

This house was the replacement for the original cottage which had burnt down in the 1930s. At that time the thatched roof was being replaced, and the old thatch being burnt nearby. But a spark flew from the bonfire and landed on the new roof. It quickly ignited. The fire brigade was called and arrived from Bangor. But their hoses wouldn't stretch far enough. While the firemen were working, neighbours helped to carry out as much as possible. But the damage had been done, and the cottage was in ruins. Over the next few months, while the new house was being built, my mother, her brother and sisters, and her parents all slept in the large workshop, which had escaped unscathed. The new house was an impressive structure. Downstairs was the parlour with its Rayburn stove, a sitting-room, a formal dining-room used only at Christmas and for funerals, a large kitchen, and a scullery. Upstairs, connected by long landings, were a large bathroom, toilet, and four bedrooms. By the time that I started visiting there were five people living there: my grandmother, my two aunts and uncle, all unmarried, and my grandmother's sister, living upstairs in a bedroom. I called her 'Tea', as I had heard my mother calling her 'Auntie'. My grandfather had died in the 1950s.

The house itself was full of dark old furniture, much of it salvaged from the fire, made by my grandfather, bought at auctions, or inherited from older family members: beds, wardrobes, chests of drawers, and sideboards. The rhythmic tick of two grandfather clocks, one downstairs, one upstairs, was a familiar sound, and there were potted aspidistras on the landing. A stuffed pheasant stood on top of the china-cabinet, and the glass lampshade in the hall still had the classic 1930s 'rising sun' motif. We often used to go and open the wardrobe in my uncle's room, and gaze at the shotgun standing upright inside. The large drawer in the sideboard in the parlour was full of pairs of spectacles; it was said that, years earlier, visitors would try them on, and if they found a pair that improved their eyesight, help themselves.

Given that there hadn't been any children living in the house for thirty years, my brother and I had to entertain ourselves as best we could, weeding in the garden, and making warships in the workshop, with blocks of wood for hulls and nails for guns. In the sitting-room was a large, glass-fronted bookcase, filled with the books that my mother, my uncle, and aunts had read as children. Underneath were numerous photograph albums. But in the parlour was a corner cupboard, and in the bottom half of that, on two shelves, were the toys that the children had played with in the 1930s. Scattered inside were a spinning-top, dominoes, dice, Snakes and Ladders, and Ludo. On a shelf a pilot sat in his tin helicopter, encased in his fuselage, three rotor blades above him, a propeller in front of him, his clockwork motor below his seat. The manufacturer's name was written near the tail: 'O. R. G. M, Germany.' Beside him, Mickey Mouse stood ready to turn the handle of a barrel-organ, a small monkey on top. Inside a large sweet tin was an impressive collection of cigarette cards, arranged in themes, fastened by rubber bands. Beside that, a rusty mouth-organ, inscribed with the words: 'Mimic Harmonica. Extra Fine Silver Reeds. Made in Germany.'

On the base of a small globe it said: 'By Appointment to the late King George V. William Crawford & Sons Ltd. Biscuit Manufacturers. Edinburgh, Liverpool & London, Great Britain.' The Empire countries were in red. In America, there was the Dominion of Canada, the Argentine, and the Falkland Island Dependencies. In Africa were French West Africa, the Gold Coast, Anglo Egyptian Sudan, French Equatorial Africa, the Belgian Congo, Abyssinia, Tanganyika Territory, Rhodesia, Italian Somaliland, and the Union of South Africa. In Asia: Persia, the Union of Soviet Socialist Republics, Siam, and Manchuria; below them the Commonwealth of Australia and the Dominion of New Zealand. Some of the names of cities could still be made out: Peking, Libreville, Bombay.

During the war there had been some serious raids on Belfast, and we saw where my mother's family had sheltered under the

stairs; bombers returning back to Germany had once shed their
loads on neighbouring fields. Once we opened up a garden shed,
locked for years, and amid the cobwebs found gas-masks, in their
original cardboard boxes. As a child growing up in the 1960s, the
Second World War still seemed very recent. Our games centred on
toy soldiers; we read stories about it in the *Hotspur* and the *Victor*; we
constructed Airfix planes and warships. Much of that furniture—
the sideboard, glass-fronted bookcase, and one grandfather
clock—and those toys are now in my own house. But there is a
sense in which this book is also partly about childhood, the everyday,
and individual and collective memory.

* * *

The evacuation has long been recognized as a major event of the
Second World War and British social history. Apart from Richard
Titmuss's official history, *Problems of Social Policy*, published in 1950,
interest was stimulated by B. S. Johnson's collection *The Evacuees*,
which came out in 1968, and Angus Calder's *The People's War* (1969).
John Rae's remarkable novel *The Custard Boys* was published in
1960, and Nina Bawden's *Carrie's War* in 1973, while Jack Rosenthal's
television play *The Evacuees* was first shown in 1975. It has often
been argued that the evacuation had a significant impact on plans
for post-war reconstruction, on attitudes to state intervention, on
ideas about poverty and social class, and on the welfare state. Much
of the writing, therefore, has concentrated on the question of how
far the experiences of the evacuees influenced wartime social
policy, including how children with disabilities were affected. It is
only more recently that there have been several collections that
have looked more at its impact on the children themselves, including
issues of trauma and abuse.

When I started to write this book, therefore, I was aware that
there had been numerous books about evacuees and the evacuation

experience. What could be said that was new? I started with different themes, but the approach was too academic, too distant from the experience of the children themselves. But this book tries to look at the evacuation story in a more child-centred and comprehensive way than previously, and has four main aims. First, and perhaps most importantly, it tries to see the Second World War through the eyes of the children and adults who were there at the time. It is undoubtedly the case that writing on evacuation has been dominated by accounts produced by novelists, poets, actors, and artists (as in the Johnson collection), many of them evacuated privately rather than in the Government scheme. Here instead I draw on narratives produced by children from predominantly working-class backgrounds, which are all the more articulate and powerful precisely because they are less polished.

But secondly, the book aims to place the stories of individual evacuees alongside those of Billeting Officers, the authors of social surveys, teachers, and civil servants in Whitehall. The book focuses on transitions across time, but also attempts to bring out regional, class, religious, and age complexities. Evacuation was a multi-layered experience, and any account needs to look at both the children and the adults; at people on the ground and those in Whitehall. I use the debates in Whitehall as the sub-plot to the experiences of the children. Thus the book aims to capture the experiences of the children as well as tracing the contours of the official debates about them. The aim is to produce a richer, more complex picture of what we mean by evacuation.

Thirdly, this book is a narrative account of the Second World War. From the early hours of 1 September 1939, the official Government scheme moved 1,473,000 children and adults from the crowded cities of Britain. The majority of these mothers and children were transferred to the Reception Areas before war was declared two days later, on 3 September. Some younger children were evacuated along with their mothers, older schoolchildren with brothers and sisters but essentially on their own, apart from their teachers and other helpers.

While the evacuation of September 1939 is the best-known, and has received most of the attention, there were two later waves. The second great exodus occurred at the time of the German raids on London, in September 1940, when about 1,250,000 adults and children were moved. It was spread over a much longer period of time, because the number evacuated rose and fell in relation to changes in the weight and geographical distribution of air attacks. Unlike the exodus of 1939, there was no mass evacuation; instead a daily or weekly stream was piloted through different channels into areas of relative safety according to circumstances. In the second evacuation, schemes operated in some new areas, as well as in the original 1939 ones. The third and final wave of evacuation came at the time of the V1 and V2 rocket attacks on London, in 1944. The first parties of mothers and children left London on 5 July. During the next few weeks all trains to the West, the Midlands, and the North were filled to capacity. But the period was much shorter than in 1940; it lasted for only two months. In this period some 307,600 mothers and children were evacuated in organized parties from London and the South-Eastern areas. A much larger number—in all about 552,000 mothers and children, old people, and homeless people—made their own arrangements to leave.

This book looks at the experiences of the main characters before the war, traces their experiences in wartime, but also follows them through into peacetime. This is the reason for the title *Churchill's Children*; clearly, Neville Chamberlain was Prime Minister at the time of the first wave of evacuation, but the emphasis on Churchill (Prime Minister from May 1940) emphasizes the narrative approach, the focus on wartime as a whole, and the sense of a generation who shaped post-war Britain.

Fourthly, the book includes London, but also tries to highlight the experience of the provincial cities. Much of the writing on evacuation and evacuees has tended to concentrate on the experience of England, on London and the South East, and on the children who were evacuated overseas, to Canada in particular. There are obvious reasons for this. More unaccompanied children evacuated in September 1939 went from London than from any other city, while the later waves of evacuation were driven by the Blitz of September 1940 and the rocket attacks of 1944. Some of those writing on evacuation have themselves been journalists, novelists, and other writers based in the capital; they have drawn on the accounts of London-based colleagues and contacts.

However, it is also the case that in September 1939 more children were evacuated from all other cities put together than from London. Apart from London, the other major centres for evacuation were Manchester, Liverpool, Newcastle, Birmingham, Salford, Leeds, Portsmouth, Southampton, and Gateshead. The Evacuation Areas in Scotland were Glasgow, Edinburgh, Dundee, Clydebank, and the Rosyth area of Dunfermline. If London evacuated 37 per cent of its children, the figure was higher in many other cities, including Newcastle, Salford, Liverpool, and Manchester. This draws attention to the fact that the evacuation experience was more varied than people realize. While we tend to think of children being evacuated by train, children also went by bus, and even by boat. In general, the experience of the provincial cities has been comparatively neglected, and England has tended to dominate at the expense of Scotland, Wales, and Northern Ireland.

* * *

The book has undergone several changes of approach, and draws on a range of sources. For I gradually moved from an academic, thematic approach to a more popular, narrative one. In earlier work I had focused on the impact of the evacuation on policy debates in Whitehall, and as reflected in social surveys. But for this book I gathered previously published eyewitness accounts and also elicited new ones through local newspapers in the cities that the evacuees went from—Belfast, Birmingham, Bradford, Edinburgh, Manchester, London, Portsmouth, Sheffield, Southampton, and Sunderland. I was overwhelmed by the response to my request for people's stories—nearly 350 written accounts, ranging from brief emails to complete unpublished autobiographies. Some were handwritten accounts on small sheets of writing paper, others type-written; some were very brief, but others very extensive; and people included treasured family photographs, newspaper cuttings, photo-copies of evacuee labels and billeting forms. I was struck that the urge to tell one's story was so strong. But equally, in some cases, it was clear that the story had been told many times before. What had prompted people to write to me? Did they want me in some way to validate their story, or to become part of 'history'? Why was it, for example, that the people who wrote invariably said they were the last children to be chosen on their arrival? What about the people who had decided, for whatever reason, not to respond? What stories would they have had to tell? Would they have produced tales of abuse rather than affection?

I at first tried to organize this material in terms of themes, but finally decided to focus on just thirteen children and adults. It seemed that about a dozen characters was as many as you, the reader, could hold in your head; but equally, that means that the vast majority of the stories sent to me have been excluded. Of the thir-teen, three had private papers that I had used in earlier archival work; three had previously published autobiographies; two had written autobiographies that had been published privately but were also sent to me; and five accounts were sent to me and had not been published previously. So the stories of thirteen individuals are featured prominently in the book. They have been chosen to provide coverage of the different aspects of the evacuation experience, including geographical variation, as well as for the intrinsic interest of their accounts. Half of both the children and adults are male, and half female. There is a deliberate bias towards the children rather than adults, and, in seeking to create a narrative that covers as much of the wartime period as possible, towards children who were away for longer periods. But it is also important to note that there are silences, and of these perhaps the most significant is that of the parents of the evacuated children.

The book is based on written accounts rather than oral interviews, and much has been written by David Vincent, John Burnett, and others on autobiography as source. But the sources here are a mix of published autobiographies, unpublished autobiographies, accounts which are not really autobiographies, and committee minutes and private papers from which a personal history can be constructed. It is arguable that written narratives may be less candid compared to oral interviews; a sympathetic, patient ear may elicit more cases of trauma and abuse. Similarly, while some of the characters were writing at the time the events took place, others were recollecting, fifty or sixty years later, things they had experienced as children. These people were seeing the experience from the perspective of an older person, and in the context of their lives as they have lived them. While some of the accounts are remarkably 'child-like', these memoirs were written at a considerable distance from childhood experience. Memory clearly needs to be understood as complex.

The process of writing the book has raised interesting challenges of historical imagination, and perhaps key among these has been how to make the experiences of the adults as vivid as those of the children. In the case of the children, on the other hand, reminiscences, whether oral or written, create difficulties in constructing a narrative. Documents that were written at the time by the adults, such as letters from Billeting Officers or memos by civil servants and others, can be dated precisely. Unlike the children, we often know what these people were doing on a day-to-day basis. With the children, on the other hand, people generally know when they were evacuated, and when they went home, but understandably they are much less certain about the exact dates of the events in between. Sometimes the season, whether spring, summer, autumn, or winter, provides the only clue. As Eileen Wilkinson, evacuated from Manchester to Bamber Bridge in Lancashire, for example, has recalled: 'Recollected memories of childhood don't seem to be time related. They are not sequential neither are they continuous. They seem to be more in the nature of kaleidoscopic images, vivid images that leap unbidden into the mind's eye.' In this way, dates are arguably more important for the story of the policy debates in Whitehall than for the experiences of the children.

Certainly, each of the 'voices' has its own register—whether poetic, prosaic, sad, comic, tragic, or quietly heroic—and one of the challenges has been how to create a picture of the war years while remaining as true as possible to individual accounts. For example, some autobiographical details are of significance to individuals, but of relatively little interest to a wider readership; their meaning is primarily personal to the writer. Overall, the hope is that the variety of voices is a strength rather than a weakness, and it will be the vividness of the stories that the reader takes away from the book.

* * *

This book, then, sets out to see the evacuation and the Second World War through the eyes of thirteen children and adults. The children evacuated in September 1939 include a boy who went from Edinburgh to near St Andrews; a 4-year-old girl evacuated from Birmingham to Leicestershire; a boy aged 11 evacuated from Southampton to Bournemouth; a boy who moved from Gillingham to Sandwich in Kent, and later to the Welsh valleys; and a boy evacuated from Manchester to a Lancashire farm. Those who went in 1940 comprise a 7-year-old girl evacuated from Ramsgate in Kent to Stafford in the Midlands; a girl who left Birmingham for Worcestershire; another 7-year-old girl who was evacuated from Southend in Essex to the Midlands; and a boy just turned 5 sent from London to Lincolnshire. The adults are a Billeting Officer in Lancaster in the North West; the head teacher of a school evacuated from London to Bedfordshire; a woman writing a social survey; and a middle-aged civil servant in Whitehall.

The book attempts to combine the narrative of the child or adult with the provocative voice of the historian. For the reader interested in significances, connections, implications, and conclusions, I try to offer some brief but incisive comments, and the Notes provide the references for readers wanting to know more. In the case of the evacuees, it looks at their departure, their experiences, and their return, and at the impact of evacuation on them. What was it like to be sent away? Did evacuation permanently alter relationships with brothers and sisters, and between children and parents? How did children feel when they finally returned home? And what was the significance of love and separation for the children's subsequent lives? In terms of the adults, the story is more about the impact of the evacuation on British society than on them as individuals. What was the wider impact of evacuation on wartime Britain? What was the influence of new experiences across geographical and class divides? And in what ways is our view of evacuation changed by looking at individual memoirs? But the primary focus has to be on the children. For it was these children— Churchill's children—who shaped Britain after the Second World War, paralleling the interest from officials, academics, and bureaucrats in the lessons from the evacuation experience.

1

'Evacuation': Just
Another Word

By August 1939 the atmosphere in London was tense with talk of war. A head teacher called Judith Grunfeld, for example, had received a letter from Stoke Newington Town Hall informing her that her school, like all the others in the capital, was to be evacuated under the Government scheme as soon as the danger of war became imminent. Meanwhile she was advised to start her preparations, and had been handed a leaflet in which all the details were set out. Her pupils were to be divided into groups of eight, each under the leadership of a teacher or voluntary helper. Each child was to be provided with a rucksack containing a change of underwear, socks, a warm pullover, soap, flannel and toothbrush, handkerchiefs, and a pencil or pen. All rucksacks were to be labelled with the name of the child, school, and group, and in addition, each child had to wear an identification disk round his or her neck. The children had to know who were their respective group leaders, and were to come to school (until further notice) with their rucksacks and outfits, ready to move once the announcement had been made. Word was to be given through the wireless when the children's exodus from London was to begin.

This was the evacuation plan, and Judith and her colleagues had hoped and prayed that it would never have to be carried out.

While the children were lined up in the playground, carrying satchels, raincoats, and provisions, and with bags and shoes dangling from their backs, the teachers examined and checked them, made lists and copied them again, and tried to smile hopefully at each other. The staff peeped into the office where the secretary had been instructed to listen to the wireless, for the code-words 'Pied Piper Today' or 'Pied Piper Tomorrow'. Monday, 28 August, Tuesday, 29 August, and Wednesday, 30 August passed without incident. Many more children had arrived from the Continent, and they had been anxious to become members of the school with the right to be evacuated to safety. Parents brought their children in fives, sixes, and sevens. There were now many who did not understand English, and so the announcements in the playground had to be repeated in German. By the afternoon of Wednesday, 30 August there were 450 children and 40 teachers in the school. Judith's own daughters were 6 and 4, and her baby boy was not yet 1. The girls had their rucksacks packed, while the baby was in the charge of a nanny, a typist who had come to England on a domestic permit. But while people prepared for the worst, they still believed that it would never actually happen. Then, on the afternoon of Thursday, 31 August, when the teachers were once more checking the labels and the tags and had stepped into the office for a quick cup of tea, they heard the words, 'Pied Piper Tomorrow'.

* * *

Although Judith was 36 years old, only five of those years had been spent in England. For she had grown up in Frankfurt, Germany, and had gone on to university there, at a time when it was highly unusual for an Orthodox Jewish woman to receive a university education. Although she had toyed with the idea of settling in Palestine, Judith had gone to work for the fledgling Jewish schools movement, in Cracow, Poland, in 1917. For the first time, girls from

Jewish backgrounds were encouraged to learn and to pursue a career in teaching, and the network of schools had expanded. This was despite some opposition from rabbis, who feared that the education of women would undermine family life and the woman's role as wife and mother. This was ironic, given that Judith was descended from rabbis on both sides of her family.

She had been born in Budapest, Hungary, on 18 December 1902, the youngest of four children of a Talmud scholar, Sandor Rosenbaum, and his wife Sarah. On 22 November 1932 Judith had married Isidor Grunfeld, a lawyer, teacher, and member of the German Zionist Federation. When Hitler came to power in 1933 Isidor was warned that, as a former student activist, he was in danger of arrest. He left for Strasbourg on the day the Brownshirts came to pick him up; Judith followed him a week later. In 1933 Isidor spent eight months in Palestine; he and Judith were reunited in London in 1934. Judith joined the staff of the Girls' Jewish Secondary School in London in 1935, and became its head teacher later that year.

The school itself had been started by Rabbi Avigdor Schonfeld in 1929; he had died in 1930, and had been succeeded as rabbi and principal by his son, Dr Solomon Schonfeld, in 1933. At first the school had been in Alexandra Villas, Seven Sisters Road, in Finsbury Park, but later more suitable premises were secured, for the boys in Amhurst Park and for the girls in Stamford Hill. Unlike Judith, Solomon Schonfeld had been born in England, on 21 February 1912, in Stoke Newington. After studying in Czechoslovakia and Lithuania, he had returned to London in 1933, where he became heavily involved in the Jewish secondary and primary schools, and in the rescue of Jewish refugees from Germany and Austria. Blessed with a dynamic personality, he was described by his father-in-law as 'an exceptionally handsome man, six-foot high, blue eyes, a renowned *shnorrer* [scrounger or fundraiser]', persuasive and affable, and willing to do everything in his power to save Jewish lives. In the previous year-and-a-half Schonfeld had brought more than 1,300 rabbis, teachers, and their families to England from Germany. He had brought a 'transport' of 200 children from Austria in November 1938, and had organized similar children's transports from other parts of the Continent, making himself responsible for the welfare of these children.

Judith recalled that one transport had been due to arrive on a Saturday night. Members of the school staff and some voluntary assistants worked feverishly on the Friday to prepare for the arrival. Each child had been issued with a special permit by the Home Office, and the permits had to be matched with the batch of photographs that had come from the committee in Vienna. Furniture, school equipment, benches, and blackboards were moved out into the yard, and the two school buildings were equipped with beds and bedding. The children arrived late at night. Judith remembered: 'It seemed that each youngster carried the imprint of his own past, of his childhood days at home with him and each one seemed to represent the programme of his own family with its heritage and special hallmark. They carried all this to the shores of a free world, there to plant new seeds.' The children had been placed with Jewish families who looked after them, or were accommodated in the hostels that had been established by various committees.

Separate courses had been organized in the school to introduce these newcomers to English, while in other subjects, like French, Hebrew, and sport, they participated in the general school curriculum. Until then the school had been fairly English in character, aiming to provide an intensive Jewish education along with secular subjects in preparation for the General School Certificate at Ordinary and Higher Level. The school itself was fighting for acceptance, and the Board of Education had refused to recognize it. A Jewish grammar school was something new. Previously, parents who had wished their children to receive a Jewish education had had no choice other than to send them to Hebrew classes, which were held in different communal centres after school hours, and on Sunday mornings. The idea behind founding a Jewish secondary school had been to give Jewish teaching pride of place and higher status, through the influence of an Orthodox, qualified staff. The school expanded in size rapidly. Many of the refugee children who arrived from the Continent between 1933 and 1939 had already attended a Jewish grammar school, and Jewish teachers also came to England.

By the summer of 1938 the teachers had known what was happening to Jewish people in Germany, and there was talk of another war. Deep down they thought it was not possible. But everyone went to the Town Hall to have gas-masks fitted, even ones with Mickey Mouse faces for the younger children. Moreover, during 1938 many refugee families had come to England from the Continent, and many organizations had brought children without their parents. Adults had parted from their children on Continental railway stations. Judith wrote that:

It was to be a final parting for many, a monstrous farewell, a skipping over the death-line. They left behind whatever had been comforting and precious in their young lives. Parents took them to the station. A last hanky was handed up through the railway window, a last warning was given not to lean against the door, not to crush the biscuits in the bag, to be sure to wrap up well against the wind. These were anaesthetics to dull the pain of the last gruelling moments of this desperate parting, the lulling, self-deceiving devices, employed to hide the abyss.

* * *

Yet the partings were not over, and it was the fears of the potential impact of aerial bombing that had dominated planning for evacuation in the late 1930s. Attention was focused on the newest and most uncertain factor in modern warfare—the damage likely to be inflicted on civilian society by attack from the air. Though the First World War had seen little heavy bombing, progress in aerial engineering, along with the experience of bombing in Spain and China, had suggested that bombardment was likely to be one of the most prominent features of any future conflict. London was regarded as being particularly vulnerable. The Government thought that a large exodus from London and other cities was inevitable; panic would send the people out, and unless the Government took firm control, chaos and confusion were bound to follow.

The perceived threat of bombing had been noted by politicians, military experts, and writers like George Orwell. Stanley Baldwin, for example, Conservative Prime Minister in 1923–4 but in 1932 President of the Council and Chairman of the Committee of Imperial Defence, had said in the House of Commons on 10 November that: 'I think it is well also for the man in the street to realise that there is no power on earth that can protect him from being bombed. Whatever people may tell him, the bomber will always get through...the only defence is in offence, which means that you have to kill more women and children more quickly than the enemy if you want to save yourselves.'

Anxieties centred on London, where some 9 million people, or one-fifth of the population of Britain, were concentrated in an area of about 750 square miles. In the House of Commons on 28 November 1934, for example, Winston Churchill, Conservative MP for Epping but (like Baldwin) out of office, had argued for rearmament. He conceded that under the pressure of heavy air attack, between 30,000 and 40,000 Londoners would be killed or

maimed, and 3 or 4 million people driven out into the open countryside. This army of people would confront the Government with
an enormous administrative problem.

The first committee to consider the problem of the evacuation
of sections of the population had been established in 1931, after
some discussion by the Committee of Imperial Defence between
1924 and 1929. In its deliberations, the issue had been seen not so
much as a problem of getting people away as one of preventing
panic flight. This led to the assumption that the police were the
appropriate officials to control evacuation. By 1933 evacuation was
being studied not simply in isolation, but as part of an integrated
system of civil defence. In 1934, for example, the Evacuation Sub-
Committee of the Committee of Imperial Defence completed its
report. It assumed that dispersal over a large area would take
place.

These fears about attack from the air dominated the plans for
evacuating civilians from the major cities which were announced
in July 1938 by the committee chaired by Sir John Anderson.
Anderson was then an Independent MP for the Scottish Universities seat, and was a natural choice, as he had chaired the Sub-
Committee of the Committee of Imperial Defence on air-raid
precautions in 1924–5. The Anderson Committee had been
appointed 'to review the various aspects of the problem of trans-
ferring persons from areas which would be likely, in time of war, to
be exposed to aerial bombardment'. It heard from fifty-seven
witnesses and also received evidence from the Air Ministry, the
Board of Education, the Home Office, the Ministry of Labour,
and the local authority Health Departments. It completed its report
on 26 July 1938. The Committee anticipated that air power would
play a much greater role in any future war than during the First
World War; large numbers of planes would be directed against

recognized military targets, along with the docks, public utilities, and important factories. The experience of Spain and China had shown what might be expected, and the Committee noted that 'no one would willingly expose children, the aged or infirm, or anyone whose presence could be dispensed with to the nervous strain entailed'.

The Committee recommended that the country be divided into Evacuation, Neutral, and Reception Areas. The elderly, mothers and infants, and schoolchildren should be evacuated in a voluntary scheme, and were to be housed in private dwellings through a billeting system. The Committee recommended that while powers should be given to compel local authorities to receive evacuees, and to oblige householders to take them in, the evacuation of children should be voluntary, and parental consent would be required. It would be necessary to make a survey of accommodation in the Reception Areas, and to ensure that welfare services were adequate. Overcrowding, for example, was a serious problem in the North of England, and, especially in Scotland, it would be difficult to find enough accommodation for the evacuees from the larger cities. The Committee recommended that although the Government should bear the cost, the evacuees should be expected to contribute towards the costs of their maintenance. It conceded that householders in rural areas would be more willing to take children than adults into their homes, but was optimistic that an evacuation would present few problems.

Meanwhile the international situation had deteriorated. In presenting the Anderson Report to the House of Commons, on 28 July 1938, the Home Secretary, Sir Samuel Hoare, accepted the Committee's recommendations. Evacuation should not be compulsory; production in the large industrial towns must be maintained; and arrangements for reception were to be mainly on the basis of accommodation in private houses under powers of compulsory billeting. The initial costs of evacuation would be borne by the Government, and special arrangements were to be made for schoolchildren to move out in groups from their schools in the charge of their teachers. This established the basic principles of the evacuation scheme. The Ministry of Health began to translate the principles of the Anderson Report into a practical plan. On 14 November, for example, it organized a conference, and in the afternoon it was announced that Sir John Anderson had invited the Ministry of Health and Board of Education to collaborate. There were meetings on 15, 24, and 30 November. The Ministry of Health appointed an Advisory Committee on the Evacuation of Schoolchildren, and this met on 7 and 21 December.

* * *

Other adults were observers rather than active participants in the unfolding drama. In London, for instance, a young Housing Consultant was at home at 11 Princes Street, just off Regent Street. She had been involved with housing in one way or another over the previous twenty years, but it was only in the past year that she had finally trained as an architect. She had just started a small practice, working from her home.

Now 45 years old, Elizabeth Denby had been born on 20 May 1894, at 95 Horton Road, Bradford, the second of four daughters of a doctor, Walter Denby, and his wife Clara. Between 1906 and 1913 she had been educated privately and at Bradford Girls' Grammar School, where she had excelled at drawing and music. Her recollections of the slums of industrial Bradford, and the contrasting pretty villages of the Yorkshire countryside, had never left her. During the First World War Elizabeth had studied at the London School of Economics, taking its Certificate in Social Science. After a period at the Ministry of Labour, and coordinating volunteer work in Kensington, in 1923 she had been appointed Organizing Secretary of the Kensington Council of Social Service, a voluntary organization that sought to coordinate social work and address welfare issues. Among the most pressing of these was the need to replace overcrowded inner-city housing. The Council's headquarters were in Portobello Road, and it had established the Kensington Housing Association, a propaganda body, and the Kensington Housing Trust, a public utility society which aimed to build new housing. Elizabeth became the Organizing Secretary of both groups.

In the slums of North Kensington, Elizabeth had responsibility for administration and fund-raising, and most importantly, had got to know the tenants and their problems. Following the Housing Act of 1930, she and her colleagues in the voluntary housing movement had publicized their agenda for urban reform through the 'New Homes for Old' exhibition, held in 1931. She had organized both this and the larger exhibition held at Olympia the following year. One of the models in the exhibition, that had contrasted a slum room with a spacious, brightly furnished flat, had caused a sensation, and had contributed momentum to the public-housing programme. In 1933 Elizabeth published a series of articles in major periodicals, and applied to the Leverhulme Trust for a research award, to visit rehousing schemes across Europe. Shortly afterwards she had written that, 'My life, my interest, enjoyment and heart, [now] lay with new building, with construction and everything it meant'. She had increasingly argued for cities rather than suburban estates or garden cities; for the designing of communities rather than individual buildings; for the rehabilitation of old properties rather than blanket demolitions; and for the provision of small terraced houses with gardens for families, rather than blocks of flats.

In the early 1930s, in fact, Elizabeth had collaborated with the modernist architect Maxwell Fry on the design of R. E. Sassoon House in Peckham, a block of workers' flats. In October 1933 she resigned from the Kensington Housing Trust Committee, to become a freelance Housing Consultant. The Leverhulme Trust awarded her the grant to study slum clearance and rebuilding at home and abroad, in eight European countries. It was these travels that informed much of her housing practice. She also now collaborated with Fry on a much grander project, a block of sixty-eight flats called Kensal House. Built in the poorest part of Kensington, not far from Wormwood Scrubs Prison, each flat had featured two balconies, one for family activities and one for clothes-drying, and these had become the hallmark of her planning. The Kensal House project was commissioned in November 1933, and opened in March 1937.

Elizabeth became a member of the Modern Architectural Research Group (MARS) in 1935, and as she had become better known, had advised the leading modernist architects Wells Coates, Erno Goldfinger, and Godfrey Samuel, as well as local authorities and government agencies. She made a speech, 'Rehousing from the Slum Dweller's Point of View', at the Royal Institute of British Architects (RIBA) in November 1936. In her writing she emphasized the need for research and planning before any major programme of slum-clearance; the adoption of the latest advances in technology to reduce the costs of production; and the need to develop new types of flats and amenities for the rehoused slum dwellers. The Leverhulme Fellowship led to the book *Europe Re-Housed*, published in April 1938, and she designed the 'All Europe House' for the 1939 Ideal Home Exhibition.

Overall, it seemed as if all Elizabeth's efforts over the previous twenty years were finally coming to fruition. Three years earlier she had been one of the founders of 'House Furnishing Ltd.', a shop near Euston Station, which supplied well-designed curtains and furnishings at a price Kensal residents could afford. Through the decade she had served on committees for the Peckham Health Centre, the Housing Committee of the London County Council (LCC), the Council for Art and Industry, and at the Board of Trade. But with the news on the wireless about the worsening international situation, it was unclear what demand there now would be for her skills as a Housing Consultant.

* * *

By January 1939, following the recommendations of the Anderson Committee, the country had been divided into Evacuation, Neutral, and Reception Areas. These had populations of 13, 14, and 18 million respectively. The main Evacuation Areas were London and the outer metropolitan areas, the Medway towns, and cities in the Midlands, Merseyside, Yorkshire, Lincolnshire, the North East, and Scotland. The Reception Areas, on the other hand, were the predominantly rural areas in the South, the South West, and the Midlands. Because it realized that the plan would not be workable if evacuation was available to all, the Government decided to restrict the scheme to certain defined groups, or 'priority classes'. These were schoolchildren; younger children, accompanied by their mothers or by some other responsible person; expectant mothers; and other adults, such as blind people and those with disabilities who could be moved. These plans were announced in a Ministry of Health circular, *Government Evacuation Scheme*, issued on 5 January 1939.

From the start, it was recognized that private houses provided the only answer to the problem of billeting 4 million people. Yet despite the recommendations of the Anderson Committee, inspectors in some areas had found that the compulsory nature of the billeting proposals had not been grasped by the general public, and householders were reluctant to take children. In Kent, for example, householders in Maidstone, who recalled the behaviour of London hop-pickers, refused to have any children billeted upon them. The National Federation of Women's Institutes had also warned that there was a strong feeling in many villages against indiscriminate billeting. A number of camps were built that could accommodate some 20,000 children in wartime. However, this did not alter the fact that billeting in private houses was the centre-piece of the policy.

The most important factor in reducing the number of billets that the Government could use was the accommodation declared by householders to be reserved for friends and relations. By February 1939 over one-sixth of the surplus accommodation in the Reception Areas, 1.1 million rooms, had been 'privately' reserved. The percentage of available accommodation which was privately earmarked ranged from 27 per cent in Buckinghamshire to 11 per cent in East Suffolk. Nevertheless, offers were made to receive and care for 2.25 million unaccompanied schoolchildren in England and Wales, and 0.3 million in Scotland. And these offers were given with the knowledge of what was to be paid for board and lodging—10s. 6d. a week for the first unaccompanied child, and 8s. 6d. a week for each additional child.

Detailed timetables had been worked out by April 1939. By May, the Government had decided to publicize the evacuation scheme in more detail, and local authorities were asked to find out how many of those in the priority groups wanted to be evacuated in the event of war. To the surprise of the authorities, the response was disappointing. Registrations were very low, not only in London but in other centres.

More generally, Local Education Authorities (LEAs) were ins-tructed to examine the schoolchildren before they set off, on the day before evacuation or on the day of departure, and to treat any ailments, such as skin diseases, which made the children unsuitable for billeting. The necessary powers for local authorities, for the Minister of Health and Secretary of State for Scotland, and to clarify the extent to which householders should be responsible for feeding and caring for any children who were billeted on them, were given in the Civil Defence Act, passed in July. A house-to-house survey, carried out in August, led to some improvement in the registration of schoolchildren, though it still varied between the main cities. For the other main priority group—mothers and children under the age of 5—around one-third had registered for evacuation.

* * *

At this time David Hodge was living in a council house in Pilton in North Edinburgh, with his mother, father, and older brother George. David was then 6 years old, and George, who had been born in 1930, was 9. David and George went to Wardie School, about half-a-mile from their home. A recent photograph showed David's father sitting on the left, in his RAF uniform; David next to him, in jacket and tie, with his hands on his knees; his mother, in hat and fur stole; and George, standing smiling on the right, arm in arm with his mother.

David had been born on 26 January 1933, and his earliest memories were of a house in the Stockbridge area of the city. The house had originally been a two-storey villa, but the ground floor had later been converted to provide offices for a garage repair workshop, and a canopy had been erected across the front of the house to cover a few petrol pumps. David's parents lived on the upper floor, and his father ran the garage and was expected to man the petrol pumps as well. At times his mother dispensed petrol. In the late 1930s there were very few cars on the roads, so the pumps were not all that busy, but in the evenings his father had to tend the pump, after the workshop closed, and serve anyone who rang the bell. Most garages closed in the evening, which was why the demand for petrol increased at that time.

David's father had been working at this garage for a couple of years, but one day, David and George had come home to find their mother packing their possessions into tea-chests. They learned that there had been a row between the garage owner and David's father, and the result was that his father had no job and no house. David never found out what caused the row; it could have been about being on constant call for petrol, or maybe his father was seen in the local pub when he should have been on duty. After a few weeks staying with a friend of their mother's, they moved into the rented house in Pilton. Pilton was a new housing estate, and all the houses looked the same, in a little block, two up two down, but quite nice inside. The only good thing about Pilton from a child's point of view was the enormous park in the centre of the estate. All the children were drawn to it, so David got to know the other kids very quickly.

* * *

Scotland had made its own evacuation arrangements. In 1936 a group charged with formulating policy for schools in the event of war had assumed that Scotland had no areas which would be subject to continuous bombing. The clear implication was that there would be no need for large-scale evacuation. However, in May 1938 the Scottish Education Department had noted that some local authorities had arranged for the evacuation of their child populations, and elsewhere parents themselves might take or send their children into the surrounding countryside. A departmental memorandum of September 1938 remarked that it was likely arrangements would be made for the partial evacuation of vulnerable areas and, 'if time permits', special arrangements might be made for the evacuation of schoolchildren. Significantly, national planning for evacuation had drawn attention to Scottish housing. The Anderson Committee observed in its report that overcrowding was a serious problem in Scotland. It would therefore be a matter of 'some difficulty to find enough accommodation in Scotland for an evacuation on a substantial scale from the larger cities'.

From late September 1938 onwards the Scottish Office began to take a more active, positive role. Initially, the Scottish Education Department was to be responsible for those children sent to the Reception Areas without their parents, whereas accompanied children were to come under the aegis of the Department of Health. Subsequently, the Department of Health was given responsibility for coordinating the scheme, and an Advisory Committee on Evacuation established. Censuses were taken of surplus housing and school accommodation in the designated Reception Areas, and of the children, teachers, helpers, and mothers of pre-school children who wanted to be evacuated. Lanark County Council's Education Committee, for example, noted in January 1939 the Government's call for details of available accommodation in the county, 'with special reference' to that for children. In January 1939 it was announced that Scotland would also, for evacuation purposes, be divided into three regions. The first was the Evacuation Areas, the cities of Glasgow, Edinburgh, and Dundee, from which it was anticipated evacuation would take place. The second was those parts of the country excluded from being Reception Areas, and termed Neutral Areas. These included large urban centres such as Paisley, and remoter parts such as most of the Western Isles. The remainder of the country was to constitute the Reception Areas. A few days later the Secretary of State for

Scotland, John Colville, noted that some 440,000 children might be evacuated (the scheme was, and remained, voluntary) and urged local authorities to participate in the national survey regarding Reception Areas.

Local authorities investigated the implications of evacuation. Edinburgh Corporation, for instance, responded positively to a Department of Health circular in March 1939. The Corporation sought to establish, by way of letters to schoolchildren and School Attendance Officers and through advertisements in the local press, how many people were eligible to be, and wished to be, evacuated. The city's Education Officer duly reported that some 37,000 people would have to be dealt with in the event of an emergency. He warned, however, that this was likely to be an underestimate, and that should war come 'these numbers would be substantially increased'. Plans were thus being made to evacuate around 80 per cent of those eligible, some 100,000 people. He concluded that 'timetables were being prepared with transport authorities on the foregoing basis'.

* * *

Back in London, civil servants at the Board of Education in Whitehall had realized, in the course of planning for evacuation, that the clothing and footwear of some children would pose problems. In December 1938, for example, a memorandum had stated that 'malnutrition and poor clothing and boots are social problems which certainly do have a special significance in relation to evacuation'. These problems came to a head when civil servants began to work on a circular about the equipment that children should take with them. Although the barefoot child of forty years earlier had virtually disappeared, in some cases that simply meant that the children wore the plimsolls that were sold cheaply in street markets. It was thought that while there were unlikely to be problems in

London, or in towns in Kent and Hampshire, there certainly would
be in cities in the Midlands and the North, such as Liverpool,
Newcastle, Sheffield, Hull, Leeds, Manchester, and Birmingham.
Under existing legislation, LEAs had powers to provide clothing
and footwear only for physical education and school journeys, and
the Board was anxious not to give them new powers in this area.
Previously there had been heated debates between the Treasury
and those LEAs which provided for children allegedly unable to
obtain proper benefit from attendance at school because of poor
footwear and clothing.

The circular issued in May 1939 had informed parents about
the assembly points, and the amount and type of hand luggage to
be taken. Each child was to carry a gas-mask, change of underclothing, night clothes, slippers or plimsolls, spare socks or stockings, toothbrush, comb, towel and handkerchief, warm coat or
mackintosh, rucksack, and food for the day. Parents were told the
children were to be sent in their thickest and warmest footwear.
LEAs in Evacuation Areas should find out the number and sizes of
coats and boots likely to be required, but there should be no
announcement of public provision, so that parents would be
encouraged to provide the children with the suggested equipment.
Instead, LEAs should find out more about voluntary boots and
clothing organizations, so that grants might be directed to them in
the event of evacuation. The circular noted that 'a proportion of
the parents will find it beyond their resources to provide the full list
for an immediate emergency, and beyond. No obligation is imposed
on the householder to remedy deficiencies.'

The practice evacuations that were held in the summer of 1939
confirmed that many children had neither warm clothing nor
strong footwear. An official from the LCC, for example, wrote on
22 June of a rehearsal at Chelsea that 'the clothing worn by many

children was inadequate, boys wearing jackets or blazers and girls very flimsy dresses; the footwear was also unsuitable, several children wore poor quality canvas shoes or plimsols [*sic*]'. In Newcastle it was reported that, of 31,000 children registered for evacuation, 13 per cent had poor footwear and 21 per cent poor clothing, while in Manchester 20 per cent of children arrived for evacuation rehearsals in plimsolls. In Leeds it was reported that the parents of the 3,000 children who received free school meals and milk would not be able to provide adequate clothing, and that voluntary organizations would not be able to make up the deficiency. All children had gas-masks, but six children in one party of fifty-seven wore plimsolls. In Bradford the Women's Voluntary Service (WVS) were making rucksacks, manufacturers were helping with clothing, and Cinderella funds were providing boots. The LEA planned to issue an appeal.

A Ministry of Health report on a successful rehearsal held on the morning of 28 August summarized the experiences of several cities. In Newcastle the children had assembled, were in high spirits, and seemed well equipped; children's packs had been improvised from pillowcases, sacking, and old army rucksacks. In Leeds the equipment brought was generally good, and all the children had come with gas-masks; 'the greatest weakness is in the supply of footwear'. The kit was also good in Sheffield, and in Bradford was 'as good as the means of the parents would allow'. In Hull it was said that the children were 'well shod, quite calm and completely equipped'. Nevertheless, civil servants realized that the success of evacuation would depend on the weather, since many parents waited for the winter before buying their children new shoes.

* * *

While Judith Grunfeld was waiting for instructions in North London, a middle-aged man was working feverishly in his office, some 240 or so miles to the north-west, in the Old Town Hall in Lancaster. This fine, two-storeyed Georgian building fronted by elaborate columns contained the city's Library and Museum, and it was its Librarian and Curator, G. M. Bland, who had been appointed the city's Billeting Officer. The Old Town Hall over-looked the Market Square, surrounded on three sides by shops, and with a fountain in the middle. The centre of this vortex of planning, the Castle Station, was about half-a-mile away. Bland had walked there from his office numerous times over the past few months: out of the front door, turn right, right again, up Market Street, across China Street, and then on up Castle Park, past the Castle and the Friends Meeting House on the right, turn right, and down Hillside to the Station.

Precise, thorough, and dedicated to his work, Bland had now been preparing for the evacuation for months—drafting the master plan, checking which local houses would be suitable as billets, enlisting home-owners willing to take in children, gaining the support of volunteer organizations, and gathering together extra equipment such as blankets and camp beds. A survey of accom-modation had been made as early as January 1939. At that time the Mayor, Hermione Musgrave-Hoyle, had written to the people of Lancaster that: 'Our geographical situation would, I hope, afford us a greater measure of personal safety than that upon which the dense populations of our great towns could count; but if we were to play the part which the Government might be compelled to invite us to undertake in receiving the children from one of these towns, we should have the privilege of sharing that measure of safety with those more dangerously placed.' In order to house the children, Lancaster had been divided into nine Billeting Districts. Each had its own team of helpers, made up of WVS staff, teachers, Girl Guides, and Boy Scouts, to ensure that homes were found for all. All this had required a huge amount of work. But many people were still unconvinced that such planning was needed; they had not believed that there would be another war.

The plan itself had been meticulously organized. Specially chartered trains were to bring children from Salford, Manchester, at hourly intervals, on 1 and 2 September 1939. On Day One, six trains were expected at the Castle Station, now termed the 'Reception Railhead', and on Day Two, five. It was a short walk from the Station to County Street, where the children would be given emergency rations. From there, the adults and children would be taken in buses to the two Reception Centres, in Dallas Road and Skerton Schools, and then smaller parties were to be taken to smaller Dispersal Centres across the city. These were mainly schools and church halls. Private cars would then take the evacuees from the 'Dispersal Centres' to their billets in various outlying areas.

In his meticulous way, Bland had set out the dates; the time of arrival of the trains; the location of the Dispersal Centres; the time that drivers should report there; the number of cars required; their registration numbers; the names and addresses of the owners; and the names of the drivers. Instructions had been prepared for the Salford teachers and helpers at the railway station:

DETRAIN ALL PARTY. CHECK NOTHING LEFT IN TRAIN, OTHER THAN HEAVY LUGGAGE. STAND CLEAR OF TRACK. PLEASE KEEP YOUR FAMILIES TOGETHER SO THAT YOU MAY BE INCLUDED IN THE SAME GROUP FOR BILLETING.

Precisely 6,117 adults and children from Salford were expected in Lancaster, 4,762 elementary schoolchildren with 476 teachers and helpers, and 799 secondary-school pupils with 80 teachers and helpers. Another 120 pupils were expected from the Domestic Science College in Liverpool. Altogether, 8,917 evacuees were expected from Salford; 6,117 were destined for Lancaster, and 2,800 for the outlying districts. Now everything was ready. Bland and his team could only wait for the evacuees to arrive.

2
Operation Pied Piper

In the early hours of Friday, 1 September 1939, as German forces moved into Poland and Warsaw was bombed, the evacuation began. Before the morning's milk had been delivered, before the daily newspaper had arrived, the quiet of towns and cities was disturbed by the hurried patter of feet and the excited voices of children. At street corners, figures in uniform had taken up position; smiling policemen wearing steel helmets and carrying respirators waved on parents and youngsters. In some districts trams and buses were in unusual demand, patient conductors and conductresses obligingly helping toddlers and mothers to board already overcrowded vehicles. Private motorists willingly offered lifts to those crowded unsuccessfully around tram stopping-places. Meanwhile special constables were marching past on their way to assist the regular police. All were converging on schools. Children only half-awake because of the overnight excitement were amazed to find that they were not the first arrivals, for there at the school gates to welcome them were police constables. Meanwhile, indoors were tired teachers who had been registering latecomers until the small hours.

Registers were marked, with frequent amendments for latecomers. Identity labels were attached round the necks of evacuees, and the names of owners were placed on an assortment of light luggage. Suitcases, attaché cases, pillowcases, rucksacks, and parcels of every shape and size had to be securely fastened and labelled. As time raced on, responsibility upon the head teachers increased. Some children were clearly without adequate clothing; should they be allowed to go? Those who lived nearby were sent home in a last effort to obtain additional clothes. Orders were given, however, that every child present, unless suffering from an infectious disease, was to be evacuated. Worse still, many of the children had been away from school on holiday, and as a result had not been medically inspected for weeks or months. Teachers knew what the condition of some of them might be, but little could be done at such short notice.

At last the registers were summarized and the numbers collected. Teachers and helpers took charge of the groups assigned to them. Following instructions, the names of the Reception Areas were announced. Posters giving the destination were fixed to school notice-boards. Teachers in charge and policemen took their places at the head of columns at the school gates. The signal for movement was given; the gates were opened. From outside the playgrounds spectators passed on the news of events in Poland. As the evacuees emerged from the schools, appeals from the teachers in charge led a rush of volunteers to carry toddlers and the luggage of mothers and children to the railway stations. Enterprising individuals suddenly produced cars to transfer luggage and infants. Older people and mothers with pre-school children were taken by buses from the schools to the stations. As the last of the groups left, the teachers at the rear of the processions waved goodbye to the schools.

* * *

While Bland and his team waited in Lancaster, several hundred miles away to the south, in Southampton an 11-year-old boy was in the middle of a column of schoolboys who were marching, three abreast, down a slight hill from the Civic Centre towards the Central Station. He and his friends were fully equipped. They wore their school uniforms, with name-tags on the lapels of their raincoats, gas-masks in cardboard boxes hung from their necks on pieces of string, and they carried paper bags that contained tins of corned beef, bars of chocolate, some sugar, and packets of biscuits. They had also each been allowed one small suitcase. The first form was in the front of the column, the second further back. They were led by one of their teachers, Mr King, who carried a large banner with the words, 'SOUTHAMPTON: TAUNTON'S'. A boy at the front had a large sign pinned to his blazer, bearing the letter 'E', denoting the code-name for the school. To their left, and in the road itself, walked a policeman in uniform who also carried a medium-sized suitcase. To the right, on the other side of the footpath and over a wall, the boy in the middle of the column could see the tops of the wagons of what looked like a freight train.

The 11-year-old was called Dave Pinchon, and he and his friend Bobby Mills had been taken to the school by Dave's parents at about 6.30 that morning. In fact, this was only the third occasion on which he had actually been to Taunton's School. The first had been to sit the entrance examination; the second to attend an evacuation rehearsal; and the third was today, the actual evacuation day. The rehearsal had involved the children running the length of the sports-field wearing their gas-masks. As the visors had misted up, it had ended in a certain amount of confusion.

Dave had said goodbye to his parents at the school gates, but the children had assumed that this was yet another rehearsal, and that they would be home by the following Monday. Before the war Dave had joined the 7th Southampton Boy Scouts, which met in the Toc H hut (Toc H was a Christian community organization, founded in

1915), at the top of Winchester Road. He had been encouraged to join by Harold Barrett, who lived opposite and who also went to Taunton's School. Bobby Mills lived round the corner, and Dave and he had shared their first pack of Woodbines in Bobby's garden shed. Now Dave felt both excited and apprehensive. For him, war meant excitement, camaraderie, gallantry, and daring-do exploits from the *Boy's Own Paper*. But Dave's parents had experienced Zeppelin raids in London during the First World War, and they knew the German dive-bombing of Guernica and other cities in Spain was a sign of things to come. Having been through a previous war, they were not among those who thought this would be over by Christmas.

* * *

Further north, in Manchester, a slightly older boy was also in a column of schoolchildren. But unlike in Southampton, the children were four abreast and they walked in the road, between the tram-tracks and the pavement. Frank Walsh had set off earlier that morning from City Road School, in the inner-city district of Hulme. He had marched along City Road towards Jackson Street. Then, all along Deansgate, typists and clerks had come to their office windows to wave to the children, as did the people walking on the pavements on both sides of the road. The children had waved back. At first there had been a buzz of conversation among the children as they had tried to guess where they were going, what would be in store for them, and how long they would be away. Some thought it would be a bit like a fortnight's holiday, while others assumed they would be home by the weekend. But later on, as they neared Victoria-Exchange Station, the children began to sing to keep their spirits up.

Frank himself had just turned 13. At City Road School, opposite Hulme Church, he was in a class in the Boys' Section, and his sister

Marjorie, who was two years younger, was in the Girls'. Mr Moss, the head teacher, had already organized evacuation rehearsals. He knew that, if war was declared, obvious targets were not far away. Trafford Park, a large industrial estate, was only two miles to the west, while the Manchester Docks were also nearby. But because Frank's mother had insisted that he and his sister should not be separated, Marjorie had always come into the Boys' Section of the school for the rehearsals. There had been four so far, but on each occasion the children had returned to their classrooms when they had finished assembling in the school playground. This time, on the fifth occasion, it had turned out to be the real thing. Earlier that morning the children had lined up in the playground with their gas-mask cases round their necks, carrying a few spare clothes in a suitcase, and with cardboard labels attached to their coat buttons with string. Written on them in ink were the names of each child, their ages, and the name of the school.

The rehearsals had certainly made a change from normal lessons. But now, as they reached Victoria-Exchange Station, it was more like a football match, with other schools as well as Frank's mingling in a large, orderly crowd, along with some of the parents who were helping. Other parents had just come along to try to find out where the children were going. No one knew, or at least they were not saying. There were a few tears as both children and adults walked along the platform to board the trains allocated to them. It was to be the end of City Road School as far as Frank was concerned.

* * *

Much further south, in Gillingham in Kent, another boy had gone to school that morning weighed down with more clothes and equipment than usual. With about 200 others he had arrived wearing his school cap, blazer, and tie, but also with a label with his name, form, and school written on it. A cardboard box containing a gas-mask was slung over his shoulder on a piece of string, and in his pocket was a postcard to send back on arrival at his new home. In the small suitcase that he carried were a change of underclothes, pyjamas, slippers, spare socks, towel, toothbrush, knife, fork, and spoon, mug, plate, handkerchiefs, mackintosh, and some food. Hopefully the food would last the day. The suitcase had been bought at Woolworths, especially for the occasion.

George Prager was 12 years old, and from the age of six months he had lived with his grandparents in Kingswood Road. His grandfather was employed in the dockyard at Chatham as a shipwright, and his grandmother looked after the home. As far as George was concerned, his grandparents were his parents, and he called them 'Mum' and 'Dad'. The rest of his family lived elsewhere locally, in the Medway towns. The previous year George had won a scholarship to the Gillingham County School for Boys. As a reward George's grandfather had bought him a Hercules Roadster bicycle, and the price represented a whole week's wages. Apart from cycling, George was keen on playing hopscotch, rolling hoops, whipping tops, and roller-skating. All of these were safe, as there were only two adults in the road who owned cars, apart from the doctor. 'Knock and run' was a popular way of annoying the other residents. Other activities included playing with cigarette cards, marbles, tip-sticks, and conkers in the autumn. In the evening, or when the weather was bad, George played indoors—marbles again, tiddlywinks, cards, bagatelle, shove-halfpenny, and board games like Ludo and Snakes and Ladders.

But it had not all been fun. George's grandparents had expected him to attend Sunday School every week, mostly at the Salvation Army Citadel, but also for short periods at the Church of the Seventh Day Adventists. Sunday School outings had been to Sheerness, on the

Isle of Sheppey. There the children had been forced to compete in races, and were allowed to paddle on the shingle beach only when the tide was in. Holidays of any length were unheard of. George's grandfather worked in the dockyard for five-and-a-half days a week, and his annual holiday entitlement was just one week. That was in August, when the dockyard was closed for work and open for 'Navy Week'. Consequently the annual family holiday was usually one day in the dockyard to see the ships and the displays, and one day at Sheerness, Herne Bay, Margate, or another Kent resort.

Despite the unpromising start at Sheerness, George had quickly learned to swim in the small pool at school. At the sports day earlier in the summer he had won the high jump. His school uniform consisted of a purple cap and blazer, worn with grey trousers. The cap and blazer were adorned with a badge which included the White Horse of Kent, and the boys were also required to wear a white shirt and purple tie. Particularly in the summer, most would remove the cap and tie at the first opportunity, and carry the blazer rather than wear it.

But on this occasion everybody was wearing their uniform. Shepherded by teachers, the boys made their way to Gillingham Railway Station. In the meantime, many parents had assembled there. Although the boys knew that they were being evacuated, they didn't know where they were going. Most considered that this was going to be a kind of holiday. Misgivings about leaving home were balanced by thoughts that at least many of their friends were going too, and it was likely to be one big adventure.

* * *

'Trainloads of excited children and anxious teachers waved goodbye to tearful parents, with nobody seeming to know where we were bound for. We were all labelled like parcels in case we got lost or even mislaid.' Maggie Quinn had only started Hope Street

School, in Birmingham, the previous Monday, 28 August. School was not far from home. Its buildings, which included the Infant, Junior, and Senior Departments, loomed over the corner shop that her parents ran. At 4, she was the youngest in the family, and it was because of her age that Maggie was being evacuated with her mother, Alice, and her brother John. Her father, James, would have to stay behind to look after the shop.

* * *

There was similar activity north of the border. David Hodge's father had served in the Royal Flying Corps during the First World War, and so was among the first to be called up. A few days after his father left, on 2 September, all the children from Wardie School were taken to Waverley Station, where they were joined by children from other schools. They were all given gas-masks, sandwiches, some fruit, and something to drink, and some children had labels tied to their buttonholes with their names and addresses. A few parents accompanied their children, to reassure themselves about conditions at the other end, and the adults included David's mother. Oblivious to the gravity of the situation, and like George Prager's companions, David and the other children regarded the experience as quite an adventure.

* * *

Like G. M. Bland in Lancaster and Frank Walsh's head teacher in Hulme, Judith Grunfeld had been preparing for the evacuation for weeks. But it was only on the previous afternoon that the instruction 'Piped Piper Tomorrow' had finally been given, signalling that the evacuation was due to begin. Judith had assembled the school that morning at 6 o'clock. The children, aged mainly from 8 to 14, had been lined up in more than fifty groups, some consisting of brothers and sisters and cousins. Judith said: 'Outside in the street the mothers were crowding; they shed tears, they waved and sent their loving encouraging smiles. They did not make a scene, they just looked and they prayed inwardly; they were as if stunned. But to see so many children marching together looked comforting, after all...The teachers appeared young and disciplined and many of them applied cheerful discipline with a smile.' There was also purposeful dignity and leadership; two boys at the head of the procession carried the Scrolls of the Law in their arms. It all looked a bit like a school outing. The weather on this September morning was sunny, and there was a strong sense of family unity. So the mothers had not cried for too long, and as the children marched out of the school yard they barely looked back.

Although she had her family with her and a nanny, Judith also did not know where she was heading for. She recalled that she thought: 'It seems that there is a machine doing all the thinking and arranging for us. It is an efficient machine, smooth and practical.' When she finally got on to her train the conductor was running down the corridor, looking for the leader of the party. Other teachers directed him to Judith. She seemed to look the part sufficiently for him to accept it without further question, without asking to see the piece of paper which gave her authorization as the 'duly accredited leader of the evacuation party'. He cupped his hands round his mouth, bent down, and whispered the secret he had to convey. He said just a few words, which at that time had no meaning for Judith at all, words which she did not even catch properly: 'This train goes to Biggleswade.' But she played her part, and nodded. She understood, although it meant nothing to her, nothing at all.

* * *

From the early hours of 1 September 1939, the official Government scheme moved 1,473,391 children and adults from the crowded cities of Britain to the relative safety of the countryside. The evacuation of such large numbers of children, along with mothers and infants, blind people, people with disabilities, their helpers, and teachers, was an immense task. Generally, the careful planning for evacuation, along with the rehearsals which had been held earlier in the summer, ensured that the evacuation was, in logistical terms at least, an unqualified success. When the evacuation began the children were guided by an array of banners, labels, and armlets, and marshalled by an army of teachers and voluntary helpers. The majority of these mothers and children were transferred to the Reception Areas before war was declared two days later, on 3 September 1939. The fact that only 40 per cent of those scheduled to be evacuated actually turned up meant that the task of assembling the mothers and children, and getting them into trains complete with teachers, helpers, food, luggage, and labels, proved to be easier than had been anticipated. The glorious weather, which many observers commented upon and which further added to the sense of a 'phoney war', also helped to make the evacuation a success.

Calculating the numbers who went is more complicated than might be thought. The total number of children and adults evacuated from England in September 1939 comprised:

764,900	unaccompanied schoolchildren
426,500	mothers and accompanied children
12,300	expectant mothers
5,270	blind people, people with disabilities, and other 'special classes'

Along with a large number of teachers and helpers, and including Scotland, this gives an overall total of 1,473,391 children and adults. If those mothers and children evacuated privately are added to the total numbers, some 3.5 to 3.75 million people moved altogether.

In terms of the numbers going, the largest Evacuation Areas for unaccompanied schoolchildren were: Manchester (84,343); Liverpool (60,795); Newcastle (28,300); Birmingham (25,241); Leeds (18,935); Salford (18,043); Portsmouth (11,970); Southampton (11,175); Gateshead (10,598); Birkenhead (9,350); Sunderland (8,289); Bradford (7,484); and Sheffield (5,338). Nevertheless, it is true that only a small proportion of those registered for evacuation were evacuated. In Rotherham, for example, only 8 per cent of its child population was evacuated, while the equivalent figure for Walsall was 18 per cent. An observer in Wallasey, on Merseyside, recorded on 1 September 1939: 'numbers evacuated in all cases below recent registrations having dropped by as much as 1 in 6 and even more.' Furthermore, the numbers leaving were a relatively small proportion of the child population of the respective cities: 76 per cent from Salford and 71 per cent from Newcastle, but only 25 per cent from Bradford, and 15 per cent from Sheffield. It seems likely that the poorer the parents, the more likely they were to agree to having their children evacuated in the official scheme.

In Scotland, the Evacuation Areas were Glasgow, Edinburgh, Dundee, Clydebank, and the Rosyth area of Dunfermline; the whole of these areas was scheduled for evacuation. On 1 September the *Scotsman* reported that in Glasgow alone some 190,000 children were due to leave over the next three days. In the event, in Scotland the total number of official evacuees was made up of:

62,059	unaccompanied schoolchildren
97,170	mothers and accompanied children
405	expectant mothers
1,787	blind people, people with disabilities, and other 'special cases'
13,645	teachers and helpers

This gives a total figure of 175,066, and Scotland thus had a much higher proportion of mothers and accompanied children to unaccompanied schoolchildren compared to England. The largest Evacuation Areas, in terms of accompanied children, were: Glasgow (71,393); Edinburgh (18,451); Dundee (10,260); Clydebank (2,993); and Rosyth (540). As a percentage of children evacuated, this ranged from 42 per cent in Glasgow to only 28 per cent in Edinburgh.

Moving some 826,959 unaccompanied children was an immense task. In London alone, for example, children were collected from some 1,600 assembly points, and those to be evacuated had to travel from 172 tube stations to 98 mainline stations. Evacuees were cleared quickly as soon as they arrived. This meant that they filled waiting trains, regardless of their destination. School groups were broken up. Therefore the Ministry of Health was unable to guarantee the number and make-up of parties travelling from London, as this would have slowed down the whole process. The main issue was to get the mothers and children out of London as quickly as possible. In fact, in an effort to reduce the strain on particular railways, some 23,500 mothers and children were taken by boat from the Thames to Norfolk and Suffolk. When it was realized, on 1 September, that the evacuees were not arriving in the numbers expected at the stations, a process of telescoping the programme was begun. Transport was particularly a problem in Scotland, where there were greater distances to be travelled, frequent stops were necessary to let small numbers of evacuees get off, and arriving before nightfall was especially important. On the other hand, compared to England the overall numbers were smaller, and there were not the same problems of putting adults and children on trains. Even so, problems with transport were also a feature of the evacuation in Scotland. There were mistakes and delays, and in Scotland too, different groups to those expected turned up in the Reception Areas.

* * *

By the afternoon of Friday, 1 September, reports on the departure of children from the Evacuation Areas had begun to arrive at the offices of the Board of Education. One observer, for example, reporting from Ealing Broadway Station in West London, had noted: 'Truly this generation of children is being brought up in the best traditions of English education; and the value of this training was never brought out more wonderfully than it was today: self-discipline, loyalty and cheerfulness passed a supreme test.' Another observer, from Manchester, had recorded that: 'In all cases the children had come to school in very good time, and well prepared. Rucksacks or paper bags had been provided in every case, and the great majority of children had their hands free. Even in the poorest neighbourhoods some attempt had been made to send them to school clean and in carefully darned clothing. Most of them were happy and quite ignorant of the significance of the occasion.' From Newcastle the reports were more mixed. The footwear and clothing of the children gave cause for concern; on the other hand, their morale had been good.

As he read these reports, Sir Maurice Holmes felt a sense of quiet satisfaction that all the planning of the previous months had been worth it. The plans had worked, and worked well. The fact that in some areas many fewer children than were registered had actually been evacuated had certainly helped. The Board's offices were at Alexandra House, in Kingsway, north of the Strand and the Aldwych. His thoughts now turned across London, to his own children, the two girls at home with Ivy at 7 Sloane Street.

It had been one of the most dramatic days in the long career of Sir Maurice, now aged 54. Born on 14 June 1885, he had gone to school at Wellington College, and had later read law at Balliol College, Oxford. On entering the Inner Temple he had seemed set for a legal career, and when he had applied to the Board of Education (which had been established by the Education Act of 1902) in October 1908, it was for a temporary position as a junior examiner. He had no training or experience as a teacher, and was about to enter barrister's chambers to gain further experience of the law. But he had worked at the Board in a range of different posts, and looking back on it, he had been destined for a career in education. His father Edmond had been the Chief Inspector of Elementary Schools for England. It was during the First World War, while serving in France, Belgium, Egypt, and Palestine, that Holmes had got married, and after the war ended he had risen quickly at the Board. In 1922 he had become Private Secretary to the President—first of all to H. A. L. Fisher and later to Edward Wood—and nine years later he had become Deputy Secretary. Finally, in 1937, he had succeeded Sir Henry Pelham, another Balliol graduate, as Permanent Secretary, and his salary had risen to £3,000 a year.

Topped off with a knighthood a year earlier, it had been a career that his own father had taken much satisfaction in. So far the evacuation had gone well, better than anyone could have hoped for. But as Holmes read those reports from London and Manchester, the trains were only arriving in the Reception Areas.

* * *

Not all adults and children were on the move in the early hours of 1 September. Mary-Rose Benton, for example, was at home in Margate, on the Kent coast. The family resided at 85 Victoria Avenue, but had earlier lived in lodgings. Mary-Rose was now 6 years old, and had been born on 20 January 1933. Her four brothers and sister, Ruby, Jack, Billy, and Jimmy, had also been born at home, within a four-year period. The children's father, Harry, had been born in 1890, in Nottingham, and came from a family that dealt in shoes; his wife, also called Ruby, was sixteen years younger. During the First World War Harry had been an army sergeant. Afterwards he had travelled to America to look for work, going to Canada and working for Wells Fargo. But shortly after Mary-Rose had been born he had gone into the sanatorium, also known as the 'Home for Incurables', and had died from tuberculosis. An anonymous well-wisher had left a box of food on the family's doorstep that night, Christmas Eve 1934.

Mary-Rose loved the sea at Margate—the taste of ice-cream and the sounds of the promenade. While the other children were at school her mother would take her to the cinema, to the Astoria or the Regal. Both she and her sister Cissie, Mary-Rose's aunt, worked as waitresses, Cissie in the restaurant above the Regal. It was Cissie who lent her sister her free pass for the cinema. Mary-Rose's mother had always been conscious of her poverty. She would send her son Jack into a butcher's shop in Margate to buy two-pennyworth of pieces of bacon, scraps from the machine, while she waited outside. Ruby carried on working as a waitress, silver service, and brought home superior leftovers for the children. But the family relied on welfare. Ha'penny dinners were pretty good, and they got vouchers for boots. At Drapers Mills School the infants were provided with slippers to wear in class, which saved on shoes and ensured that the children did not sit in wet footwear in the winter. Jumble sales were a rich source of practical goods—a carpet-sweeper for a few pence, and a trunk for a shilling—and the British Legion helped out with jumpers and other garments. As the civil servants had noted, it was shoes that were the main problem.

* * *

Further along the coast to the east, in Essex, a 7-year-old girl had found that the local beach was covered in barbed wire. Her mother had almost been shot by a soldier, who shouted: 'Halt! Who goes there?' when she tried to get on to the sands. Juliet Norden had been happy living near the sea; there was hardly a day when the family didn't go down to the beach, to play on the sand or swim. Even on schooldays during the summer, the children would meet their mother there in the lunch-break. She would bring a picnic, which they would devour after they came out of the sea. Juliet's father, who was a keep-fit fanatic, swam in the sea every day when he was around.

Born on 6 August 1932, Juliet was the baby of the family; her brother Bryan had been born in 1929, and her sister Myriam in 1930. But her surname, 'Norden', gave a clue that Juliet's father, Julius, was not English. In fact he was a German Jew, fluent in most European languages, who had begun to teach the family German. Although a naturalized Englishman, who had lived in England for many years, he had never lost his German accent. A few weeks earlier he had been in a hotel in Cracow on business; on looking out of the window, the sky had suddenly darkened with an enormous flock of crows, which he had taken as a bad omen. So he had returned home to England immediately, just before the German invasion of Poland.

Juliet's mother Violet had been working as a nurse when she and Julius got married, and was twenty-two years younger than her husband. Previously the family had lived in Harpenden, near St Albans in Hertfordshire, and at that time they had a comfortable existence. They had a large Minerva car, imported from Belgium, Bryan attended a prep school, and Juliet and Myriam the Montessori (one of a number of schools using a child-centred, alternative educational method based on the child-development theories of Maria Montessori). However, in 1937 the hat business owned by her father in Luton had failed, and in order to find a less expensive lifestyle the family had moved to the Westcliff area of Southend-on-Sea. Julius had discovered that the education system in Southend was one of the best in the country. During the previous months the family had all been issued with gas-masks, identity cards, and ration books, and Julius had built an Anderson Shelter in the garden. But it was not a happy marriage, and wartime would test it to destruction.

* * *

Eddy Rowley was also at home, in the terraced house that her parents owned: 60 Grace Road, in Sparkbrook, Birmingham. Christened as Edna, everybody called her Eddy. Born in 1934, she would be 5 next December. She had two older sisters: Joyce, born on 20 January 1928, and Jean, born on 15 April 1932. Eddy lived right opposite Montgomery Street Primary School, and had been due to start her education in the Infants Department that September. She was longing to go to school. However, because of reasons unclear to Eddy the school had not opened.

* * *

A boy who was even younger than Eddy was at home that day in Great Peter Street, in Westminster, London. Carl Coates was not quite 4, having been born on 16 September 1935. His parents, Richard and Sarah, were officers in the Salvation Army. His father had been born into a poor family in Hartlepool in 1895, while his mother came from Birmingham. In fact both Carl and his sister June had been born in the Salvation Army's 'Mothers Hospital' in Lower Clapton Road, in Hackney, East London. The headquarters of its social work for women was in nearby Mare Street. At the time of Carl's birth his parents were the officers in charge of the men's hostel in Middlesex Street, close to Petticoat Lane and Liverpool Street Station. But by September 1939 the family was living in the Salvation Army hostel in Great Peter Street, close to Millbank and the Houses of Parliament. Carl's parents were in charge of the large men's hostel there.

* * *

Like these children, the Housing Consultant Elizabeth Denby, at home in Princes Street, would also play a part in the evacuation, even though she was not to know it in September 1939. If it had been a long day for the adults involved in the evacuation—Billeting Officers like G. M. Bland, teachers such as Judith Grunfeld, and Sir Maurice Holmes and other civil servants—it was even more so for the children. Dave Pinchon in Southampton, Frank Walsh in Manchester, George Prager in Gillingham, David Hodge in Edinburgh, and Maggie Quinn in Birmingham were all on their way. But for both children and officials the day was not yet over. In most places, it was only by the afternoon that the children would arrive at the Reception Areas.

3

The Railway Children

There was a contrast between the plans being made in Evacuation and Reception Areas, for departure and arrival. But in the Reception Areas too, like Lancaster, willing helpers had been busily engaged. Billeting Officers had hurriedly revised their lists of available accommodation, and cars had been assembled for transport. Local doctors were now enrolled to carry out medical inspections, at the cottage hospitals maids had scrubbed and polished to make everything spick and span, and at the railway stations, nurses and members of the St John's Ambulance Brigade and Red Cross Voluntary Aid Detachments were ready to render assistance if required. Strenuous hands had been dismantling boxes of emergency rations, while others had been industriously filling carrier-bags with tins of corned beef and milk, and packets of chocolate, to be ready for distribution. The WVS had been collecting bedding and crockery and serving them out to householders to augment their supplies. Farmworkers were perspiring as they made up pillowcases and mattresses. Active helpers were making halls ready for the visitors, collecting food, and preparing tea to be served on the arrival of the evacuees. Householders were shifting furniture, making up beds, and all the time wondering how their new families would behave. Special constables, donning their official armlets, patrolled the streets, swapping yarns about the last war and discussing the new rules

about the blackout. Meanwhile Boy Scouts were bustling about
on railway platforms ready to convey the light luggage, and Girl
Guides were eagerly waiting to carry the evacuated babies. At
station gates boys and girls had assembled to catch the first glimpse
of their new schoolmates.

*   *   *

On the journey itself, teachers and helpers had had no time to relax.
The children kept bobbing up and down. At one moment it was
cows in a field, at another a colliery, woods, and rivers, or rabbits
scurrying to their burrows. All these created a stampede of eager
sightseers from one end of the carriage to the other. Then the children remembered the food and bottles of lemonade they carried.
Someone found a toilet at the end of a corridor. Yet gradually the
journey began to lose its interest, and comics were thrown aside.
Grimy and tired, the children became fractious. Babies began to
fret, and mothers to worry. Sharp words were spoken, and tempers
became frayed. Helpers took charge of the babies, while the teachers
started community singing, announcing that the destination was
near at hand and that possibly tea would be awaiting them. At last,
as the train slowed down, the children crowded to the windows to
see what the place was like. Fields everywhere, a few cottages, then
streets and shops. Finally the train stopped. The carriage doors
were opened, and after stepping out on to the platform exhausted
mothers and wearied children fell into their respective groups to
await instructions. All were tired. On Friday, 1 September, the rush
had been too great. Rain was falling, and rumbles of thunder heard
on the journey caused alarm, being mistaken for gunfire. On
Saturday, 2 September, people were perturbed by the imminence of
war. On Sunday, 3 September, even on trains conveying evacuees,
news spread that war had been declared.

*   *   *

In Lancaster, the children from Salford had arrived. They were given their emergency rations at County Street as planned—a tin of corned beef, a Kit Kat, a tin of condensed milk, and some biscuits. They also got a pre-paid postcard so that they could write home and give their new address to their parents. The children went to the Reception Centres in Dallas Road and Skerton Schools, again in line with the plans, and then on to the Distribution Centres. But although the foster-parents were prepared, the children had not been allocated homes beforehand. Selection seemed to be arbitrary, and according to chance. In some cases families came to the halls to choose the children they wanted; in others, children were marched through the streets to their new homes and were picked on the doorstep. Many who had been told by their parents to stay with their brother or sister were often left until last.

It was an ordeal that the children themselves were not to forget quickly. Kathleen Faunt, for instance, who was 9, later remembered: 'We were taken to Greaves School and from there were walked around to find homes. I was the last one—with another girl, Peggy O'Neil—and the lady shouted "Doesn't anybody want them?" Mrs Crosby said "I'll take them" and she took us straight off to Morecambe on the bus to see if the illuminations were still on.' Alexander King, aged 11, recalled that: 'We were dumped at a roundabout with our labels on. People pulled and tugged at the children they wanted. It was a bit like a cattle market. The Billeting Officer was supposed to sort it out but people just waded in. I went with a lady and her daughter—she was like a second Mum.'

Kathleen and Alexander were chosen by kind people, but Albert Shaw, also aged 11, had a particularly traumatic experience:

We were taken to Dallas Road School, placed in a classroom, from which we were called out individually and dispersed to billets with families in the town. All, that was, except me. I was not on the list for billeting. The school went silent as darkness began to fall. The only faint sound coming from traffic in the street, as I sat waiting to be called out. Then I risked switching on the room light. It didn't come on, so I ventured into the next room…then the next…until I found every room empty and no lighting at all. I was alone in this strange stone school, from which there was no escape—for I soon discovered I had been left, locked in darkness. Increasingly afraid I began to cry and shout for help. Eventually a passer-by heard me wailing and called the Police, who came to my rescue. Released, I was taken with my parcel and gas mask to the Police Station beneath the Town Hall, given some sandwiches and a drink, chatted with and finally bedded in a cell with a wish for a quiet night. I felt safe at last and slept soundly. In the morning I was given food and drink and was told I would be taken to join my classmates.

Margaret Charnley, who was 6, recalled that:

We were taken to a school hall in Bolton-le-Sands so we could be found homes. I was an only child and, because of this, I wanted to be with the other children. I refused someone who wanted to take me because she had no children. I was told I couldn't go with a family on a farm in Nether Kellet because they had six children and I was told I would not be able to cope with this—not being used to it. In the end I was the last child there. I was taken by Mrs Hutchence who had a twelve-year-old daughter called Gwen.

School rolls for 2 September indicated that some 3,550 children from Salford were now in Lancaster. The evacuation of the children had been supervised by the Education Department in Salford, and its officials were present at the station there when the children left. The condition of the children, as far as their clothing was concerned, was considered to be reasonably satisfactory, bearing in mind the conditions that prevailed. But G. M. Bland telephoned the Director of Education in Salford shortly after the children arrived in Lancaster. According to him, there were urgent cases of children requiring clothing. Authority was given to purchase whatever was necessary, and bills totalling £240 were later sent to Salford from Lancaster.

On the Sunday, Bland listened to a radio broadcast by Walter Elliot, Minister of Health. Elliot surveyed the work of evacuation, expressing thanks to helpers, parents, and children and giving advice for settling down in the Reception Areas. The Minister went on: 'The first bit of the task is over. The move has been made. That was the work of the organisation. Now we have to tackle the second half—that is the adjustment and settling in. That is infinitely important, and can be done by no organisation. It has to be done by the people themselves, and only the good will and imagination of the newcomers can really make it succeed.'

Elliot thanked the parents for their calm and foresight; the children for their steadiness, trust, and cheerfulness; and the teachers, 'who have been repaid, I like to think, in this one weekend with a deep and scarcely hoped-for tribute of confidence and affection for their years of devotion'. He also paid tribute to the Reception Areas—the local authorities who had planned the survey and reception arrangements, the voluntary helpers, including those in the WVS, and the householders, 'without whose goodwill this movement could never even have begun, much less been completed'. He added:

Now we have to look for the points of friction and clear them up as far as possible. To the children I would say, 'Be brave, be kind to each other, give your obedience readily to those in whose charge you are, and show that you are responsible persons by proving yourselves fit to be trusted with the use of other people's homes and other people's possessions'. To the grown-ups I would say, 'It is a great change for you to have changed your surroundings, but do not forget that by your very coming you have made a change as great if not greater in the surroundings of those with whom you now are'. Did I not say three days ago that we would show the world what could be done by a free people which put its back into its work and its heart into its job? And haven't we done it?

Nevertheless, despite Elliot's reassuring tone, Bland's correspondence with his counterpart in Salford showed the real tensions that evacuation had created.

* * *

Judith Grunfeld had discovered, as her train left London, that its destination was Biggleswade in Bedfordshire. After an hour the train stopped, and she and the children got out. As they left each child was handed a brown paper bag containing a tin of corned beef, biscuits, and tinned milk. Judith looked around for her baby, and took him in her arms. It was when she approached a newspaper kiosk to buy a postcard to send home to her husband that she found out that Germany had invaded Poland, and Warsaw had been bombed. She later wrote: 'Goodbye outing; goodbye adventure. This was the first cold grip on our heart. We hold the brown paper bag. It suddenly turns into a khaki bag with weapons of war in it. The sunshine loses its brilliance, while our eyes become sterner, the grip in our heart tightens.' The teachers and children marched out of the station, and in the Station Square found eight large buses; fifty to sixty children were put in each, then they set off through the Bedfordshire countryside.

After about three-quarters of an hour the buses stopped. The children and adults stretched themselves, picked up their rucksacks, and got out. They found themselves in the Market Square of what seemed to be a small village. It was crowded with people in their Sunday best, older women, sturdy farmers and their wives, and young women with little children by their sides. They all seemed to have been expecting the evacuees. And now they gave the arrivals from London a welcome, quiet, reserved, and friendly. Judith recalled: ' "I would like to have four little girls", we hear one woman say, and four girls are escorted away by Mrs Mitchell. "I'll take six" ... "I'll take three" ... "I'll take one" ... The Rector's wife took seven boys, all grown up, to the Rectory in the car in which the Rector had been patiently waiting.' Quickly the children were chosen by the men and women, and very soon the Market Square was empty. The Billeting Officer said that this was as many children as Shefford could take; the other children had gone to the neighbouring villages of Clifton, Stotfold, and Meppershall.

This was the first time that Judith had heard the name 'Shefford'. It meant nothing to her, just a name, a geographical label. But the situation lost something of its strange character. However, Judith also suddenly realized that her nanny and 1-year-old baby had gone. A man with a pipe in his mouth said that someone had come back from Meppershall and said that a foreign girl with a baby had ended up in the bakery, and seemed to be rather miserable as she had lost track of the group she belonged to. The man volunteered to drive Judith there to look for her. She recalled: 'Side by side in the car with the farmer, who hardly spoke but seemed to know the countryside very well, I was left to my thoughts. I felt rather uncomfortable. Looking for one's baby in the cottages of the Bedfordshire countryside was an unexpected situation quite outside my life's programme.' Judith found the girl and her baby in the back room of the bakery; the baby had spent the time rocking a sack of flour. Then they went back to Shefford.

Back in the village they found the school's Principal, Solomon Schonfeld, who had just driven there from London. The local vicar had agreed that the children could use the church hall. Dr Schonfeld then went back to London, and Judith, the girl, and the baby were billeted in the vicarage. When Judith walked down the road she could see her school's pupils everywhere. She had a meeting with her staff on the corner of the High Street. Some foster-parents were annoyed that the children seemed unappreciative; they had not touched the unfamiliar food put in front of them. The teachers went to every house to try to explain the situation and clear up any misunderstandings. The adults and children celebrated the Sabbath in the church hall. Then, after the meal and prayers, they went back to their houses. But at the homes of the rector and the vicar the phones would not stop ringing. In the pub too, the topic of conversation was the same. The villagers had not expected to have a group of Jewish children billeted upon them.

* * *

Dave Pinchon was also arriving in an unfamiliar town. After having been in the column of schoolboys on the way to Central Station in Southampton, his next memory was of sitting with Bobby Mills on top of a rapidly emptying yellow double-decker bus as they went round Bournemouth. Eventually the bus arrived at a house that would take two children, and they disembarked.

Their new home was 16 Soberton Road, in the suburb of Boscombe. The two boys were shown up to an attic room, and then met the family. Mr and Mrs Playdon were a middle-aged couple. Dave later recalled that: 'Mr Playdon could have been a role model for Captain Mainwaring of "Dad's Army" fame. He was portly, shortish, glasses, moustached and had a very important air. He was a Bournemouth councillor and when attending a Council meeting or going to church he wore a winged white collar, black coat, and striped trousers.' Mr Playdon had owned a confectionery shop in Christchurch Road before he sold up and retired. For health reasons he took a small dose of bicarbonate of soda and Epsom Salts in his first cup of tea at breakfast. Mrs Playdon, on the other hand, was tall, erect, well-dressed, and gracious. She reminded Dave of Miss Havisham in *Great Expectations*. The third member of the family was their daughter Freda, hard-working, kindly, and loyal, who lived at home, caring for them and the house. She was a classic unmarried daughter, dutifully and uncomplainingly looking after her ageing parents. Dressed in her wrap-round overall, and with her well-scrubbed face, she seemed to be totally absorbed in her life of cooking and cleaning. The Playdons' married son lived in a flat above a gentleman's outfitters in Christchurch Road.

The house itself was substantial and well equipped. Breakfast was a family affair in the large kitchen; the Sunday breakfast of sausages and onion gravy was a memorable meal. Dave and Bobby had the use of the kitchen and the morning room, which was equipped with a half-size billiard table that they were allowed to play on. The garage had been converted into a proper snooker room, with a full-size table where Mr Playdon would entertain his friends in the evening. Sometimes the boys were allowed in to watch for a short while; they were never allowed to play. They were also allowed to use the clock golf which had been set up on the lawn. In order to provide a means of directing the energies of the boys, the Playdons had bought a punchball. The family and the boys attended Sunday morning service at St John's church in Christchurch Road every week. If the boys went on their own, they were questioned about the sermon when they returned home.

* * *

Some 140 miles to the east, George Prager had left Gillingham Railway Station. His journey was short in terms of distance, but still took a long time. Finally the train arrived at Sandwich in Kent, where the teachers and boys were met by local dignitaries and townspeople who had offered to take in evacuees. In the Town Hall, next to the Market Square, they were served with light refreshments before a start was made on sorting out who was there. There was a problem because there were only boys; many of the towns-people had wanted girls. But eventually they were prevailed upon to accept the boys, and their hosts took them away in ones and twos. George and a boy called Norman were adopted by an attractive woman. They were in the last four, and she seemed reluctant; George later thought that they were taken initially on trial.

The two boys climbed into the back of a large car, their belongings were deposited beside them, and they were transported to a large house, Sandown Lodge, situated quite close to St George's Golf Course. It turned out that the woman was a film star called Judy Gunn, and there were several other film stars living nearby. She had appeared in a romantic comedy directed by Michael Powell, *The Love Test*, in 1935, and in *The Last Journey* in 1936. Her husband was a member of the River Police, Thames Division, and he spent only occasional weekends at home. He drove an Austin Seven, but in the garage was a large American car. George and Norman were looked after by Judy, along with a cook and a young maid. The other residents were a very young baby, a Pekingese dog, and a black cat.

* * *

Like Judith Grunfeld, Maggie Quinn was finding out her destination, and in her case it was Leicestershire. The train stopped at Nuneaton to enable the evacuees to collect 'iron' rations; the children were marshalled off, and queued round a room filled with trestle tables. Each child was issued with a bag, and they collected items of food from the tables as they processed round the room. Much of the biscuit and chocolate ration did not make it to the billets; that was asking too much of inner-city children, some of whose parents could barely feed their families from week to week.

Maggie was accompanied by her brother John, who was five years older, and because she was so young her mother had come as well, to see her settled. On arrival in the village of Groby, 4 miles to the north of Leicester, they were taken to a school, where the children and the fosterparents were matched up. Because there were three of them, the Quinns were the last to be chosen. A Mrs Morris said she would take them, and they went to a farm managed by Mr and Mrs Tweddle on the outskirts of the village. To her shame, Maggie remembered crying, because the fresh milk straight from the dairy did not taste like the sterilized milk sold in her parents' shop, and which she was used to at home.

* * *

In Manchester, Frank Walsh had been soon on his way, the children ten or twelve to a carriage along with a teacher or parent helper. They eventually arrived in Preston, where they were put on buses and taken to a large room in a school, there to be given carrier-bags filled with emergency rations—tins of corned beef, small packs of butter, tea, and sugar, and large bars of chocolate. Like Maggie Quinn, Frank and the other children began eating the chocolate even before they got back on the bus.

A single-decker bus took the children to a small village called Catforth, just outside Woodplumpton and halfway between Preston and Blackpool. Trees, hedges, and fields with cows in them surrounded the village. There was a small village hall, a tiny post office-cum-general store, a pub called The Running Pump near the post office, and a church on the outskirts. Most people in the area lived on the farms that surrounded the village. Trestle tables with benches to sit on had been put up in the village hall. These were laden with sandwiches, cakes, and drinks for the children, and cups of tea and sandwiches for the teachers and helpers. After drinking their tea, the helpers got back on the bus and returned to Manchester, leaving the children, including their teacher Mr Evans, to stay in the village.

Some of the villagers were standing round at the back of the hall, while others helped to distribute the sandwiches and drinks to the evacuees. When they had finished eating, various farm-people came over and began to choose the children that they wanted. Because Frank's mother had said he must not leave his sister Marjorie, he had to turn down offers from farmers who wanted a boy to help on the farm, and who only had enough room for one evacuee. He even had to refuse Mr Allan, the head teacher of the local school.

After a while, only Frank, Marjorie, and a few local people were left in the hall. The children felt unwanted, and even thought they might have to be taken home again. Finally a farmer's wife said that she would take them, but Marjorie would have to share a bedroom with her and her husband. They had really wanted two boys, because of the accommodation that they had available. The farm, Clarkson Green Farm, was owned by Mr and Mrs Cornall. They had two grown-up daughters, Phyllis and Annie, living at home, a grandson Ronnie aged 9, and a farm labourer. In addition, the farm had 300 cocks and hens, 32 cows, 20 pigs and numerous piglets, 3 cats, 2 geese, 2 dogs, a bull, and a horse. There was some amusement in the farmhouse when the children handed over their rations in the carrier-bags, particularly the condensed milk and corned beef, which Mr and Mrs Cornall had not seen before. After a good meal and a wash, they all went to bed. Frank had discovered that everyone went to bed early because they would have to be up at six o'clock the following morning for an early breakfast before starting work on the farm.

* * *

In Scotland, David Hodge found that attempts had been made not to split up brothers and sisters, and for the children to travel in family groups. Their destination was St Andrews in Fife, where they were collected and delivered to various people who had been selected to provide accommodation. The number of children taken depended to a large degree on the size of the house and the number of rooms available. On the train David had noticed children who were, for the most part, very scruffy and poorly dressed, and who came from deprived areas of Edinburgh. On arrival in St Andrews these children all went to stay at the Priory. However, David suspected that they were not looked after very well; even after months in the town, he could pick out a Priory child at a glance.

David, his mother, his brother George, and another boy about George's age called Peter Holland were collected by a man and driven a few miles outside St Andrews, to a place called Burnside Farm, Boarhills. The man was John Brown, a farmer, who was married and had three daughters aged from 8 to 10, and two sons aged 12 and 14. Mr Brown had earlier been given a copy of the official Defence Regulations form, dated 2 September 1939 and signed by the local Billeting Officer, that required him to provide accommodation for the Hodge family. Mr Brown's instructions were:

You are required to provide, until further notice, in the premises described above [Burnside Farm, Boarhills], accommodation, consisting of shelter and reasonable access to water supply and sanitary conveniences, for the persons hereby assigned to those premises [Mrs Hodge, George D. Hodge, David C. Hodge]. *Should you fail to carry out this requirement you will commit an offence.*

In return, John Brown would receive payment at the rate of 11*s*. a week, being 5*s*. a week per adult, and 3*s*. a week for each child under 14. Payment was to be made weekly, in advance, at the post office. The form stated that occupiers were not required by law to provide cooking facilities, but it was hoped that they would do so.

*   *   *

As with the reports from the Evacuation Areas, reports from the Reception Areas were now arriving on the desk of Sir Maurice Holmes at the Board of Education offices in Whitehall. An observer reporting on the arrival of children in Sussex, for example, had written that: 'The children themselves appeared very cheerful and obviously many of them looked upon the expedition as great fun. Even among the younger of them, and some were not older than four, I saw very few signs of distress, and certainly none of alarm.' In Surrey it was much the same. Here it was reported that: 'The story is the same everywhere, plenty of voluntary helpers, first-class organisation and everything going like clockwork. The way in which teachers especially and other laymen have rallied round is striking.' The same observer reported that, on his way home, it was clear that the town children were already taking kindly to the country, and the country to them. Exploring had already begun. Outside most houses there were mixed groups of Cockneys and countryfolk, and he hoped the children could get to know one another as school playgrounds became social centres.

In some places fewer evacuees than expected had arrived. The *Portsmouth Evening News*, for example, reported that in Ryde, on the Isle of Wight, 4,000 evacuees had arrived, although plans had been made to transport three times that number. Similarly, the *Folkestone, Hythe and District Herald* had recorded that the numbers arriving in Kent had been far below those expected and provided for. One train had brought fewer than 400 passengers, compared to the 722 that had been anticipated. Further north, in the village of Hemsworth, south-east of Wakefield, only 280 children had arrived on the first train from Leeds compared to the expected 750, while the second train brought only 282 rather than the 743 that had been planned for (or around 40 per cent). Nevertheless, it was reported of Hemsworth that the children were treated with the greatest kindness. It seemed as if the whole village had turned out to welcome them. On the other hand, there clearly were problems with some of the other Leeds children. In the village of Kirk Sandall, north of Doncaster, it was reported that the children had smeared chocolate over their bedsheets, and had driven some of the local people into the streets because of their bad behaviour.

To the south things had run more smoothly. An official reported of children evacuated from Southampton to Poole and Wimborne in Dorset that, 'as to the smoothness and efficiency of to-day's proceedings there can be no doubt'. Similarly, in Reading in Berkshire it was reported that:

In better class residential roads, where children are not so frequently seen in peace time, a useful system of exchange and supply of stored and outgrown garments has been established on a simple and informal basis. Once the idea got going, people dug out from wardrobes, supplies of clothes, stored and forgotten. This led to thoughts of amusing the children (no light matter to elderly retired folk) and jigsaws and painting boxes etc have rapidly emerged, and this evening lawns which have hitherto not been trodden by children are now occupied with groups from several houses engaged in sorting out the oddments which have been contributed. Pets of the normal residents are in great demand, especially toy dogs, and the few children who normally keep cavies [guinea pigs] and tame mice are holding receptions for the benefit of the billeted children.

In Abingdon, Oxfordshire, where mothers and children were arriving from Ealing in West London, it was reported that the town square was crowded with cars to collect the evacuees, ranging from modest Austins to large Rolls-Royces.

* * *

Although the children had initially been excited by the train journey and seeing the countryside for the first time, the experience proved difficult for many children and their accompanying adults. The journeys were long, the weather hot, most children quickly became bored, and many needed to go to the toilet. In one case, 400 mothers and children were sent from Liverpool to Pwllheli in Wales, a distance of some 120 miles, in a non-corridor train. Many children didn't arrive until the evening, and although numbers were fewer than expected, there was often confusion at the receiving end. Children underwent a selection process, and were chosen by people who wanted them; the younger children, or family groups, were last to be chosen.

In terms of the number of children received relative to numbers expected, the figures ranged from Suffolk East (at 59 per cent) to Wales (at 32 per cent). The largest wholly Reception Counties, in terms of numbers arriving, were: Sussex East (72,527); Wales (56,987); Somerset (46,532); Northamptonshire (42,529); Sussex West (41,656); Suffolk East (38,842); Bedfordshire (37,163); Berkshire (36,832); and Buckinghamshire (31,345). But in some of the smaller Reception Counties the numbers arriving were much smaller than expected: the Soke of Peterborough (15 per cent); Lincolnshire (Kesteven) (7 per cent); and Cornwall (3 per cent). Overall, the population of the Evacuation Areas decreased from 1,914,000 to 1,179,000 people, and the population of the Reception Areas increased from 1,958,000 to 2,693,000. In the words of Richard Titmuss, the official historian, evacuation henceforth 'ceased to be a problem of administrative planning. It became instead a multitude of problems in human relationships.'

4
Living Out of a Suitcase

On Christmas Eve, 1939, arguably the most famous novelist of his generation was at the home of his parents-in-law in Somerset. But he was not happy. When war had been declared he had abandoned what he hoped would be his most successful book. Instead he had secured a commission in the Royal Marines, and since November had been at Chatham Barracks undergoing officer training. At 36, he was the oldest recruit in the Marine Infantry Brigade, a crack battalion skilled in the techniques of amphibious landing and sabotage.

Evelyn Waugh had already published five novels: *Decline and Fall* (1928); *Vile Bodies* (1930); *Black Mischief* (1932); *A Handful of Dust* (1934); and *Scoop* (1938). Born in 1903, Waugh had been educated at Lancing College and Hertford College, Oxford. At Oxford he began to devote himself to a life of pleasure and socializing, obtained a third-class degree, and went down with huge debts and no choice but to return home. Subsequently he became a schoolmaster in North Wales, Buckinghamshire, and London. In 1928 he had secretly married Evelyn Gardner, but this marriage was annulled in 1936; he married Laura Herbert on 17 April 1937.

It was from the Herbert family home, Pixton Park, that Waugh wrote to Diana Cooper on 24 December 1939. He had already lampooned the household as Boot Magna Hall in *Scoop*. The house had also taken in some evacuees: 'Well I am having a spot of leave

at Pixton; it is a rough transition from the comfort & order of
barracks but there was no alternative ... Pixton is full of slum children; eight professional spinsters, ironically termed "helpers" sit
down to dinner with Mary. I eat on a tray in Laura's room. It is all
highly disagreeable.'

* * *

Waugh was later to draw on this experience for his portrait of the
Connolly family in *Put Out More Flags*, published in 1942, and his
comment highlights the variety of the evacuation experience. For
children were evacuated both to families of higher and lower social
status than their own. In Sandwich in Kent, for example, George
Prager was struck by two incidents that took place on the day after
his arrival, Saturday, 2 September. First, 'dinner' was served in the
evening, not at midday as was usual in his own home, and after the
meal he and Norman were introduced to coffee, very strong, black,
and syrupy, with a thin slice of lemon, served in tiny bone china
cups. Secondly, when the maid cleared away the dishes at the end
of the meal and prepared to wash them, she dropped a milk-bottle
on the red tiled kitchen floor. But instead of the bottle shattering
into pieces, it bounced off the floor and she succeeded in catching
it. George could still remember the look of relief on her face.
George and Norman were usually required to take their meals in
the kitchen, but they were allowed into the lounge in the evenings,
provided that they were well behaved. On the Sunday war was
declared, and the whole household assembled in the lounge to hear
Neville Chamberlain, the Prime Minister, broadcast to the nation
on the wireless. An air-raid siren sounded immediately, and the all-
clear about two minutes later.

   School started on the Monday. However, pupils from both the
Gillingham and the local schools could not be accommodated,
and this resulted in shift-working in the classrooms. A variety of

buildings—local Methodist and Congregational church halls, large rooms in private houses, the Salvation Army's offices, a scout hut, and, ironically, a shop that had been the headquarters of the local branch of the Fascist Party—had all been pressed into service as temporary accommodation. These were spread over about two square miles, and this sometimes caused delays between lessons as the members of staff moved from place to place. Whenever there was a lack of space for lessons, the boys were taken for walks around the area, including on free half-days. George visited the cattle market in town, the Town Hall, the Butts, the Toll Bridge, and churches in Worth and Woodnesborough. Walking beside streams, fishing for sticklebacks, and visiting the beach in Sandwich Bay via the golf course were all activities that he tried and enjoyed. He also picked blackberries, especially those that grew through the chain-link fence of a garden near his new home.

George and Norman became friends with a boy called Gordon, the son of the steward of St George's Golf Course, and they learnt the rudiments of the game. They borrowed two or three clubs from one of the members, and were allowed to play on a practice hole of about 200 yards, which had a tee and a green of sorts at both ends. They spent many happy hours playing on this hole, backwards and forwards, and became quite expert at hitting the ball. The catering for the members of the club was excellent, because food was not yet rationed. Often in the club dining-room there would be food that was surplus to the needs of the members, and occasionally the boys would be allowed to sample some of the dishes. Gordon was a favourite of one of the waitresses, so the three boys were frequently treated. It was here that he tasted salads with fresh salmon for the first time.

* * *

Others had experiences that were less comfortable. In Bedford-shire, Judith Grunfeld had found on the evening of her first night in Shefford that, while the children themselves were sleeping peace-fully, the villagers were angry at having to accept Jewish evacuees. Judith became dimly aware of the difficult situation for both the children and her immediate family. Many of the schoolchildren who had been entrusted to her care were billeted beyond her reach and influence in four different villages. There were no schoolrooms where the staff could start regular teaching, and she was in charge of 450 children, with a staff of 20. She was cut off from the London school office. Meanwhile her baby and nanny were exhausted after a sleepless night; her two little girls were billeted with a school-mistress who had made it clear she was not prepared to keep them much longer; she knew her husband Isidor was alone in London; and her mother-in-law was waiting with relatives in Wales. All this created a sense of panic. By lunchtime, Judith was in a state of considerable anxiety. When she thought about it, there were two main problems: first, how to overcome the resistance of the local people to the Jewish children and ensure the Jewish laws could be kept; second, how to gather her own family together again.

Nevertheless, on 3 September the sun shone brightly, and it was a normal peaceful Sunday morning. The children assembled for a roll-call at St Michael's Hall. Judith, leaving them in the charge of the teachers, set out in search of those who had been billeted in the neighbouring villages of Clifton, Stotfold, and Meppershall. Parents had arrived from London to check on their children, and this caused a revival of the antagonism which had been starting to fade. Some parents decided to evacuate themselves to the country-side and take their children into their own homes as soon as possible. Judith hired a bicycle and cycled to Clifton, where sixty of

the children were settled. It was here that she learned, from a landlady listening to the radio in her cottage, that war had been
declared. Judith later said, 'the bomb had fallen here in the house
with the rose bushes, with the purring cat, with the flapping knitting needles, with me, feeling my heart drop right down to the
ground with a thump.'

She was filled with foreboding, and got back on her bicycle,
realizing what was ahead of her. She would now have to organize
the school on a more permanent basis. While she cycled the five
miles to Stotfold, she had to come to terms with this new reality.
She recognized that she could no longer take the apparent picture
of peace seriously. Cycling along the empty road, she was alone
with these thoughts. When she arrived in Stotfold she found eighty
children there. On the way back to Shefford, she got lost—all the
signposts had been removed from the roads in order to confuse
German spies who might be dropped by parachute. She left her
bicycle behind with a note in the basket, and hitched a lift back to
Shefford. There was a surprise waiting for her. Among the many
visitors who had arrived during the afternoon was her own
husband. It seemed a long time since they had parted, three days
earlier.

Judith undertook to find accommodation for her own family in
Shefford. The teachers assembled with the children every morning,
and the roll-call and assembly lasted an hour, followed by prayers,
walks, sports on the meadow, and the communal meal. Nobody
could concentrate on serious studies yet. The children became
acquainted with the fields and meadows, the paths and the river,
became friendly with the postmaster and the newsagent, invaded
the sweetshop, and investigated the village railway station. There
was plenty to look at and listen to. Judith could be spared to find a
home for her family of seven. After meeting the local Billeting

Officer, she found one in the village of Campton. The house had neither electricity nor a telephone, but it stood among meadows and was comfortable, neat, and homely. They moved in on the following Friday. With her own accommodation problems solved, Judith could devote herself to the administration and organization of the school community. There were many things to be done. The children had so far not received much tuition; schooling had to be organized for each age-group; and there were still children who did not get on with their foster-parents. Judith found a house that became her headquarters, consulting room, and school post office. It was here that the children's letters and postcards home were censored by the teachers. The office became very busy indeed.

* * *

In Lancaster the children had settled down in their billets. However, one problem was that the Salford parents often visited at weekends, were entertained at the expense of the foster-parents, and then took the children back home with them. G. M. Bland wrote on 25 September to John Hartley, the Director of Education in Salford, noting: 'The usual batch of returns to Salford yesterday. I counted seven motor charabancs from Salford at three centres in the City, and doubtless there were others.' Bland argued that something would have to be done about these visits, which were particularly a problem on Sundays and to a lesser extent on other days. They were threatening to upset all the arrangements that had been made so carefully. Lancaster could not consider receiving any more evacuees while these problems persisted. Good billets were being closed by the dozen, because people were tired of having to entertain large groups of relatives, sometimes seven or more of one family expecting two meals, who then went back to Salford taking the children with them. The Lancaster householders felt that the whole enterprise was a waste of time.

Bland also asked Hartley whether anything could be done to stop the growing habit of allowing children home at weekends, which was being experienced in all Reception Areas. There was no reason to suppose that Salford was any safer from aerial attack on Saturdays and Sundays than on any other day of the week. Bland wrote again to Hartley on 2 October about the Salford children, noting that some who had come only ten days earlier, whose parents had appeared willing to leave them in Lancaster, had already returned home. As before, the children had been unsettled by the weekly visits of their parents. Bland wrote: 'A waste of money and time, and a loss of good billets, as householders, having in some cases twice experienced this treatment, are not accepting more evacuees.' But he thought it would be useless to send any children who had returned to Salford back to Lancaster. Everything had been done to discourage the return, and householders who had been put to great inconvenience and annoyance, often more than once, had refused to accept evacuees again. This action on the part of the parents meant that the doors of hundreds of potentially excellent billets in Lancaster were now firmly closed.

Moreover, he asked whether more sturdy clothing and footwear could be supplied for the Salford children. He and his colleagues were now faced with the onset of winter, and the supply of clothing and footwear available at the WVS centre, based in the Old Town Hall, was insufficient to meet demand. This was even though they had, through the generosity of the Lancaster League of Help, already used the supply of clothing collected for the use of the city's own children. By 23 October school rolls showed there were only 2,438 Salford children in Lancaster and the outlying districts, compared with 3,550 on 2 September. Bland again advised parents that the money spent on their frequent visits would be better used to buy footwear and clothing for their children. He wrote that: 'It is very desirable to give the children every opportunity to settle down happily in their new surroundings; and for this reason parents will be wise not to visit their children too frequently. The money spent in such visits would be better spent on thick country footwear, raincoats, overcoats, or warm underclothing for the children.'

As well as friction, though, there was evidence of altruism. Voluntary organizations had again been active. The Salford Necessitous School Children's Clothing Society, for example, agreed on 23 October to clothe 1,500 of the evacuees, and it issued an appeal. An anonymous donor had made a gift of 100 coats and 100 pairs of boots, and the Mayor's Fund had contributed £246 15s., including grants from the Education Committee and the Salford City Treasurer. This money had been spent on overcoats, mackintoshes, wellington boots, nightwear, and clogs. Women from the WVS had done the typing for the appeal, and had knitted jerseys and stockings. Overall, the Society provided 2,971 garments and 1,315 pairs of footwear in the year 1939–40. Officials were critical of the behaviour of some parents, but there was evidence of generosity, too.

* * *

About twenty miles to the south, Frank Walsh had only been on the farm a few days when his adopted family also all gathered round the wireless to hear Chamberlain announce they were at war with Germany. Not a lot was said, but everyone had different thoughts, and after a short time the farmer's wife, Mrs Cornall, said they should all say a prayer together. This they did. More generally, the Cornalls were very affectionate, and treated Frank as if he were one of the family. The only problem was that when the evacuees went to school they were classed as townies, and there was a bit of animosity at first. One of the local boys at school was a fairly big lad, and Frank had a confrontation with him. Everyone was standing around, and Frank kept shouting at him, 'Step over that line, go on, step over that line.' If he did, Frank was going to say, 'You're on our side now'. But the boy backed off, and Frank and his friends never had any trouble after that.

Frank was also learning about life on the farm. The farmhouse was plagued by a swarm of wasps in early September. These were countered by punching a hole in the lids of nearly finished jam-jars and leaving them on windowsills and other places. The wasps crawled through the holes in the lids, but after feeding on the jam could not escape until the jar became full. The jam-jars were then immersed in a bucket of water. The farm had a large pear tree in the field next to the house, and an apple orchard some distance away. The wasps' nest was eventually traced to halfway down towards the orchard, on the side of the path the cows took on their way from the cowsheds to the grazing fields. Frank rolled his school socks up above his knees and tied his short trousers at the bottom with string. He hung a large hairnet over his face and wedged it under his hat, as a makeshift form of protection. Thus equipped, and wearing gloves, he ventured down the path. He dug in with a spade at the entrance of the nest, but when he began to lever it up literally hundreds of wasps poured out and followed him in a swarm as he ran, as fast as he could, towards the farmhouse outbuildings. Suffering from numerous stings on his legs, Mrs Cornall began administering 'dolly blue'. Frank handed over the task to the farm-hand who, after a short wait, poured a mixture of petrol and paraffin down the hole, then gave it a second dousing before stuffing rags in the hole and setting them on fire. It seemed to do the trick: the number of wasps was reduced considerably.

In some respects, being 13 and unexpectedly introduced to farming customs taught Frank a lot about life in general, and about the cruelty inherent in nature in particular. In the cowsheds, pigsties, and other outbuildings on the farm, for example, there was a warren of rat runs. The rats ate the pigswill out of the troughs, and in one sty ran along a wooden joist. The local rat-catcher paid for each rat-tail, to encourage the extermination of vermin. In the farmhouse was a double-barrelled shotgun that the children were forbidden ever to touch, but one day, when Mr and Mrs Cornall went into Preston, Frank had the idea of shooting a rat with the gun as it ran along the wooden joist in the sty. His plan was to kill the rat, cut off its tail, and claim the reward. Frank stealthily loaded the gun and rested it on the lower part of the door, aiming at a particular spot on the joist, just waiting for the rat to pass by:

The cumbersome gunstock rested against my shoulder, the rat duly appeared, the trigger was pressed, and the recoil knocked me backwards on to the farmyard floor along with the gun. Picking myself up, I looked over the half open door in horror. There, where there should have been a solid wooden wall, was a large gaping hole about two feet square where the spreading shot from the gun had shattered the wooden boards, leaving a shot-peppered beam running across the middle of space where you could see the open fields beyond. There was definitely no sign of the rat or its tail in sight.

More generally, the farmworkers laid cage-like traps with home-made cheese to tempt the rats inside. These were collected each morning from various parts of the farm and taken to the horse-trough to be immersed, the rats still in the cages, until they drowned. When the rats were held over the water they emitted a high-pitched scream, as though they had a premonition of what was to come next. Their tails were cut off and the bodies buried in the dung-heap. On the next farm the farmer kept a ferret in a cage to combat rats or any weasels that ventured near the hencotes. Weasels always killed indiscriminately once in the henhouse, twenty to thirty birds at a time. Once the weasel's lair was found, the ferret had a length of string, knotted at one-foot intervals, tied to its back leg and was sent down the hole to kill it. The knots on the string were then counted, to ascertain the distance from the entrance of the hole. Digging then commenced in order to retrieve the ferret and stop it staying in the warren to eat its prey.

To feed the ferret and keep it alert, it was occasionally placed in a barrel with wire netting covering the top. A captured rat from one of the cages was then dropped in. Once the rat saw the ferret it started running round the wall of the barrel like a motorbike on the 'Wall of Death', while the ferret sat in the middle, watching it run but never moving. Eventually the rat began to tire, and had to stop from sheer exhaustion. Once this happened the ferret pounced, killing the rat with one bite to the throat, tossing it from side to side to make sure it was dead before feeding off the carcass. To teach terrier pups the art of 'ratting', one of the young rats caught in the cage had its back legs tied together with wire, and was then attached to a rope strung over a pulley and pulled up to near the top. The pups were waiting and yapping down below. Eventually the rat gnawed through the rope and dropped to the ground stunned, whereupon the pups killed it. An unencumbered, fully grown rat would probably have attacked the pups and killed them, or at least made them afraid of their ferocious adversary.

Once a year, all the surrounding farmers and helpers gathered at one farm to have a cull. When it was the turn of the farm where Frank was staying, the rat holes were blocked off, apart from two. A hosepipe was put down one of the holes, while the farmworkers formed a double line at the exit of the other. All had sticks and cudgels, and at the very end of the line sat the dogs. After a short time a number of rats began to emerge, one by one, running down the line, with everyone trying to hit them with their sticks and cudgels. If the rat did manage to run the gauntlet without being hit, stunned, or killed, then the dogs would finish it off. Up to thirty rats were caught that day, and of course the farmers and the children benefited by selling the tails to the local rat-catcher.

* * *

David Hodge was also on a farm. But he found that whereas Mrs Brown and the girls were friendly and nice, Mr Brown was surly and remote, and the two boys hostile and aggressive. They were resentful of the attention being paid to the new arrivals by their mother and sisters. One day the sons grabbed George, submerged his head in the farmyard horse-trough, and held him under. Fortunately for George, his mother had seen the incident from one of the farmhouse windows and quickly came to his rescue. Even after her intervention, though, the sons were reluctant to let go, and she was forced to get physical before they released him. Shortly after this, while out walking along the riverbank near the farm, David, his mother, George, Peter, and one of the farmer's daughters encountered the two sons on the opposite bank. The sons proceeded to bombard them with stones until they retreated out of range.

Although David's mother returned to Edinburgh, the water-trough and stone-throwing incidents meant that she worried about the safety of the two boys. A few days later David, George, and Peter were collected by a chauffeur-driven car and taken to a farm a few miles away, on a small estate called Balmungo. The estate was owned by a Mr and Mrs Nish, and Miss Meldrum, Mrs Nish's unmarried sister, also lived there. They had no children, and were aloof and patronizing. The children did not speak unless spoken to, and that happened rarely. Everyone on the estate worked for the Nish family or for Mr Murray, the farmer who leased the farm. The Nish family lived in a large house which stood in a clearing in a wood; almost all the wives of the men who worked on the estate worked at the Nish home, usually on a part-time basis as cleaners or servants.

Close to the Nish house was a walled garden about 200 yards square, and all the fruit and vegetables for the estate were grown there. David found that his new hosts were Hendry Ballantyne and his wife. Hendry worked as a gardener in the walled garden, and was also the Nish chauffeur when they went out; his brother-in-law, Jim Ridley, worked as a gardener and gamekeeper. The boys' new home was positioned very close to the farm. It was a stone building, comprising two double bedrooms, a living-room, a large kitchen, and a small lavatory. There was no electricity and no hot water; all the food was cooked on the living-room range along with two primus stoves. The lighting was supplied by a Tilley lamp, other paraffin lamps, and candles. David, George, and Peter shared a double bedroom upstairs, which was really the attic but was nevertheless quite comfortable.

* * *

In Bournemouth, Dave Pinchon had already left the Playdons' at Soberton Road. By early 1940 a combination of Mrs Playdon's chronic sickness and the realization that the war would not be over by Christmas brought the boys' stay to an end. Instead, Dave moved to stay with Mrs Clarke, at Holdenhurst Road. This was a transport café-cum-bed and breakfast, and was known locally as 'Clarke's College'. It seemed to be used as a clearing house for about a dozen evacuees. At the time Dave was there, between eight and ten boys of various ages were in residence. Order was maintained by two or three school prefects who were also living there. When a bout of measles hit some of them, they were all placed under quarantine and confined to the café. This coincided with end-of-term exams, which they all completed under the supervision of a prefect. A recess in a corridor housed an old man who slept on a ramshackle, evil-smelling sofa. The other memorable smell at the café was created by one of the boys smoking herbal cigarettes. They smelt like a garden bonfire, but were supposed to help his asthma. None of the other boys were tempted to join him. Dave's friend Bobby Mills returned home to Southampton about this time. But it was at Holdenhurst Road that Dave first met Jimmy Allott, who was to become a firm friend.

* * *

When she was evacuated to Groby in Leicestershire, Maggie Quinn had initially been billeted with the Tweddle family on their farm. But this was only a temporary arrangement. Maggie's mother could not stay long, and she was anxious to get a billet in the village nearer to the school. This was not easy to arrange, as she was concerned that Maggie and John should stay together. However, finally they moved in with Cyril Burdett, his wife Louisa, and their daughters Betty and Joyce, who lived at 'The Rookery'. Louisa's sister, Amelia, also lived with them. Like many of the men in the village, Mr Burdett worked in the local quarry. He was also an accomplished singer, with a beautiful tenor voice.

Maggie was a frail, sickly child, and after a couple of months she went home with her mother to Birmingham. She needed to have her tonsils out, but doctors said she was not strong enough to withstand the operation, and that if her parents did not get her out of Birmingham she would be dead within a year. So Maggie went back to Groby, but this time to live with Cyril Burdett's parents, Mark and Sarah Ann Burdett, their daughter Amy, and her husband Ernest Sedgley, who all lived in a house in Markfield Road which is now called 'Penny Cottage'. Amy and Ernest worked in the nearby city of Leicester, Amy as a cutter in a clothing factory and Ernest for a manufacturing chemist. Amy worked first of all for Corah's, and later for another company; she had huge, very sharp shears. Ernest's company paid Maggie and her friends for collecting rose-hips (to make rose-hip syrup) and foxglove leaves. Maggie called the family members 'Grandad', 'Grandma', 'Uncle Ern', and 'Aunty Amy'. She later wrote: 'they gave me as much affection as if I had been their own, so I had the privilege of having two loving families.'

Mark Burdett had bought the property in Markfield Road, which comprised two cottages, when the Bradgate Estate was split up and put on the market. At that time it had a thatched roof, but the thatch was removed and the roof raised and slated. There was one large living-room with a connecting passage to the kitchen and pantry. Upstairs there were two bedrooms, and Maggie slept in the corner of Mark and Sarah Ann's bedroom. They had electricity and running water, but no indoor toilet; they used one outside, halfway up the garden. A visit to the toilet on a winter's night meant donning shoes and coats and taking a torch which (because of the blackout) had to be pointed directly at the ground. The garden was mainly given over to fruit and vegetables, but there were some flowers, a lilac bush, and a Victoria plum tree.

The Burdetts let the smaller cottage, which was constructed of wattle and daub and was still thatched; it was occupied by a Mrs Polly Branson. Her own husband, Jack, had tried to kill her, and had been committed to the Narborough Asylum for the rest of his life. Polly was extremely deaf, and never heard the air-raid sirens. Forgetting about the blackout, she would come out at night to admire the stars, leaving her door wide open with light streaming out—almost a criminal offence, and a great worry to everyone. There was no water or electricity in her cottage; she fetched her water in a bucket from an outside tap just outside the fish shop.

* * *

George, Frank, Dave, David, and Maggie were settling down. However, more generally in September 1939, as the anticipated heavy bombing failed to materialize, there was an outcry in the national press about the behaviour of the evacuees, both children and mothers. Letters in local and national newspapers alleged that large numbers of evacuees had head lice, wet the bed, had never seen farm animals before, and had appalling table manners. *The Times*, for example, published on 12 September a letter from a Major E. F. Oakeley, who complained that 'some of the women evacuated arrived in a verminous condition, which has contaminated bedding and wallpaper in the houses where they have been billeted. Surely steps might have been taken to prevent this.' Another correspondent wrote on 22 September of: 'Stunted, misshapen creatures, only capable of understanding the simplest language and quite incapable of thought, moved by impulses at the best sentimental, at the worst brutal...War has lifted the flat stone—these disgraces to our educational system have been forced out into the light.' There was particular anger that householders had to provide clothing and footwear for the city children.

The debate moved from the press to the political arena. In an adjournment debate in the House of Commons on 14 September, for instance, many of those who spoke were Labour MPs representing Glasgow constituencies, including George Buchanan, MP for the Gorbals and John McGovern, MP for Shettleston, as well as Frederick Pethick-Lawrence, MP for Edinburgh East. Others represented London, such as Dr Leslie Haden-Guest, Labour MP for North Islington, and Reginald Sorenson, Labour MP for Leyton West. More conventional Conservative figures were Ronald Tree, MP for Market Harborough, Nancy Astor, MP for Plymouth Sutton, and Commander Sir Archibald Southby, MP for Epsom. Clement Davies, Liberal National MP for Montgomeryshire,

George Tomlinson, Labour MP for Farnworth, and Sir Henry Fildes, Labour National MP for Dumfries, also spoke in the debate. It covered such issues as the evacuees' clothing and footwear, poverty, bedwetting, and head lice, and the fact that many had rapidly returned home. The Labour MPs, particularly those from Glasgow, rejected many of the comments made about the evacuees as slurs on the working class. For example, George Buchanan said: 'I am not having the children whom I represent slandered, not even by an officer. They are as good as yours, and I am not having them slandered in a superior tone. They are my folk and I know them, and they are the only folk that ever I knew.' Later in the debate he said: 'I hope that one result that will emerge from this business will be that people will get to know something more about the slums, and that they will seek to end the slums of Glasgow and other cities.'

The debate adjourned at 10.45 p.m., and so it was almost midnight when Harold Nicolson finished his diary entry for that day. Nicolson had been elected National Labour MP for Leicester West in 1935, but writing was on his mind, as he had just begun a weekly column, 'Marginal Comment', in the *Spectator*. Nicolson had been born in Tehran in 1886, into a minor patrician family with an established tradition of public service. Following Wellington College (which he hated) and Oxford, Nicolson had joined the diplomatic service. On 1 October 1913, he had married Vita Sackville-West, and it was at their home, 'Long Barn' near Sevenoaks, that the Nicolsons laid the foundations of their reputations as successful gardeners and writers. Nicolson resigned from the diplomatic service in September 1929, and it was then that he began his public life. In the spring of 1930 the Nicolsons moved to Sissinghurst Castle. Out of a job, Nicolson was thrown onto his resources as a writer; he also became an MP. It was also from New Year 1930 that Nicolson started keeping the diary for which he would be remembered.

In his entry for 14 September 1939, Nicolson wrote that there had been discussions in the House about the evacuation. When children had been evacuated with their teachers there had been no problems, but there had been trouble with the mothers. Many children had head lice, the mothers refused to help, evacuees had drifted back to London, and there was much ill-feeling. Nevertheless, evacuation had also exposed poverty in the cities. Nicolson wrote: 'The interesting thing is that this feeling is not between the rich and the poor but between the urban and the rural poor. This is a perplexing social event…But the effect will be to demonstrate to people how deplorable is the standard of life and civilisation among the urban proletariat.'

* * *

Neville Chamberlain, the Prime Minister of the day, also commented on the evacuation and its problems. He had written to the Archbishop of Canterbury on 5 September that, 'I pray the struggle may be short, but it can't end as long as Hitler remains in power'. He disliked the role of war leader. Chamberlain had been born on 18 March 1869 at Edgbaston, in Birmingham, the only son of Joseph Chamberlain and his second wife, Florence. Following Rugby School, Chamberlain had been apprenticed to a firm of accountants, and between 1887 and 1916 he had established himself as a leading figure in the industrial life of Birmingham. This formed his entrée into local government; he had been elected an alderman in 1914, and in 1915 he became Lord Mayor. Elected in 1918 as the MP for Birmingham, Ladywood, he made an immediate impression as a backbencher, and he had become Minister of Health in March 1923. Out of office in the late 1920s, he had become Chancellor of the Exchequer in 1931, and finally Prime Minister on 28 May 1937.

Chamberlain wrote to his younger sister Hilda on 17 September, three days after the Adjournment Debate, that:

The stories I hear about evacuees are awful and there is no doubt that the dwellers in the country districts have had a shocking revelation of the manners [and] customs of their town cousins. Dorothy heard of [a] child who wrote home, 'There are no bugs in this house we have got rid of all our fleas', another who had never before seen a bed made up with sheets & didn't know how to enter it, others who had never sat up to table to have tea. And she tells us of how one hostess said to her, 'I never knew that such conditions existed, and I feel ashamed of having been so ignorant of my neighbours...For the rest of my life I mean to try & make amends by helping such people to live cleaner & healthier lives'. It certainly is a disappointment that all the care & money spent in the schools has not produced a better result, but however bad conditions are I am still convinced that they are infinitely better than they were 20 years ago.

Evacuees could provoke reactions of hostility, sympathy, and complacency. Shock was the main reaction of the businessman and politician Oliver Lyttelton at his home at Wittersham in Kent. Lyttelton was now 46 years old. Born in 1893, he had been educated at Eton and Trinity College, Cambridge, but his university career had been cut short by the outbreak of the First World War, when he served in France continuously from 1915 to 1918. In 1919 Lyttelton had joined a banking firm, but then, after a brief apprenticeship, he had served as General Manager of the British Metal Corporation, and later as Managing Director. He had also become Chairman of the London Tin Corporation, and joined the boards of a number of foreign companies. On the outbreak of war, because of his business background, he had been appointed Controller of Non-Ferrous Metals. His extensive network of personal contacts and intimate knowledge of the mining industry promised to secure for Britain vital supplies of metals at highly advantageous rates. Apart from this war service, Lyttelton had offered to take in ten evacuees at Wittersham. In fact, instead of the ten, the LCC had sent thirty-one infants aged between 4 and 5 from the East End, along with some junior nurses. Lyttelton recalled:

They duly arrived, some suffering from childish illnesses and one or two from impetigo. I was afraid of infection spreading amongst them, but we did our best and packed them in. I got a shock; I had little dreamt that English children could be so completely ignorant of the simplest rules of hygiene, and that they would regard the floors and carpets as suitable places upon which to relieve themselves. I was still more surprised when some of their parents arrived in motor-cars to see them at the week-end.

* * *

The children themselves, of course, were oblivious to all this. When war was declared on 3 September, Mary-Rose Benton, for example, was at home. As soon as the air-raid warning sounded her mother took the gas-masks to her brothers Jack and Billy at school, where they were at choir practice. They hadn't heard the siren—it had been drowned out by the hymns. She insisted they put the respirators on. But when she left the boys threw them to one side, and carried on singing. Meanwhile, Mary-Rose stood at the doorstep, expecting the Germans to arrive at any moment, and wondering if the gas would damage her skin.

The children no longer played on the sands; the beach was covered with barbed wire and heavily mined. At their home in Victoria Avenue the children helped Mr Bailey, the lodger, to dig the pit for the Anderson Shelter; they were issued with an advice list on what to do when the bombs began falling, and they were fitted with gas-masks. In a hall in a district confusingly called Reading Street, Mary-Rose's brother Jimmy's terrified screams rang out when they put the gas-mask on his face. He thought they were trying to suffocate him. Billy, too, thought they were up to no good, but was too stubborn to let on. None of this affected Mary-Rose at all—yet. Children respond to different threats. With Mary-Rose, it was noise; with Jimmy it was having something put over his face, the sinister smell of rubber, and the talk of being gassed to death.

The children had air-raid drills at school, and practised putting on their gas-masks. But it didn't feel like a war, and everybody thought it would be over by Christmas. Pranks went on, Jack remained detached from the rest of the family, and Mr Bailey answered their questions and gave Mary-Rose money to spend at the corner shop. It was about this time that she decided to become a carpenter. It seemed that boys had more fun, even if they got smacked more often.

5
The Official Response

If letters about the evacuees appeared quickly in newspapers like *The Times*, they were also published, albeit more slowly, in medical journals. The *British Medical Journal*, for example, published a letter from a Dr Kerr, who wrote: 'I do not think it is using language any too strong to say that in many cases the scum of a town has been poured into a clean countryside with a most callous disregard for the consequences and apparently without the most elementary safeguards for the public health.' Another letter noted that a large percentage of children suffered from impetigo, head lice, and scabies, and that these were most common among those who had 'an inherent dislike for soap and water'. A doctor from Aylesbury in Buckinghamshire was similarly resentful, writing that: 'We have learnt by very uncomfortable contact how the other half of the world lives, and we have seen that the other half appreciates us as little as we appreciate them. Town mothers shot into the country are not grateful, and the rising tide of country resentment matches the objections of the unwilling guests.'

In an editorial, the *Lancet* noted that bed-wetting had turned out to be a major problem, and 'some of our country towns have lately come to have a Continental look; for every morning every window is filled with bedding hung out to air in the sunshine'. There had been bound to be misfits, because of different standards of conduct, language, and diet. But nobody had foreseen that country life would be so unbearable as to send town-dwellers back to town in their thousands. The *Lancet* noted of a series of articles in the *Scotsman* that, while doctors must have been aware of the true state of child health, these revelations had come as 'an unpleasant shock to many rural and suburban hosts', and this should stimulate a combined effort to improve housing, education, and supervision by doctors and nurses. Editorials in the *Medical Officer* provide evidence of a shift in opinion, and of a desire for change. It had previously noted that lice and fleas were unlikely to cause problems, since in many of the towns in the Reception Areas they had been eliminated by public-health measures. Similarly, scabies, ringworm, and impetigo had ceased to bother local Public-Health Departments. A large proportion of children would be expected to wet their beds, and while the physical state of the evacuees was below that of their hosts in the Reception Areas, it was far superior to the average condition of children thirty years earlier; children were well nourished, clean, and well brought-up. But now the journal commented that 'eventually good will result if this wartime experience draws attention to the persistence of verminous conditions in the homes of the poor as a social scandal'.

* * *

Full-length articles took slightly longer to appear. A typical early report was that by J. E. Haine, Medical Officer of Health (MOH) for Guildford, Hambledon, and Haslemere in Surrey, published on 7 October. Some 6,800 evacuees from London had been billeted there, mainly from Fulham, Wandsworth, Battersea, Earlsfield, and Putney. At the three railway stations used as arrival stations, First-Aid rooms had been manned by the Red Cross and the St John's Ambulance Brigade. But few cases had required attention. Haine noted that 'the excellent showing of these children not only as regards cleanliness and general care, but also their healthy appearance and

quiet, calm behaviour excited universal comment'. Medical examinations had been conducted by teams of nurses led by health visitors, and every evacuee had been examined. The main problem
had been 'dirty heads', as children were not so free from head lice
as might have been expected given inspections in schools, and adults
and pre-school children were also infested. Psychological problems
had been encountered from the start, and impetigo had led to
epidemics that had remained localized, but had proved difficult to
control.

In a letter, W. R. Dunstan, the Medical Officer (MO) for Lewes
in Sussex, recorded that the trainloads that he inspected had
varied greatly; the worst cases filled him 'with a more intense
depression than did the fact of war, and I found myself wondering
just exactly what we mean by the word "civilisation". They were
not unhappy, they showed remarkable endurance and an envi-
able patience, but their squalor was undeniable.' The town of
Spalding in Lincolnshire had received 2,500 evacuees from three
different districts, and reported 228 cases of head lice; after six
weeks very few children required further cleansing. The local
MOH, W. G. Booth, reported that almost three-quarters of the
mothers and children of pre-school age had gone home; evacuated mothers used to life with cinemas, cheap food, and other
attractions were unable to adapt to life in a quiet country town or
village. On the issue of head lice, he blamed the legislation
governing school medical inspection. Booth wrote that: 'Whilst
head teachers depend upon attendances for their status and
resent exclusions for "a few nits", whilst we are forced to crack
the pea nut of the social problem group's incapacity to look
after its own children, and whilst children are compelled to be
educated but not to be clean, it is obvious that the problem must
remain unconquerable.' The journal *Public Health* suggested that

'evacuation has brought into the open a state of affairs which many members of the public had not realised, because it had hitherto been segregated. The revelation is quite a useful corrective to a certain complacency which has crept into official reports.'

Writing of children evacuated to Darwen in Lancashire, the local MOH, R. C. Webster, produced an interpretation that was predominantly conservative. He reported that the average nutrition of the evacuees was below that of the local children. However, he argued that, given that Darwen had suffered from a prolonged depression in the cotton trade, poverty per se was not the key factor. Impressions gained in clinics and at school medical inspections suggested that 'unsuitable feeding' was the most important cause. Most mothers did not breast-feed their infants, and the evacuated mothers who had applied to the Welfare Centre had asked for dried foods rather than liquid milk. One mother, for instance, who had enough money, thought that a pint of milk a day was enough for herself and four children aged 8, 6, 3, and ten months. While fresh fruit was cheap and abundant, children were given tinned fruit instead, and dummies were a useful way of distinguishing the evacuees from the local children. Webster concluded that 'even the poorer children of small urban and rural areas have the advantage of fresher air and sunshine, and this has perhaps a general dynamic action on the nutrition and vitality of the child'. Bed-wetting had been common and had been found to be a condition of long standing. Moreover, 'dirt diseases' were surprisingly prevalent, and scabies and impetigo were also common; together these indicated 'a poor standard of parental care coupled with bad environment'. It was clear that public-health measures would have to 'make headway against much ignorance, apathy and criminal neglect'.

Social surveys took longer, and were slower to appear than the reports in the medical journals. One of the first was by the

Association of Architects, Surveyors, and Technical Assistants. It had grown out of the Architects' and Technicians' Organization, formed in 1935, and which (in contrast to the more apolitical MARS) had seen its efforts as part of a radical movement dedicated to building a better future. Published on 14 October, the report noted that the evacuees were not evenly distributed in the Reception Areas, many areas had received only a fraction of those expected, and those evacuees who did arrive were generally not those planned for. For example, a group of evacuees heading from West Ham to Somerset in a non-corridor train had found that the call of nature proved too strong, and so they had been deposited in Wantage in Oxfordshire. Many mothers and children had quickly gone home. Education had been disrupted by evacuation, and the shift system in schools was unsatisfactory. The report said that the greatest need was for social facilities for those mothers still in the Reception Areas. Some evacuees had been put up in outbuildings, and even stables. But the report was also cautious, warning that information about the extent of dirt and infection was not easy to obtain. One case of impetigo could be the talk of the village. Moreover, the number of real complaints was much lower than might at first appear. Taking a more structural or environmental line, it argued that children were the future of the nation, and that 'our treatment of them is the sort which might be expected in a pauperised Balkan state, but is scarcely in accordance with the resources of the richest country in Europe'.

*   *   *

At the Board of Education in Whitehall, Sir Maurice Holmes was also grappling with a range of related issues. Initially, the main concern of the Board was simply to keep existing services going. Cecil Maudslay, for example, an Assistant Secretary, was nearing the end of his career. Born in 1880, he had been educated at Clifton

College in Bristol, and Exeter College, Oxford. He had entered the Board of Education as a Junior Examiner in 1904, and was subsequently Private Secretary. Maudslay wrote on 11 September that the discovery of malnourished children was so important an aspect of the work of the School Medical Service that it should be continued even with reduced staffs, and should take precedence over routine inspections. The experience of the First World War suggested that, although there would be individual cases in which families would become impoverished, unemployed men would be absorbed into industry to replace those called up for military service, and this would reduce the number of families in poverty. Maudslay hoped that the development of school meals and milk, whether free or for payment, would continue during the war.

But Holmes was also receiving letters on a range of other issues. One woman, for instance, had suggested that it would be useful to have talks on the radio for evacuated mothers, on such matters as cooking, laundry-work, sewing, and darning. She wrote: 'In some cases cleanliness and good habits seem to be lacking and in the fresh air of the country these mothers would have an excellent chance of training their children in better ways.' In fact, the President of the Board, Earl De La Warr, did liaise with the BBC over the text of Sunday talks by 'Mr Middleton', its gardening expert. Although these tried to interest both evacuees and parents in school gardens, the subtext was to persuade parents to keep their children in the countryside. In one, 'Mr Middleton' said: 'I cannot imagine any devoted mother wanting to rob them of this opportunity, by bringing them back to the drabness of London just now...the winter will pass, and when the buds begin to burst, and the violets and primroses colour up the hedgerows, and the lambs are skipping about, then the children and their parents will be glad that they remained there.'

Herbrand Edward Dundonald Brassey Sackville, the ninth Earl De La Warr, had been born on 20 June 1900 in Bexhill in Sussex, the only son and youngest of the three children of Gilbert George Reginald Sackville. 'Buck', as he was universally known, was educated at Eton and Magdalen College, Oxford. In 1915 he succeeded to the earldom, and in 1918 had joined the Royal Naval Volunteer Reserve, as he was a conscientious objector. He was perhaps the only Able Seaman to sit on the steps of the throne in the House of Lords—the place reserved for peers who had succeeded as minors, and who could not take their places in the chamber until they were 21. After coming of age De La Warr had actively supported the Labour Party, and served both in Ramsay MacDonald's second Labour administration and in the National Government. He had become Lord Privy Seal in May 1937, and President of the Board of Education in October 1938. This was considered a demotion. But as Mayor of Bexhill between 1932 and 1935 he had persuaded the local council to finance an entertainments pavilion. Built to the design of Erich Mendelsohn and Serge Chermayeff, the De La Warr Pavilion was considered a landmark in the history of modern British architecture.

* * *

There were other problems, that were more religious or cultural than economic. Arthur Hinsley, the Archbishop of Westminster, for instance, wrote to Sir Maurice Holmes on 9 October that he should appoint staff to deal with those evacuees who were Catholics. Hinsley recommended that they should be removed from scattered villages and concentrated in new centres. This had been particularly a problem in the case of children evacuated from Liverpool and Merseyside to North Wales. It was further alleged that what was termed 'freemasonry' created problems of school management. Of the 80,000 children that had been expected in North Wales from Liverpool and Birkenhead, only 40,000 had actually gone. But of these, 25 per cent were 'filthy' and had to be medically treated, and 30 per cent had already gone home. Lord Portal, Regional Commissioner for Civil Defence in Wales, wrote on 25 October that 'the condition of these children, and the behaviour of many of the mothers, has completely dissipated the goodwill and welcome accorded to them by the Welsh people, whose hospitality is proverbial'.

Some of the Reception Areas continued to complain that the arrangements for clothing and footwear were impractical; in many cases, parents seemed irresponsible. The Labour MP for Clay Cross, near Chesterfield, wrote that it was a serious problem: 'private assistance will provide a good deal, but in some cases it can provide hardly anything. The vast majority of my constituents have no margin. They are short themselves. At the best there will be a need which must be met by the Treasury.' However, more typical was the response of Lily Boys, County Organizer for the WVS in Lincolnshire, who wrote to Earl De La Warr that children had come to her county from Leeds, Grimsby, and Hull. She had seen various references in the press to the effect that the problem of head lice had been exaggerated, but that had not been her experience. Householders had been shocked at the conditions in which some people lived, and it was unfair that the Reception Areas had to clothe the children as well as clean them. In response, Earl De La Warr wrote that the responsibility was that of the parents, or the state in the case of those receiving unemployment assistance or public assistance. The Board remained keen to limit state responsibility, and had never expected that the WVS or householders in the Reception Areas would be responsible for boots and clothing.

Holmes and his colleagues were increasingly concerned about reports of juvenile delinquency. On 24 November Sir Arthur Mac-Nalty, the Chief Medical Officer, wrote to Holmes and Maudslay that he shared the anxieties of Walter Elliot, the Minister for Health, that 'the London "street arab" type of child, whose disappearance is a comparatively recent social event, will speedily reappear in numbers to present a thousand problems of behaviour and disease, if some degree of proper supervision of all children of school age be not resumed'. In an attempt to counter the alleged rise in juvenile delinquency, efforts had been made to reopen schools in the Evacuation Areas. MacNalty's comment on 'street arabs' showed how the official response to the evacuees tended to focus on particular 'problems'.

While Walter Elliot had urged that all children should be deloused at least once a month, Earl De La Warr wrote to him on 20 November that it was unlikely that all children would be back at school before January or February 1940. This would damage their education, but also lead to a lack of medical care and treatment. One option was to use First-Aid and decontamination centres. He wrote that, 'here our difficulty is to get hold of the children particularly those who must need it who, being of the lowest type, might be the last to go'. Another possibility was to use the school-attendance laws, or some form of compulsion. De La Warr wrote that: 'I can't help feeling that if we could do something of a really thorough character that ensured virtually every child in Evacuation Areas being cleaned up between now and the time of reopening the schools, it would have a tremendous effect both in terms of usefulness and of politics.'

However, Sir Maurice Holmes replied that, while Elliot wished to be helpful, his suggestion that parents should be compelled to submit their children to medical inspection and treatment would require legislation, would be controversial, and ran counter to the policy of the Board. There was discussion among the civil servants about the wording of a circular, and Cecil Maudslay wrote on 5 December that:

Dr Glover [the Senior Medical Officer] and I are, however, very doubtful about including this sentence [on monthly baths]. On the one hand parents whose children live in good home conditions and have frequent baths at home might resent the idea that their children need a monthly bath at a cleansing station while on the other hand it would probably be argued that a bath once a month is not of much use for children who live in bad home conditions.

Meanwhile, Dr Kenneth Mellanby, an entomologist who was then Sorby Fellow of the Royal Society, had from October 1939 been conducting research on head lice, following advice from a colleague at the London School of Hygiene and Tropical Medicine. Mellanby had found that admissions to hospitals in Sheffield suggested that official statistics on head lice were inaccurate. He suggested to the Board in early December that there should be an investigation. Mellanby had been born on 26 March 1908 at Chapellfield, Barrhead, Renfrewshire, into a brilliant family. The son of Alexander Lawson Mellanby, then Professor of Mechanical Engineering at the Royal Technical College, Glasgow, and his wife Annie; Kenneth's uncle John was Waynflete Professor of Physiology at Oxford, while his uncle Edward directed the Medical Research Council. Kenneth was educated at Barnard Castle School, then read natural sciences at King's College, Cambridge, where his interest in medical entomology began. In 1930 he moved to the London School, where he studied for a PhD on the susceptibility of human parasites to desiccation and overheating, and became interested in cockroaches and bedbugs. Mellanby had been the only British delegate at an international conference on

23 August 1939; as this was on the eve of the outbreak of war, this shows him to have been both a determined researcher, and a headstrong character.

Civil servants now debated whether the Board should commission an independent investigation on head lice from Mellanby. Cecil Maudslay wrote that, 'if the results show percentages of verminous children similar to those already found by Mr Mellanby it might be undesirable to publish them and thus give an opening for German propaganda'. But although the findings were likely to be worrying, it seemed safer for the Board to discover and publish the position rather than that others should do so. The sensitivity to public criticism was in part a legacy of the debate over malnutrition in the 1930s.

*   *   *

Most of the anger over the evacuation of mothers and children was directed not at the Board of Education, but at Holmes's counterparts over at the Ministry of Health. In that department too, reports were flooding in from the Reception Areas on the behaviour of the mothers. The County Inspector of Schools in Northumberland, for example, had written that many of the evacuees had left home very poorly provided for winter conditions. Thick coats or waterproofs and stout boots or clogs would soon be urgently needed. There were many needy cases where parents had been unable to provide adequately for their children. But there were also many cases where parents had exploited the generosity of householders. One observer said that the women from Leeds had head lice, were dirty, refused to wash themselves or their children or to make their beds, and terrorized the farmers and their wives on whom they were billeted to such an extent that they feared to come home in the evening. Some mothers had gone back to town because their husbands were unused to preparing food for themselves, or it was impossible to buy food in the shops after a day's work.

Walter Elliot, the Minister for Health, had made a radio appeal for clothing on 8 September. Elliot had been born on 19 September 1888, at Markgreen in Lanark, the son of a livestock auctioneer. His mother had died four years later, and the children were partly brought up by their maternal grandmother in Glasgow. Elliot had studied medicine at Glasgow University, and had served as a Medical Officer during the First World War; in April 1917 he was awarded the Military Cross. He was elected as MP for the Lanark division of Lanarkshire, and then for the Kelvingrove division of Glasgow. In the late 1920s Elliot had been involved on the Research Committee of the Empire Marketing Board, and in providing free milk for schoolchildren. He had also promoted the Board's support for documentary films. In September 1932 he had been appointed Minister for Agriculture and Fisheries, and again had expanded the provision of milk in schools, through the Milk Marketing Board. In 1936 he had been appointed Secretary of State for Scotland; he had also been involved in the setting up of the WVS.

The Ministry of Health issued a circular on 12 September. It acknowledged that in some areas the influx of people 'in a dirty or verminous condition', or suffering from skin disease, had presented 'a somewhat serious and distressing problem'. The circular accepted that it had become apparent that the clothing and shoes of some children were inadequate, but noted that the responsibility remained with the parents. The majority would have no problem in providing the necessary clothing, and the radio appeal had been intended for the relatively small number of 'necessitous' cases. Sir John Rowland, Chairman of the Welsh Board of Health, had reported to Sir George Chrystal, the Permanent Secretary, that in some areas the clothing of the children was so dirty and

infested with lice that it had to be burnt, and the children had to
stay in bed until new clothes had been obtained. But Chrystal told
Rowland that the most needy cases would be met through the radio
appeal, and it was important not to weaken the responsibilities of
parents.

Nevertheless, reports continued to come in from the Reception
Areas. In particular, Lily Boys, who had already written to Earl De
La Warr at the Board of Education, wrote of women evacuated to
Lincolnshire that 'the low, slum type form the majority of the
mothers, some out for what they can get, most of them dirty, many
of them idle and unwilling to work or pull their weight'. These
mothers, who were used to dirty homes, were unhappy and could
not settle in the cleaner houses, whose occupants resented 'their
dirty ways'. Boys suggested they should be put into camps or
hostels. Furthermore, there had been a huge percentage of 'dirty
and verminous' children arriving into country towns and areas.
Overall, the arrival of the evacuees from Leeds and Hull had been
an eye-opener and an unpleasant shock to the inhabitants of rural
Lincolnshire, who had no idea that such 'terrible' conditions
existed.

Reports from Wales suggested that the footwear and clothing of
evacuees were poor in most areas, and it was thought that the need
would become more urgent as winter approached. There were
urgent and deserving cases in all areas, and the response to the
radio appeal had been negligible. Lord Derby wrote to Sir Samuel
Hoare, Lord Privy Seal, on 3 October that: 'The state of the children both from the point of view of clothing and of cleanliness,
when sent away from various areas to be evacuated, was really
disgraceful.' Meanwhile, representatives of the WVS complained
that foster-parents, often on wages far lower than those of London
families, were being put in an intolerable position. Either they had

to see the children under their care going to school without boots or coats, or else they had to pay for these expensive items out of their own pockets. The National Council of Social Service (NCSS) said there was growing discontent among 'country dwellers' at the fact that the Reception Areas were still expected to provide clothing for the evacuees when the rural children were not getting similar help.

The Ministry of Health issued another circular on 7 November, and this again stressed that the primary responsibility for providing children with the necessary clothes rested with the parents. Those who were unemployed could apply to the Unemployment Assistance Board (UAB) or to public assistance, where they could get a cash payment, an order to a tradesman, or the issue of the actual clothes. Voluntary organizations such as the WVS had an important role, and there should be cooperation between teachers and the representatives of local Welfare Committees. If this was not successful, head teachers should report cases to the Director for Education for the relevant Evacuation Area. The circular recommended that the setting up of working parties for the repair and manufacture of boots should be part of the development of community activities. It was said that the Minister of Health 'has no doubt that "make and mend" work of this kind will make a special appeal to the mothers of young children from the evacuating areas who are living in these districts'. The circular offered £1 for every 200 children to be evacuated, and £5,000 was given to the LCC as a small emergency fund. But no publicity was to be given to this arrangement, in order to encourage assistance by voluntary organizations and parents.

* * *

Some investigators were only starting to carry out their research. The outbreak of war had brought to an end the six years of activity since Elizabeth Denby had launched herself as a Housing Consultant in October 1933. Plans for all but one version of her 'All Europe House' had been shelved, and the slum-clearance scheme on which she had been working as an advisor for Paddington Borough Council had also been abandoned. Elizabeth was afflicted at this time with a first bout of serious illness. But once her health recovered she went to the work that was available, and adapted herself to do whatever was required. One body was the Women's Group on Problems Arising from Evacuation, part of the NCSS. An early pamphlet had declared that:

I think we are all conscious of something lacking in the outlook that so many women have had until now towards the duties and responsibilities of citizenship. Of course, in every area, even in that of the smallest rural district authority, there will be found women of character and personality who could be natural leaders in building a new social order, but there will also be found, I am afraid, a dead weight majority of women who do not regard it as their particular responsibility to concern themselves with social questions.

On 6 November 1939 a letter from Margaret Bondfield, Chairman of the Woman's Group, and W. Thompson Elliott, Chairman of the Churches Group, was published in *The Times*. Bondfield was a trade-unionist, campaigner for women's interests, and politician. Born in 1873, the daughter of a foreman lace-worker, she had become a shop assistant at the age of 14, and later a social investigator. She joined the National Union of Shop Assistants, and did investigative work for the Women's Industrial Council. In 1899 she had been the only woman delegate to the Trades Union Congress, where her speech had made a great impression: 'small in stature, with dark hair, wide brows, and bright dark eyes, she reminded her hearers of a courageous robin as, in her clear, resonant, musical voice, she told them that the unions must get together for political action if they were to achieve their larger aims.' Bondfield had been elected Labour MP for Northampton in 1923, was later MP for Wallsend, and had been appointed Minister for Labour in 1929. Although she lost her seat shortly afterwards (in 1931) she continued with her trade-union work.

In their letter, Bondfield and Elliott noted that an earlier letter from the Archbishop of York and others had made important points for all those, particularly local authorities, religious, and voluntary bodies, who had tackled the evacuation. They wrote that: 'The time for long-term planning has now arrived, and the questions are being widely asked, how can the maximum advantage to the nation be secured of this great dispersal and what combined action can be taken to solve some of these urgent problems of education and leisure time, health and happiness, of the hundreds of thousands of families affected in town and countryside?' Many of the solutions lay in the hands of the Government and local authorities. But voluntary organizations also had an important role to play. The Women's Group had recently been established, to pool the experience and resources of various other bodies. It had concerned itself with practical problems, and hoped to exchange information on local experiments and services. But its main efforts were directed towards 'the wider long-term problems affecting all sides of home life'. One of the most urgent was education, and the 'proper' use of leisure time.

* * *

The minutes of the Woman's Group for 7 November recorded that it had formed a sub-committee on Water Supply, Sanitation, Manners and Customs in the Home. It was convened by Amy Sayle, who had earlier written on public libraries and housing, had been involved in the Women Public Health Officers' Association, and was a member of the Women's Health Enquiry Committee. Hettie Haldane represented the National Federation of Women's

Institutes, and Dora Ibberson was a civil servant. The day after the letter appeared in *The Times*, Elizabeth Denby wrote to the Group's Secretary, Letty Harford, at its offices at 26 Bedford Square, that this was something in which she was particularly interested. When Elizabeth's letter was handed to Margaret Bondfield, she wrote back asking: 'I wonder if it would be possible for you to come in and take an active advisory interest in one of our sub-committees which has particular reference to housing. If it would be convenient for you to call here I should be so glad to explain what we are trying to do and we shall greatly appreciate your practical help.'

Subsequently, Amy Sayle wrote on 15 November to notify Elizabeth that the first meeting of the sub-committee was to be in a couple of weeks time, on 28 November. Irene Barclay, who worked for the St Pancras Home Improvement Society, was now on the Group, as was Letty Harford, of the NCSS. Now called the Sub-Committee on Rural Sanitation, Water Supply, and Personal Hygiene, its terms of reference were 'to explore the problems of water supply and sanitation, and of manners and customs in the home, that have been raised as the result of evacuation'. Elizabeth Denby offered to find out about personal cleanliness among school-children in London, Liverpool, Bolton, and any other large towns, and in Derbyshire and Hampshire. Notes were then circulated to Elizabeth and the other members of the committee to help them in their work. Dora Ibberson, for example, laid out some of the issues to do with 'Hygiene in the Home and Person':

The problem before the Committee is that of the ways of living of the town mother. It seeks to examine how the homes of the past have turned out certain girls who, as mothers, are insanitary and offensive in their personal habits and in the habits imparted to their children and how education has failed to correct the influence of the homes; what in short, are the defects in the social and educational services of the present time which appear to have permitted the continuance of a substratum of the population in eighteenth century conditions.

In the meantime, letters had poured in to Margaret Bondfield, at the head office of the Group. A Billeting Officer from the village of Calcot, near Reading, for example, had written that there were no 'outrageous' cases in the village, no drunkenness after the first night, no bringing in of men to bedrooms, but 'a few nice decent women who fitted in to the best of their power and tried to bear with country conditions'. In a radio broadcast on 12 December Bondfield's more overtly political stance was in contrast to the more conservative position of some members. She said that the Group was painfully conscious of the criticism in the Reception Areas of a 'small minority of dirty, ill-mannered, and destructive elements which have given such a bad name to sections of our cities'. But everyone should face up to their responsibility for this past neglect. They had not cared enough that poverty, unemployment, and ill-health had made havoc of people's lives. Now that they were feeling the consequences, it might make people keener to build a new social order. Thus, Bondfield ended her talk by saying: 'Let us now face the fruits of our neglect with courage and determination to end poverty, ignorance and slums. Unless we can win *this* fight on the home front, the end of the War may find us defeated indeed.'

6

A Winter on Welfare

In March 1940 arguably the best-known society hostess of the day was living in a house in Bognor Regis loaned to her by her mother. Diana Cooper had been born in 1892 in London. She received no formal education, but had been educated at home by governesses. In 1910 she came out as a debutante and took her place at the centre of a so-called golden generation. When the First World War broke out Diana had trained as a member of the Voluntary Aid Detachment at Guy's Hospital. In 1919 she married the diplomat and soldier Duff Cooper, who was to enter Parliament, as Conservative MP for Oldham, in 1924. In 1937 Duff Cooper had been appointed First Lord of the Admiralty, and it was at Admiralty House that Diana displayed her outstanding talent as a hostess. During the war they lived at the Dorchester Hotel and at the house in Bognor, and it was from the latter that she wrote in March 1940:

The Stately Homes in my radius were all gutted of their fine trappings and turned into maternity homes for mothers from crowded areas. Aubussons had given place to linoleum, and rows of hospital beds were the only furnishings. Heirlooms, pictures and their own children had to make way for cradles, charts and nurses. In the brilliant sun of last September, exhausted and cumbersome women lay panting in last-word Fortnum & Mason garden chairs, staring at turquoise bathing-pools. They were not happy. They learned of new pests, like wasps. They yearned for their street of neighbours and familiar surroundings, however squalid. One mother said that she could stand anything but the trees; they really got her down.

* * *

Like many commentators, Cooper focused on the evacuated mothers rather than the children, and was less sympathetic towards them. The debates about evacuees of whatever age had taken up much newspaper and journal column space in the autumn of 1939. But although some of the reaction was translated into animosity at the local level, the children themselves were largely oblivious to the furore that the evacuation had provoked. In any case, statistics showed that many evacuees had only stayed in the countryside for a brief period, and had returned home very quickly. Figures from the Ministry of Health and Department of Health for Scotland for fifty of the eighty-one Evacuation Areas, for example, showed that by 10 December 1939 those returning comprised:

206,000 of 630,000 schoolchildren (33 per cent)
246,000 of 383,000 of the mothers and young children
(64 per cent)

The percentage ranged from 55.2 per cent in Sheffield, to 21.1 per cent in Croydon.

This return home accelerated after Christmas. Another evacuation count was taken on 8 January 1940. This showed that about 900,000 evacuees, out of a total of about 1,473,000, or around two-thirds, had returned to the Evacuation Areas. In England, those that remained in the Reception Areas at that point comprised:

420,000   unaccompanied schoolchildren   (55 per cent)
56,000   mothers and accompanied children   (13 per cent)
1,100   expectant mothers   (9 per cent)

2,280	blind people, people with disabilities,	
	and other 'special cases'	(43 per cent)
43,400	teachers and helpers	(49 per cent)

Overall, 522,780 children and adults (40 per cent) remained in the Reception Areas. In Scotland the figures for those remaining were:

37,600	unaccompanied schoolchildren	(61 per cent)
8,900	mothers and accompanied children	(9 per cent)
40	expectant mothers	(10 per cent)
160	blind people, people with disabilities,	
	and other 'special cases'	(9 per cent)
3,100	teachers and helpers	(23 per cent)

Overall 49,800 children and adults (28 per cent) remained in the Reception Areas.

By 4 February 1940, 44 per cent of the evacuated schoolchildren and 87 per cent of mothers and young children had gone home. The rapid return home of the mothers and accompanied children, and (to a lesser extent) of the unaccompanied children was hardly surprising given the problems in the Reception Areas in September 1939. As with the proportion of children sent away in September, the proportion still away in January 1940 varied between the major cities, from London (66 per cent) and Liverpool (62 per cent) to Birmingham (56 per cent) and Glasgow (25 per cent). At the other end of the scale, Rotherham, Sheffield, Walsall, Derby, Coventry, and Dundee all had less than 10 per cent of their children still away. The proportion of children returning to the poorer areas of East London was higher than that for children returning to the wealthier areas of West London. But there were many other reasons that helped to explain why the evacuees returned home.

In his survey of the evacuation in Scotland, for instance, the educationalist William Boyd found that between September 1939 and May 1940 the evacuees had returned in waves. Half the children evacuated from Clydebank and Glasgow under the Government scheme had returned by October, and three-quarters by Christmas, but children evacuated privately returned even more quickly. Children from Clydebank returned more quickly than those from Glasgow, and the Catholic children from Clydebank returned more quickly than the Protestant. Most of the Clydebank evacuees had been taken to parts of Dunbartonshire accessible by bus, whereas the Glasgow evacuees had gone further afield. Boyd found that the factors affecting the return of the evacuees were, on the evacuee side: the number of rooms in the home; the number of children of school age or under in the family; the age and sex of the evacuee; the character of the evacuation group; and the frequency of visits. On the receiving side, they were: the character of the receiving household; the number in the billet; and change of billet.

The parents generally were responsible for the children's homecoming. Therefore Boyd argued that if any conclusions could be drawn, they were: 'that not only religious difficulties but difficulties of any kind, including bedwetting and verminous condition, were much less serious than the current complaints generally suggested. On the side of the hostesses, there was a good deal of human sympathy and helpfulness, and on the side of their guests in a large proportion of cases a reasonable standard of behaviour.' Boyd concluded that evacuation 'has brought about an appreciable improvement in socially desirable conduct and a firming up of personal character, but that apart from a slight increase in timorousness, it has left unaffected the emotional life of the children'. Overall, it seemed that differences were inevitable, depending on the choice

of billets and foster-mothers, and the poverty and homes the
children came from.

* * *

More generally, through the early months of 1940 depressing news
on the international front was echoed by the weather, as the winter
was one of the worst in living memory. Heavy snowfalls covered
much of Britain, many villages and small towns were cut off, and
schools were closed. In Bedfordshire, Judith Grunfeld found that
she also had to prepare for the arrival of Rosh Hashanah, the
Jewish New Year. The senior boys did most of the preparation,
gathering all the things that were necessary for the service in the
traditional style. They borrowed or bought the white-paper cover-
ings for the tables, and white skullcaps for the boys. The traditional
food for the festival—apple and honey, carrots, and so on—was
also found. It helped that the head teacher of the school, Dr
Abraham Levene, had a vast knowledge of English literature and
culture. Judith could not attend the service for very long; she had to
visit a home where two boys had wet their beds. Then she set off
for Meppershall. When Yom Kippur, the Day of Atonement,
arrived there was no great feasting at the beginning of the fast, and
no special dinner for the children when they returned to their
billets. A very meagre meal had to suffice. But all the children
walked through the village that day, while onlookers peeped into
the church hall to watch the children at prayer.

The beginning of the evacuation had coincided with the most
concentrated religious season of the year, the Jewish month of
Tishri, and Judith later conceded that it could not have been easy
for the villagers of Shefford. But gradually astonishment faded into
respect, and the more intense the religious life of the school became,
the more goodwill there appeared to be. Meanwhile the autumn
winds had begun to blow, the fires in the houses were lit, and parcels

containing winter coats, warm underwear, and pullovers arrived daily for the children. The teaching had been organized in separate classes according to ages and standards. In each of four different church halls two, three, or four classrooms were accommodated. Schoolbooks and other educational equipment had been sent from London, and the old cinema hall was also taken over. Part of it was used as a canteen, part as a school office. Long after the children had gone home, the adults sat in the corner of the empty hall and talked about the events of the day or problems that they shared. Here, under the glow of the paraffin lamp, all their activities were planned and ideas discussed.

On Sunday mornings, as well as on Saturday afternoons, the children were taught in groups. Although the cinema hall was not comfortable, it made the community more creative. The pressure of space, along with the makeshift and dire emergency arrangements, proved to be an electrifying influence. The meals prepared in the kitchen were tasty and nourishing, the groups under youth leadership flourished, and the school syllabuses were revised and planned in the utility office. A great concert was organized on Hanukkah, and with the blackout curtains screening the children from the world outside, the Festival of Lights was celebrated.

One morning at 7.30, in February, when she was in her house in Campton, Judith heard a knock at the front door. From an upstairs window she could see that one of her senior boys had arrived on a bicycle. Why would anyone want to disturb her at such an early hour? The boy said calmly: 'Something unpleasant, something went wrong with the stove in the cinema hall. There was a fire in the middle of the night.' Without waiting to ask any more questions, Judith was already on her bicycle. They travelled the mile down the country lane that separated Campton and Shefford, into the High Street, then round the corner to the cinema hall. The archway was still there, the yard was full of people. On the ground were charred chairs and benches, books thrown into a heap, and the cinema hall itself was a mere shell. The roof was gone. The belongings that had been saved were scattered on the ground, and village people were gathered around in groups.

At that moment, when Judith jumped off her bicycle, all eyes were on her. She had a feeling of guilt and failure, of having stolen and of having been robbed, and of confusion as to what to do next. And here among the onlookers was the cinema-owner who, some months ago in an impulse of generosity, had given her the use of the hall. Judith hoped the ground would swallow her up before he saw her, but Bruce King seemed unperturbed, and simply said, 'I would ask the Liberals if I were you. They have a hall for their meetings, they might help you out. Here is the address.' Then off he went. With that, the matter was settled. Benevolence, sympathy, and help were extended from all sides. The local fire brigade, which had been called during the night by neighbours, had broken into the cinema hall and taken out of the blazing fire the Scrolls of the Law, the prayer-books, and the Hebrew bibles. They were all undamaged. The typewriter was burned, as were the boxes of food, but the Scrolls of the Law had been saved from destruction.

So now here they were with a heap of books, charred tables and chairs, blackened pots and pans, but without a communal hall or an office. The key to the cinema hall was still in Judith's pocket, but the shell of the building was now open to rain, wind, and snow. Snow was now falling in soft white flakes, covering up the site of the fire. Quickly the boys carried away the books and Scrolls, and got them under cover. The children were taken away in buses to the small canteen that had been established at the beginning of the stay, in Clifton, a mile from Shefford. Together with the Clifton children, they had to eat in several shifts. Judith cycled round all day to interview local clergymen, the chairman of the local council, and the heads of various local social groups, in the hope of finding a new home for her school. Taking a copy of the local newspaper with the headline, 'Evacuation Home of Jewish School Scuttled', she went to London and called at the offices of various wealthy business-people. When she returned to Shefford late that night, she at least had a bit of money at her disposal, and was able to go to an estate agent and rent some premises where she could continue running the school.

* * *

In Bournemouth, Dave Pinchon spent the early months of 1940 at 'Clarke's College', the transport café-cum-bed and breakfast on Holdenhurst Road. Then, on 17 March, he moved to stay with Mr and Mrs Brock at 500 Charminster Road. As with his previous move, this marked a dramatic change. The Brocks were a youngish couple with one small child. Mr Brock was a well-built young man who was a glazier by day and professional boxer by night. Dave was aware that, even in those days, there were certain regulations regarding the frequency of fights. Mr Brock overcame these restrictions by travelling to another part of the country and fighting under an assumed name. He must have been quite a skilful boxer, because Dave could not remember seeing him badly marked.

The big incident during Dave's stay with the Brocks occurred when a rude remark was discovered written on the outside lavatory wall. Following a handwriting test and a grilling by the Revd Smith, who taught Scripture and English, Dave was exonerated. After suspicion and pressure on the other evacuee living there, the boy eventually confessed. It was completely out of character and inexplicable. However, Dave was also steadily losing weight at the Brocks. His parents contacted the school and insisted he change billets. He would shortly be moving yet again.

* * *

In Kent, George Prager and his friends found they were still required to play rugby on the school playing fields and go on cross-country runs even after a heavy fall of snow. One day he and a friend set off early to visit the beach at Sandwich Bay, crossing the golf course as a shortcut. On the way across, George disappeared into one of the snow-filled bunkers, almost up to his neck. Undeterred, and having extricated himself (much to his friend's amusement), they continued to the beach where George decided to take a dip in the sea. As they were the only ones in the bay, George stripped off and plunged into the water. Gasping for breath with the shock that he had experienced, he came out faster than he had gone in. Running up and down the beach in an effort to get warm and having to get dressed again in wet clothes, he was very uncomfortable. Slowly his clothes dried on his body, and he experienced a warm afterglow. He felt warm for the rest of the day, but his clothes were a sorry sight, and had to be washed to remove the salt.

In March George made a sightseeing trip into the town of Deal, and having some money left from when he had left home, decided to buy a camera. It cost 5s. from a chemist's shop, and started a fascination that grew over the years. He took several pictures of Judy Gunn, the baby, and the Pekingese. Since no air-raids had occurred at Sandwich or Gillingham, many of the boys had returned home. George and Norman had to leave Sandown Lodge because of a change in the domestic circumstances of Judy and her husband, who had to move to the London area where he was stationed. Instead the boys were moved to the golfcourse clubhouse, to live with their friend Gordon's parents.

* * *

In Leicestershire, Maggie Quinn had found that Mark Burdett was a very efficient weather forecaster. 'February fill dyke, either black or white', meant a very wet month, whether it snowed or rained. The sky could be too high for rain, or it might be too cold for snow. As well as red skies at night and in the morning, if it was a very bright, clear morning it was well known that this would not last the day. A 'mackerel' sky meant impending rain, and if the weather-vane on the Old Hall pointed to Desford, you could be sure rain was on the way. If the dog's coat thickened they were in for a cold spell, and if she started to moult, a hot one.

There was great excitement when the Groby Pool 'bore', which meant it was sufficiently frozen for people to skate on it and make slides. The locals were joined then by people from other villages and from Leicester itself, and there were huge, long slides made by youngsters and older adults following one another in very rapid succession. The pool might only be frozen over for a few days, so everyone took advantage of it when they could. In the winter months the schoolroom was heated by a furnace surrounded by a strong metal grille so the children would not burn themselves. The room was bitterly cold most of the time, and the mid-morning milk was frozen. The third-of-a-pint bottles were brought in to stand by the fire, but it seemed to have little effect on them.

* * *

Frank Walsh also found in Lancashire that the winter was a very bad one, with lots of snow. One morning the family opened the back door to find the house covered in snow from the roof to the ground. When they looked outside there was just a white wall. Luckily, at the front it was only about two feet deep. The snow had drifted in the wind, and as well as piling up on one side of the house it had settled between the high hedges. On the roads, the snow was level with the hedge-tops, lying about five to six feet deep. The village of

Catforth was cut off for a week, and the only means of transport was by hitching the horse to the two front legs of the large, upturned oak table from the kitchen. This was used like a sledge, and the hedges had to be broken down between the fields to allow access to them. This was the only way to travel between the different farms, or to the post office, pub, and the few houses situated on the very outskirts of the village, where eggs and milk and other necessities were taken to help out. All other forms of transport had ground to a halt.

Although food rationing had begun in January 1940, with butter, lard, sugar, bacon, ham, and eggs, people on farms seemed better off than those living in towns and cities. The odd pig was secretly slaughtered, cut up and salted, and distributed to neighbouring farmers. Sunday lunch always consisted of chicken, which was killed the day before, a process known as 'necking'. Once, the farmer asked Frank and Ronnie to pick a hen, 'neck' it, and pluck and clean it ready for the Sunday lunch. Very nervously, Frank managed to hold the bird firmly under his left arm, gripped the neck, and proceeded to pull and twist as hard as he could. The bird fluttered and struggled hard, until eventually it escaped from his grasp. The boys chased it, caught it again, and a second unsuccessful attempt was made. Not to be thwarted again, Ronnie held the bird's neck over a wooden block, whereupon Frank chopped its head off with an axe. The boys rushed away as the blood spurted and the headless hen ran round and round, in what the boys thought was pursuit of them. Eventually they mastered the technique.

When he had first arrived at the farm Frank had been given an old hat to wear when he was in the 'shippon' or cowshed, and very quickly he had become adept at milking, sitting on a three-legged stool, with the bucket resting on one heel and held between his legs, and his head on the side of the cow. He had three cows to milk before school, and the same three when he came back home in the afternoon. Later, an automatic milking system was installed, but when the teats were disconnected they still had to finish the cows off by hand to make sure all the milk was out. Each cow produced between half and three-quarters of a bucketful at every milking. The cows were brought in twice a day, the dogs being used to round them up. When the milking was finished, Frank and the farmhand had to clean out the cowsheds using hosepipes and brushes. The cows all had individual names. There was only one that gave any trouble, and she was always milked by the farmhand, as she was prone to kicking out. In order to speed up the cleaning, the boys would run behind the cows as they were being milked, holding a bucket to stop the manure splashing on the cowshed floor. But one night, before the boys were going to be taken out for the evening, Frank was standing behind the cow with his bucket ready to catch what was ejected. The cow coughed. That was the end of his night out. He ended up covered from his waist to the top of his head.

In the winter of 1940, Frank and the family still had to milk the cows in the morning and the afternoon, but because there were not enough milk canisters they distributed some milk to other households along with food, then had to throw the rest away down the drains. All the farmers helped each other, and began digging in shifts, clearing the snow by hand. It was seven or eight days before the gangs digging from the Preston area linked up with those working from Catforth village. No one in living memory had experienced such a heavy snowfall, or one that disrupted their everyday routines to such an extent. All the ponds and canals in the area were frozen solid. With the school closed, the children were free to enjoy skating—the metal bases on the clogs they wore were ideal for this—snowballing, and building snowmen. There were bruised bottoms and elbows as skaters lost their balance, but luckily no broken bones. The only real casualties were the swans that became trapped as the water began freezing. Once the ice became thick enough, people released them by breaking it away from their feathers.

* * *

David Hodge had noted in Scotland that both Hendry Ballantyne and his brother-in-law Jim Ridley were paid very little, and lived in houses owned and maintained by the Nish family. They were permitted to take fruit and vegetables from the garden for their own use, and Jim was allowed to sell any woodpigeons he shot by way of keeping their population down. The birds were very destructive in the garden, and Jim kept a gun handy—any pigeon or crow that landed within sight was dispatched.

Hendry Ballantyne was a very quiet person, but his wife had a nasty streak at times. David's brother George was a tall, good-looking extrovert, and soon became the favourite of both Mrs Ballantyne and Jim Ridley. This came as no surprise to David, as George had been the favourite of all his aunts and grandparents at home. Most of the time, David did not mind his brother's popularity, but it could be annoying when he got preferential treatment from Mrs Ballantyne. David, though, was fortunate to become the favourite of Hendry himself. This stood him in good stead when Mrs Ballantyne turned nasty.

Like Frank Walsh in Lancashire, the boys all became good at rounding up the cows and taking them back to the farm for milking, which they helped with as well. The milking was done by hand, so every pair of hands counted. The boys also became good marksmen under Jim's tuition. His employers expected him to keep all vermin under control, and as far as Jim was concerned anything that ate seeds or the produce of the garden qualified, as did any animal that ate game, birds, eggs, and chicks. Rabbits were plentiful and destructive. As well as shooting rabbits, Jim kept ferrets. He and the boys visited rabbit warrens and staked nets over most of the holes. Then down went the ferrets, on rope leads and collars. The rabbits charged out of the burrows into the nets, where they were clubbed to death. Although other rabbits were killed by the ferrets, this could prove troublesome. Once the ferret made its kill, it was very reluctant to be separated from its prey until it had eaten its fill; it sank in its teeth, and wouldn't let go. The ferrets had to be dragged out using the leads round their necks. In spite of being half-choked, some emerged still holding on to the rabbits.

* * *

Compared with those of the children, the activities of the adults were more prosaic. In Lancaster, G. M. Bland was dealing with evacuees that had gone home. For example, a Mrs Burgoyne wrote to him on her return to Bury, north of Manchester: 'I should like to express my thanks to you for all your kindness. My stay in Lancaster was a very happy one and a really wonderful experience. Everyone in school and billet seemed only too willing to help St Luke's children and one could wish that the parents had acted differently. Our experience has made us all a little wiser.'

The issue of clothing for the Salford children had become more pressing. Bland wrote to the head teachers still in Lancaster on 19 February that he had been in conversation with the Area Officer of the Unemployment Assistance Board in Lancaster. He was obtaining clothing and footwear for children whose parents were unemployed and receiving assistance from the UAB in Salford. He agreed to send direct to his colleague in Salford the particulars of the cases submitted. Bland asked if the head teachers could let him have a list of such children, their full names, Salford addresses, ages, heights, specific needs, and shoe sizes. To ensure parents were receiving assistance from the UAB, he would forward the particulars to the Area Officer who would forward them to his colleague in Salford for verification. This would make the process quicker than in the past.

* * *

Debates about the evacuees continued both in the popular press and academic journals. There were articles, for example, by A. D. K. Owen and William Robson in the *Political Quarterly*. Born in 1904, Owen had been educated at Leeds Grammar School and the University of Leeds. He had earlier worked on surveys of unemployment and housing in Sheffield, and had been Co-Director of the Pilgrim Trust survey of unemployment, in 1936–7. By 1940 he was Lecturer in Citizenship at the University of Glasgow. Owen wrote that the experience of evacuation showed that the suspension of the School Medical Service during the summer holidays had resulted in a falling away in cleanliness and in the attention paid to minor ailments. The evacuation had been a success, but while stories of head lice and bad behaviour had been exaggerated, there was sufficient truth in them to create great concern among householders and officials in the Reception Areas. He argued that if institutional billeting had been adopted for cases of bed-wetting from the start (such as in school camps), much of the acrimony that surrounded the evacuation scheme would have been avoided.

In contrast to Owen, Robson had left school at 15, and had worked as a clerk at Hendon Airport before studying at the London School of Economics and specializing in administrative law. He had been one of the main founders, with Leonard Woolf, George Bernard Shaw, Kingsley Martin, and Beatrice and Sidney Webb, of the *Political Quarterly* in 1930, and had become a joint editor in 1931. Later, his interests had spread into local government and city planning, and his book *The Government and Misgovernment of London* had been published in 1939. Robson argued that the evacuation had profound sociological and political implications, and represented a complete reversal of historic trends. Town and country planning should have higher status, and should be placed in the hands of a strong central department, capable of directing the location of industry, and formulating a national plan for the whole country.

There were comments in other journals. In the *Quarterly Review*, for instance, Frederic Evans argued that evacuation had been successful, but would have important social repercussions. Mothers and young children had posed particularly difficult problems. Clothing the evacuees had been a challenge, as had head lice. Perhaps a new 'mode of life' might emerge out of the war, and a 'brave new world' might be built. In the journal *Social Work*, Marjorie Cosens quoted from the experiences of Care Committee workers, head teachers, Billeting Officers, and social workers, and argued that the evacuation could force people to accept a levelling up of the income of the poorer sections of society.

* * *

Some of the early reports on the evacuees noted psychological problems, and in debating this issue Cyril Burt was to prove a major figure. Born in 1883, he had been educated at Jesus College, Oxford, and had become involved in Francis Galton's anthropometric survey and in the world of eugenics. Appointed as psychologist to the LCC, Burt had published *The Young Delinquent* in 1925, and had chaired the Child Guidance Council. As an educational psychologist, he had contributed to policy-making at the Board of Education, and in 1932 had become Professor of Psychology at University College London. Considering the evacuation of children from London, Birmingham, and Liverpool, Burt argued that evacuation had not altered the amount of 'serious' nervous disorder, though it had increased 'mild' and temporary nervous disturbance. These 'anxiety-states' included home-sickness, bed-wetting, and the exaggeration of grievances. But what was more impressive was how little the children had been affected; Burt said this was testimony to the adaptability of children and the care shown by foster-parents and teachers.

Others were more concerned about the effects on children of early separation from their mothers. Along with Emanuel Miller and Donald Winnicott, the psychiatrist John Bowlby had argued in 1939, in a letter to the *Lancet*, that the separation of small children from their mothers could lead to 'persistent delinquency' in later life. Bowlby, born in 1907, had been educated at Trinity College, Cambridge, qualifying in medicine, and going on to specialize in psychiatry. At the time of his letter he was in charge of the Child Guidance Unit at the Tavistock Clinic, London. In March 1940 Bowlby, by then at the Child Guidance Centre in Cambridge, argued further that a high proportion of the nervous, difficult, and delinquent children seen at such clinics were found to have had unsettled home conditions during the first few years of life. These children were likely to grow up into discontented and difficult adolescents, and to be 'chronic social misfits' in later life. Thus the separation of mothers and children during evacuation should be avoided; mothers, or at least friends or neighbours, should go with them; children should not be placed in large groups under the care of a matron.

* * *

In some cases School Medical Officers (SMOs) who in the 1930s had been isolated critics of the School Medical Service now felt vindicated. Reflecting on the condition of the evacuees and the earlier efforts that had been made, Dr Hugh Paul, the SMO for

Smethwick in Birmingham, for example, argued that 'it is not now a question as to when or whether we should get back to normal, but whether our pre-war efforts were adequate'. The legal framework for dealing with 'persistent uncleanliness' would have to be strengthened. W. C. V. Brothwood, Chief Assistant Medical Officer of Health (MOH) in Lancashire, conceded that in some Reception Areas insufficient staff, inadequate facilities, and the too-frequent arrival of trains had meant that it was only possible to do a hasty inspection of the evacuees, and some children who should have been removed to hospital had been admitted to private homes. He argued that the problem of head lice had been exaggerated; some children were affected, but not to the extent that the general public had been led to believe. The nutrition of the evacuees had improved while they were in the countryside. Bed-wetting was linked to psychological factors, and scabies was introduced to county areas where it had not been known; in some cases householders became infected, causing an uproar. Brothwood reflected that while some of the evacuees had head lice, 'at the same time I do not think they were appreciably dirtier than a sample we ourselves could have provided from certain of the county districts which are thickly populated and industrial in type'.

In the *Lancet*, it was reported that of children evacuated from London to Chelmsford, in Essex, one in seven required free milk, as against one in twenty of the local children. Children evacuated to Kent, on the other hand, were reported as being superior in height and weight to the local children, perhaps not surprisingly as they came from better-class schools in South-East London. Some places had foreseen early in 1939 that head lice would pose a problem; in Bootle on Merseyside, for example, a list of 'recidivists' (those who regularly had lice) had been drawn up, updated, and forwarded to the MO in the Reception Area. If generally adopted, these lists might have avoided much recrimination, since the main complaint of the Reception Areas had been that they had not been told what to expect. In Leicestershire, another doctor now reflected that the strength of a medical service was not gauged by numbers treated, but by the proportion of people who received its benefits. Similarly, an MOH argued that it was a problem of the whole community and not of schoolchildren alone; he conceded that official reports claiming a low incidence of 'uncleanliness' had to be treated with scepticism. The evacuation meant that these came under more scrutiny than previously. Noting that statistics for London for 1938 seemed to show that 98 per cent of children were free of head lice, and only 86 children out of 170,000 examined had been found with body lice, the *Lancet* argued that these figures had to be reconciled with what was found in the evacuees. One explanation was that evacuation came at the end of the summer holidays, when the children had been unsupervised for some weeks. Employing a military metaphor, the journal concluded that 'the main battlefield is adequately manned by the School Medical Service, but the enemy is continuously reinforced from the adult population'.

* * *

In London, Elizabeth Denby was grappling with many of the same issues in her work for the Hygiene Sub-Committee. At the meeting on 12 January 1940 she reported she had made a study of the MOH reports for Manchester, Liverpool, Derbyshire, and Hampshire. She had looked particularly at the incidence of disease; at the number of toilets; and at disinfestation and 'verminous' conditions. She had found it difficult to draw any firm conclusions, as there were no uniform standards or methods of tabulating the results of inspections. Letty Harford was to look at the reports for Sheffield for the period 1936–8, but the women agreed the next step should be a short questionnaire, to be distributed in various London boroughs. Elizabeth would deal with Paddington; Amy Sayle with Battersea and Shoreditch; and Irene Barclay with St Pancras and Stepney. They also agreed that the theme of 'Hygiene in Schools' should be added to their terms of reference, meaning by this both the teaching of hygiene and the provision of sanitation and washing facilities.

Just over three weeks later the Sub-Committee met again. At this meeting the members discussed Elizabeth's memo on cleanliness statistics in Derbyshire, Hampshire, Bolton, Huddersfield, Hull, Liverpool, Manchester, and Newcastle. Sayle also reported on her enquiries in Battersea and Shoreditch; Elizabeth on Paddington; Barclay on St Pancras and Stepney; and Harford on Sheffield. Together they recommended that the Ministry of Health should reconsider its policy on housing, complete its schemes, and resume slum clearance. Letty Harford agreed to obtain other pamphlets on evacuation, including one recently published by the Fabian Society, and one on evacuation to Cambridge.

By now the pace of work had accelerated, and the Hygiene Sub-Committee was meeting at fortnightly intervals. Irene Barclay was later to write of this period that 'we spent whole days on the job, taking a brief luncheon interval. We studied a vast mass of reports, books and articles.' Between 15 February and 9 May the sub-committee interviewed some twenty-seven witnesses, mainly female Billeting Officers, head teachers, social workers, and other voluntary workers. On 13 March, for example, Joan Clarke, an Assistant Children's Care Organizer in St Pancras, Hampstead, and Holborn, said that she believed the 'problem families' were not usually the larger families; there the older children were able to help with the babies, and in fact the most difficult children were from broken homes. The Sub-Committee had received an offer of additional voluntary assistance; and a member was investigating the potential usefulness of rubber sheets and books on the teaching of hygiene in Sweden. On 26 February the members heard about the personal habits and personal hygiene of schoolchildren, while on 13 March the women agreed to look further into slum clearance and building schemes, and on ways to overcome the lack of timber. Following a resolution from the Ling Physical Education Association, they agreed to get more information about the teaching of hygiene. Although they deferred consideration of the replies to a National Council of Women's questionnaire on evacuation, they heard about the experience of schoolchildren in Eastbourne. Amy Sayle recommended the Toynbee Hall Housing Association's book *Growing Up in Shoreditch*, which had been published in 1939, and the women wondered if they had information on where the six schools featured in the book had been evacuated to.

* * *

Several streets away, in Whitehall, Sir Maurice Holmes was urging that welfare services for schoolchildren should continue in wartime. In a pre-Christmas circular, issued on 14 December, the Board of Education had argued that provision should be made for the treatment of skin diseases such as impetigo and scabies; the experience of the Reception Areas had shown that the condition of some schoolchildren after the interval of the summer holidays was far from satisfactory. It hoped that school clinics would be available for children in need of treatment, that school meals and milk could be continued in the Evacuation Areas, and that surveys could continue in the Reception Areas, since the circumstances of many families had worsened as a result of the war. There were regional variations in the extent to which the school health services were functioning, and the circular asked LEAs for a statement of the current position. These services had been built up over thirty years, and, 'must not be allowed to lapse because of the stress of war'.

The previous day, the Board had noted a recommendation by the Advisory Committee on Nutrition that each child should have one to two pints of milk a day, but admitted that the amount of school milk normally consumed was much smaller than this. It had been assumed that children would get milk at home, but among poorer families the amount consumed at home was very small indeed, especially in households with several children. In January 1940 the Milk Marketing Board, representing producers, noted that the evacuation had led to a 30 per cent decline in the consumption of milk in schools. It argued that every effort should be made to restore the amount sold to schoolchildren, and there should be an extension of free school milk. Those who needed milk most were children under 5, those of school age, and nursing and expectant mothers from poorer homes. Nevertheless, the provision of cheap milk without an income test would amount to a direct food subsidy, and this could not be justified.

Although it seemed obvious that city children would benefit from their stay in the countryside, the Board of Education was supporting a statistical survey of the heights and weights of children in school camps. The particularly bad winter weather meant that, for evacuees still in the Reception Areas, the issue of clothing and footwear had become more pressing. Grimsby's Director of Education, for instance, supported by numerous other LEAs, urged the Government to offer 100 per cent grants for the supply of footwear and clothing. Margaret Bondfield had written suggesting that classes should be formed in schools, under properly qualified instructors, to repair boots and shoes.

Because of the debate over head lice, the Ministry of Health published two memos in January, *Scabies* and *The Louse and How to*

Deal With It. The first emphasized prevention through vigilance, and with an emphasis on early diagnosis. If the patient was a child it was likely that other members of the family were infected, so the whole family should be treated and their belongings disinfested at the same time. The second pamphlet noted that lice multiplied rapidly in favourable conditions, such as when people did not wash or remove their clothes. In 1938 school medical inspections had found that 444,967 schoolchildren had head lice. All children should be inspected once a term; all those cleaned should be reinspected at weekly intervals. Homes should be visited, and parents instructed in the cleaning of children.

* * *

In a House of Lords debate on 7 February, Lord Addison, a former Minister of Health, admitted that the lack of 'cleanliness' in the Reception Areas was a pity: 'it was really most disappointing and if it meant anything it meant that our school inspection and school medical services and nursing services and the rest required not scattering to the winds but augmenting.' Meanwhile, the investigation by Kenneth Mellanby into the incidence of head lice was under way. By March 1940 he was checking hospital records in the Midlands city of Leicester, close to where Maggie Quinn was living. Mellanby reported that the local people complained that the children evacuated from London were the worst they had had to deal with. However, he noted that everywhere he went the people said, 'But have you been to Liverpool?', as if that was the home of the head louse.

More generally, the experience of September 1939 had led to calls for an inquiry into the School Medical Service, and these drew a response from the Chief Medical Officer. Born in Westmorland in 1880, Sir Arthur MacNalty had spent his early boyhood in the Lake District. Educated privately, he had later studied natural sciences at Corpus Christi College, Oxford, and had taken the Diploma in Public Health in 1927. However, his career was an unusual one, in that he had chosen to work at the Ministry, unlike many of the leading figures in public health, who had risen through service in the local authorities. MacNalty had initially been interested in chest diseases, and was involved in the development of tuberculosis services. He had been a member of staff transferred to the new Ministry of Health in 1919, and had succeeded Sir George Newman in 1935.

MacNalty conceded that the evacuation had revealed 'an unexpectedly high incidence of pediculosis and bad habits among school children'. However, he also claimed that the School Medical Service had not been stagnant, but progressive and constantly expanding; it was alive to, and responded to, constructive criticism. It was a partial service, hedged around with artificial boundaries imposed by statute and regulation, and reinforced by the desire of Parliament to prevent educational funds being used for health purposes. But when the handicap imposed by these legal limitations was borne in mind, its record was one of growth and achievement. MacNalty wrote to Holmes on 16 February that:

It has been shown that the criticisms relating to the social habits and misfits of certain of the evacuees concern the home conditions and are no reflection upon the School Medical Service. It was inevitable in this national game of general post that difficulties and criticisms should arise. The articulate voices of complaint naturally outweigh the silent satisfaction and contentment that have been felt in numbers of homes with regard to evacuated schoolchildren.

Thus the School Medical Service should not be blamed for the poor health of the evacuees; the root cause lay in the home. MacNalty said it was clear that 'slum clearances still lack completion; that low standards of living persist, and that the lessons taught in the school and clinic and good social habits do not always survive the pressure of bad home circumstances when young people have passed from supervision'. An investigation by outside experts was therefore not necessary, and in any case could not be completed satisfactorily under war conditions.

When Sir Maurice Holmes wrote to Earl De La Warr the same day, he acknowledged that the volume of complaints about the uncleanliness of the evacuees must have come as a shock to everyone, whether they were familiar with the education system or not. A natural reaction was to assume that there was something wrong with the School Medical Service. But Holmes echoed MacNalty, in writing that: 'The School Medical Service does not enter into the homes of the children, where the source of the trouble so often lies, and the shock to public opinion is in itself a measure of the success with which in normal times the School Medical Service counteracts the effects of bad home conditions.' Any inquiry would need to cover a wider field, including housing, and the problem of the 'dirty school child' was not one that could be solved by an investigation of the School Medical Service itself.

7
City and Countryside

In the spring of 1940 German air attacks, from April onwards, anticipated the Battle of Britain, which would carry on into the summer and autumn. The Norway debate, on the failure to prevent the German invasion of that country, took place in the House of Commons in May, signalling the end of Neville Chamberlain's premiership. Discussions about the health and welfare of the children evacuated in September 1939 continued, as did the work of local voluntary organizations. But lessons had been learnt. Arrangements had been made for the medical examination of children in the event of future evacuations. For example, when children were evacuated on 2 June, from towns on the East Coast to Wales, MOHs received satisfactory reports from the Reception Areas. These lessons were extended to other movements of people. Those deemed to be refugees were examined at the ports where they landed, and at Reception Centres in Greater London.

A range of general studies of evacuation were published in this period, including those by Tom Harrisson and Charles Madge (for Mass Observation) and by the National Federation of Women's Institutes. Born in 1911, Tom Harrisson had spent his early years in Argentina, where his father was an engineer. He was educated at Harrow and Pembroke College, Cambridge. He organized various expeditions, including to Sarawak, in northern Borneo, and to the

New Hebrides, and his book *Savage Civilisation* had been published
in 1937. Charles Madge, born in 1912, was educated at Winchester,
and Magdalene College, Cambridge. In the thirties he joined the
Communist Party, and became a poet. In 1937 Harrisson and
Madge had founded Mass Observation, to do 'anthropology at
home' and let ordinary people speak for themselves, publishing
Britain by Mass-Observation in 1939.

In their book *War Begins at Home*, published in 1940, Harrisson
and Madge included a chapter on evacuation, and quoted Billeting
Officers, mothers, and schoolteachers from a variety of locations
including Blackpool, Liverpool, Wales, and Scotland. Mass Observation personnel had recorded eyewitness accounts of both the
departure of the evacuees and their arrival in the Reception Areas.
One teacher, for example, observed that while her school was in a
poor district, the mothers had tried hard to provide the necessary
equipment. While one child in twenty did not have all the articles
listed in the Ministry of Health's circular, half had new pyjamas,
soap, toothbrushes, plimsolls, shirts, and knickers. Harrisson and
Madge quoted a teacher who had helped with the evacuation
arrangements:

One mother stood by while I examined the luggage of her son and
daughter. She was shabby, thin and very anxious. She said, 'It's a dreadful
thing having to send the children away like this, but I want to do the best
I can for them. I've told them it's a holiday, because I didn't want to
frighten them'. Then as I began to take the articles out of the neatly
packed new rucksacks, she said, 'I don't want them to be any bother to the
people they're going to, Miss, so I've given them each an extra pair of
stockings so there won't be so much darning. I've given them extra soap
and toothpaste too'. She had also provided them with two pairs of substantial new pyjamas, and two new pairs of warm underwear, and two large
thick new towels. She glowed with pride when I congratulated her on the
way she'd equipped her children.

Harrisson and Madge were sympathetic to the different habits of the working-class mother. A survey by the National Federation of Women's Institutes, *Town Children Through Country Eyes*, also published in 1940, compiled similar anecdotes about evacuees from London, Leeds, and Liverpool, but was less sympathetic to the evacuees, whether mothers or children. It commented particularly on their table manners and clothing. The author of a report on evacuees from Bermondsey in London, for instance, concluded that, 'after this experience I think England ought to be proud of her country women for their cleanliness, good housewifery and decent standards'.

*   *   *

At the local level, some evacuees found that, as the weather improved, they were able to experience the countryside for the first time. Their foster-parents taught them the names of trees and wild flowers; they went fishing in local streams and rivers; and they were able to roam in the country's relative freedom. Others were hard at work on local farms, where they enjoyed the cows, pigs, horses, hens, and ducks, but where they were also introduced to the realities of birth and death.

In Leicestershire Maggie Quinn had found that Groby was a small village, with a few shops. There was the Co-Op, Chaplin's the butcher's (where she used to play in the walled garden with another evacuee called Irene), the post office, Clara Clement's shop on the corner of Newtown Lane, Letts' on the corner of Ratby Road, and Alf's cobbler's shop nearby, where Maggie's shoes were patched at the back when they got too small. Sarah Ann Burdett bought as much as she could from the Co-Op, maximizing the dividend she received as a member. The Co-Op butcher called twice a week, on Wednesdays and Saturdays, but from January 1940, with rationing, the choice was very limited. However, with five children and adults in the house the family managed a joint of some kind or other for Sunday lunch. This was served up cold on Mondays, with perhaps bubble-and-squeak followed by rice pudding. This was a typical Monday washday lunch for many families, when the weekly laundry took a good half-day to complete. The weekly visit to Leicester meant tripe and pigs' trotters from the tripe shop.

There were three farms in the middle of the village—Mr Biggs in the Old Hall; Mr Ball whose farm was up Chapel Hill; and another farm at the bottom of the hill, on the junction of Ratby Road. Because of the urgent need to grow food in wartime, a lot of the land which was fallow had been ploughed up for cereal crops. Maggie went gleaning in the fields. The family kept poultry for eggs and meat, and any corn they could collect was very welcome as feed. The adults and children were not allowed to do this until the fields had been raked, which took place after the crop had been carted and stacked.

A lot of the social life of the village revolved around the pub and the British Legion Club, which were the only places that had rooms suitable for social events. Concerts were put on to raise money for specific projects, and talented local people sang, danced, and generally entertained. They nearly always ended with community singing, and there was usually a piano-accordion player and other instrumentalists. Cyril Burdett was a soloist, with 'Take a Pair of Laughing Eyes' a favourite in his repertoire. In spite of his tenor voice he had been rejected from the BBC Choir, so stayed on in the village as a pitman and later as a foreman. Not too many people had cars, and most travelled by bus. There was the Midland Red, which went to Coalville and Ashby, Brown's Blue and Smith's from Groby—all running between Leicester and calling at other villages. Maggie later wrote: 'One bus sticks in my mind. That was the one with the miners being bussed back to Leicester. I can still remember all their dirty faces looking out of the windows—literally coal-black—no pithead showers in those days.'

Although the Burdetts were 'chapel' people, the church loomed quite large in the life of the family. Living so near the church, Mark Burdett loved to sit in the window on Sundays with his jug of pre-lunch beer and watch the churchgoers returning from morning service. Every so often there was a parade, with the Home Guard, National Fire Service, Scouts, and Guides forming up in the pub car-park and marching up the hill, flags waving, to church. These were often on National Prayer Days, during the darker days of the war, when the whole country was asked to pray for the dire state of the nation and the difficulties of wartime. During the earlier part of the war the church bells had been silenced, but the funeral bell was allowed. When someone died, one bell was rung in a sequence to tell everyone in the village there had been a death, two chimes for a man and three for a woman. Everyone drew their curtains on the day of the funeral, and usually there was only the hearse in the cortège, with all the mourners walking in twos following on behind. The big car crawled up the hill at walking pace, followed by everyone in their dark clothes, right down to hats and gloves. The same sequence of chimes, either two or three, accompanied the funeral.

* * *

Farm life opened the eyes of town children to many experiences that were everyday occurrences to countryfolk. For Frank Walsh this included watching a new foal being born in a field without any assistance from a human. Its mother licked it all over before it tried to stand up on splayed legs, falling back a few times before eventually managing to stand up and walk. All this happened in a matter of minutes. On one occasion the members of the family were all roused from their beds in the early hours of the morning to help the vet who had been called out urgently. A cow giving birth was in difficulties, and the calf had to be extricated. Frank could never forget the sight of the vet's arm plunged in up to the elbow, withdrawing a leg and then pulling as hard as he could on a rope tied to the back legs of the calf, until it was dragged from the womb of the mother, who was bellowing loudly with each tug. The sound was echoing within the confines of the straw-strewn floor and whitewashed walls of the cowshed, while the cow began to lick its newly born offspring as if nothing untoward had taken place. Then the family all crawled back into bed, sipping a warm drink, following a discussion of other similar incidents that had occurred in the past.

All this was a revelation to an innocent boy from Hulme. On another occasion, Frank had to look for a young calf that had gone missing. A tour of the farm's fields had been unsuccessful, so the search was widened to those of neighbouring farmers. There was a hollow in one of the fields on the next farm, and lying at the bottom of the incline was what Frank assumed was the missing animal. Gripping his stick firmly, he rushed down the slope and gave what he thought was the calf a few hefty swipes on its backside to make it stand up. It stood up all right, but turned out to be a fully grown bull, complete with a ring through its nose. For a moment bull and boy stood face to face just a few feet away from each other, mesmerized. Frank turned away intending to run, but his legs would not respond to the commands given to them by his frightened brain. Pure terror had by now taken hold of his senses, as he quickly dropped to his knees and began to try and scramble, as best he could, to the top of the slope. When he looked back, the bull was staring at him in sheer amazement. Some years earlier the farmer had been gored by his own bull, and had spent time in hospital. In his overwrought imagination Frank could visualize himself tumbling through the air after being tossed by the bull, and landing back on its horns.

But apart from incidents like these, Frank's sojourn on the farm was mostly enjoyable. One of the large wooden henhouses, that was nearly new and had never been used, was turned into a makeshift theatre, where the children put on home-made plays. This helped to occupy some of their playtime. Riding the pigs in the orchard was another pastime, the winner being the one that could stay on the sow the longest. This was not very long, as there was nothing to hold on to, and the sows bucked and jumped once anyone landed on their backs. Better results were obtained with the farm horse and a makeshift circus ring, a plank, and a bale of hay. One child led the horse, while others took it in turns to run up the plank and jump on, holding on to each other. As there was no saddle, the first one on tended to start sliding as each extra rider was added, and ended up hanging on to the neck, upside down, afraid to let go and fall to the ground because they would probably end up getting trampled.

The horse was used for ploughing, which Frank was allowed to try out, but not very successfully—shouting 'augh' if you wanted the horse to go to the left and 'gee' to the right. Riding it bareback to have new shoes fitted at the smithy and driving the cart during haymaking were also experiences that Frank relished. Many new jobs were undertaken during his evacuation—muck-spreading, tarring the henhouse roofs, taking calves and cows to Preston market to sell, buying new stock, and collecting eggs from the geese. These last were much larger than hen eggs, and a lot harder to obtain. The goose had to be shooed off its nest situated on a small island in one of the ponds, and then kept at bay, along with the gander, while the eggs were collected; he'd get a nasty nip from one or the other if he was not quick off the mark.

* * *

In Scotland, the school in St Andrews that David Hodge and his friend attended was about 3 miles from Balmungo. They had to walk to school and home again. The walk home usually took a long time, and in season the boys picked the wild strawberries and blackberries that grew at the roadside. When they got bored with that, they stopped at a blacksmith's that stood where the road forked, left to Crail, and right to Anstruther. If the blacksmith wasn't shoeing Clydesdale horses he would be repairing farm machinery. He knew everyone on the Balmungo estate, and was always very tolerant of the boys. In turn, they enjoyed visiting him.

When the boys first moved to Balmungo they went to school in a gas showroom for a few days, moved to the Fisher School for a while, and then went on to the Burgh School. Here David was in the same class as his brother George, even though George was three-and-a-half years older. It was run by a teacher called Miss Buckip. She had a large class of between thirty and forty children, with an age range of 6–12. She gradually brought the younger children up to the standard of the older ones, and then taught them all as one class.

At lunchtime most children had sandwiches, and many went down to the harbour to eat them. There they would encounter the children that had also been evacuated from Edinburgh but who stayed at the Priory. They were generally scruffy in appearance, with very worn clothes with holes, but they always seemed happy enough. Most of them carried old syrup tins with wires across the top so that they could be lifted on and off a fire with a stick. Some would collect driftwood from the beach and light a fire, while others collected winkles from the rocks. These were boiled in the syrup tins on the fire and eaten, using a bent pin to remove the winkles from the shells. David could not help wondering what the food was like at the Priory.

*   *   *

Following the fire at the old cinema hall, Judith Grunfeld found that the Olde White House, in North Bridge Street in Shefford, was vacant and to let. It had once been an antique shop, and had two large front windows. All the rooms were small, but the house was attractive. So Judith rented the house, signed the agreement, and her staff moved in. Every corner was used. The entrance hall served as a cloakroom, assembly hall, and debating platform; there was a pantry where food could be stored under lock and key, and there was a separate kitchen, dining-room, and welfare room, as well as two rooms for the housemaster and his family, and another room where some boys were accommodated. There were also several rooms for lessons, and even a bathroom.

The children only slept in the homes of their foster-parents, leaving these at 7.30 in the morning to have breakfast, lunch, tea, and dinner at the Olde White House. A lot of negotiation had to be done with landladies or foster-parents. It was agreed that they would keep 5s. of the official billeting allowance, and that the rest, which ranged from 10s. 6d. to 18s. 6d., depending on the age of the child, would go to the school. In return, the landladies were relieved of the burden of feeding the children and looking after them during the day. It was a satisfactory arrangement, but it needed a good liaison officer, Mr Moser, to make it work. Every single head of the village households had to be contacted. But these household contributions were not sufficient to cover the canteen expenses. So every month Mr Moser went to London to collect donations. The senior boys established a Shefford Fund in order to buy Jewish books, with the money coming from pupils' relatives and friends, and from ex-pupils.

It was at this time that Judith learned to appreciate the comfortable homeliness of small interiors. Whoever came to her office felt at home. Even the small window, showing the derelict corner of the back garden heaped up with broken benches, became a friendly sight when viewed through the flowers on her table. Sometimes other Jewish children, who had been evacuated to non-Jewish schools and houses, came to the office to ask to join the school. In some cases the children's parents had sent them to England, and the children had not seen them since. The last living contact had been the parting embrace when they had left home on the *Kindertransport*, when their mothers' tears had fallen on their cheeks and their fathers' trembling voices had told them to remember to be good. The very last sight of them had been the flutter of the handkerchief, waving goodbye when the train left the station carrying hundreds of children away to safety.

Judith's office was the nerve centre of the school community. It was here that the canteen orders were written out, school reports drawn up, correspondence carried on, and parents, foster-parents, teachers, helpers, Billeting Officers, welfare workers, and pupils interviewed.

* * *

In Lancaster, G. M. Bland was still finding it difficult to recruit householders who were willing to take in evacuees. Although 13,000 leaflets had been given out to householders, only 400 had been returned, and 20 per cent of these were refusals. On 18 April he wrote to the Town Clerk, R. M. Middleton, that, 'as far as I can see, there appears to be a spirit of general resistance to further evacuation at both ends, as I believe that Salford returns of parents willing to register their children for a new evacuation scheme have been very poor'. In the event of a second evacuation, he hoped that a hostel or hostels would be available for children who required medical treatment, and for the temporary accommodation of what were termed 'special cases'.

Bland was so depressed about the evacuation that he began to consider whether some sort of compulsory system should be established. In May he wrote that, 'in general the evacuation scheme is the only part of the Government ARP [air-raid precaution] plans which so far has completely functioned, and as most of us now know much of the theory was found defective in actual practice'. Householders were reluctant to register for the reception of further evacuees. Bland admitted that there were hundreds who had had such unpleasant experiences in the past eight months, both from parents and in some cases from the evacuees themselves, that it was impossible to persuade them to go through it again. Meanwhile, although the weather had improved, the question of footwear and clothing was still taking up a lot of Bland's time. In the early days of the first evacuation, in September 1939, a clothing store had been established at the Old Town Hall. Since then, some 2,300 garments and pairs of boots had been issued, and much help had been given by the WVS. Bland had also kept in touch with the Lancaster UAB, in order to speed up the delivery of clothing and footwear to children in Lancaster whose parents were receiving assistance in Salford.

In June, the Mayor of Lancaster received the Queen's message, to be sent on to the city's citizens:

I wish to mark by this personal message, my appreciation of the service you have rendered to your country in 1939. In the early days of the War you opened your door to strangers who were in need of shelter, & offered to share your home with them. I know that to this unselfish task you have sacrificed much of your own comfort, & that it could not have been achieved without the loyal co-operation of all in your household. By your sympathy you have earned the gratitude of those to whom you have shown hospitality, & by your readiness to serve you have helped the state in a work of great value.

One wonders how this was received, given people's reluctance to go through the experience again. Nevertheless, as the weather improved in the spring of 1940, some of the Salford evacuees were discovering the joys of the countryside. Albert Shaw, for example, aged 11, found that the Lune was a salmon river, where the weirs had been equipped with ladders to enable the fish to make their way up to the spawning-grounds. He and his friends spotted the odd salmon on the riverbank behind fishermen, but never saw one landed. A special sight was to watch the salmon jumping in the evenings, as they made their way upstream near the weirs below the aqueduct. On the canal they once saw a man catching fish with almost every cast. He showed the boys how he was using a silver metal spoon with hooks attached, to attract young pike. There were quite a number already stowed in his rucksack, all intended for his family's dinner. Albert's mother began sending a 6*d.* postal order every week, and Woolworths were selling rods for exactly that amount, so he was soon away catching his first perch. His next catch was an eel, which he stored in a tin box in the shed.

On other occasions, the children took packed lunches to school, and had lessons in the open air. Since all the road-signs had been removed because of the threat of invasion, Albert found that using a one-inch Ordnance Survey map became second nature. The children had geography lessons while potholing, science on the riverbanks, and history at Roman sites in Lancaster and Halton. He took to helping out in the Junior Library in Lancaster, collecting and later shelving books once the staff were satisfied he was reliable. During this period he read every book he could find on astronomy and bees. Another evacuee, Enid Lindsay, discovered that the family she was billeted with had cows, and the children used to help with the milking. They had to empty their wellingtons first in case of cockroaches. Sometimes her foster-father made them sit in a field with their jackets over rabbit-holes waiting to catch them. They never did. Enid thought he just did it to keep them occupied. One day her sister got a bird's egg and pricked a hole in it. Unfortunately she sucked instead of blowing. She was very sick.

* * *

Debate continued in the medical journals. Correspondents in the *British Medical Journal*, for instance, continued to compare the incidence of head lice among the evacuees and the local population. It remained unclear whether there was any truth in the statement that head lice were always a bigger problem after the summer holidays. As in the *Lancet*, the statistics generated by school medical inspections were now viewed with suspicion; commentators wondered how the statistics were collected, and at what stage of the school term. In an editorial, the *Medical Officer* admitted that the results of inspection were disappointing. The same children, the same families, were found to 'be unclean', and the same degree of dirt was recorded at successive inspections. Teachers often claimed that, before inspections, they could list the worst offenders from their own knowledge of children and their homes. The journal noted, therefore, that:

We must admit that the problem of infestation and uncleanliness is deeply rooted. It has taken a war to probe our complacency; the social upheaval of the September evacuation forced us to view uncleanliness not from the depressed standard which we associate with the working-class child, but from the standpoint of reception into middle and upper-class homes. Our previous standards were too low and we are faced with an evil which cannot be corrected overnight to save the face of the powers that be.

The journal claimed that the problem was a social one, bound up with the standard of home life, and it called for the education of parents and children, better housing, and for higher living standards.

In the *Lancet*, a doctor in Derbyshire noted the greater incidence of
nits and head lice in children evacuated from Birmingham and
Manchester compared to the receiving households, and asked why
children couldn't have been cleaned in their home towns; the
system of school hygiene seemed to have failed. In the journal
Social Work, a writer argued that the experiences of the previous six
months had shown the need for a revision of the administration of
social services, and a greater insistence by local authorities on their
statutory duties and powers.

*   *   *

In London, Elizabeth Denby and her colleagues in the Women's
Group Sub-Committee were pressing on with their social survey.
They met again on 2 April. A list of books on the teaching of
hygiene had been circulated, but the women were unable to use the
information from the National Council of Women's questionnaire
on evacuation; the replies were too brief. The pace of their work
was again accelerating. The Sub-Committee now planned all-day
meetings on 22 April, 29 April, and 9 May, when they would take
evidence from witnesses. Meanwhile Amy Sayle was getting information on the Shoreditch evacuees, and Letty Harford was to try
to collate the MOH reports on housing and disinfection. Dora
Ibberson was to get information on the hygiene of girls attending
Ministry of Labour training centres, and Margaret Bondfield was
to approach the Ministry of Health for access to reports on evacuation. A few days later, Dora Ibberson asked a Miss Leslie for
advice as a person of 'great experience of housing conditions & the
habits of dwellers in poor property'. Ibberson asked various questions about sanitation, environment, and education. She admitted
that 'we have heard a number of witnesses without really getting
much light on the sanitary habits in their homes of the mothers &
children who made a scandal in the countryside'.

There was a new Drafting Committee. At the meeting on 31 May (which Elizabeth was unable to attend), the women agreed its procedure for drawing conclusions from the expert evidence that it had heard; Letty Harford should analyse this under the heading 'Facts, Causes, and Remedies'. They also agreed the title for their report, and the main subject headings. Thus, the section 'Facts' included personal hygiene, the presence of 'vermin' and the lack of cleanliness, dirt diseases, clothing, 'sanitary habits', urination, and defecation. The sections 'Causes' and 'Remedies' covered such issues as economic insecurity, housing, health, education, and 'character'. Cicely McCall of the National Federation of Women's Institutes reported on a study on the Education Acts; the women had wanted to discover what the education system lacked in terms of the teaching of mothercraft and housecraft. As we have seen, the Women's Institutes had published their own study of evacuation, *Town Children Through Country Eyes*. The two organizations agreed to keep in close contact. In general, the Sub-Committee planned the outline of their report, and arranged for the subediting of each section. Subsequently Letty Harford prepared a summary of the evidence from the twenty-seven witnesses, and this was considered at a meeting on 25 June. Dora Ibberson agreed to draw up a draft of the report, including some recommendations.

* * *

In Whitehall there were some signs of a more sympathetic approach to the evacuees on the part of Sir Maurice Holmes and his colleagues. This was partly in response to organizations such as the South Wales Children's Nutrition Council, and writers in the journal *Education*, which had continued to point out the condition of the evacuees and the inadequacy of Government circulars. In the Evacuation Areas, the School Medical Service had been slow to resume work; by April 1940 only half the pre-war

clinics and hospitals had reopened. In the same month Herwald
Ramsbotham had become President of the Board of Education,
following the resignation of Earl De La Warr. The position was
still regarded as a political backwater. But unlike his predecessors,
who had been keen to move on to more prestigious positions,
Ramsbotham remained at the Ministry and initiated important
reforms. Born in 1887 in Cholsey, Berkshire, Ramsbotham came
from a distinguished Lancashire family noted for public service.
He had been educated at Uppingham School and University
College, Oxford, and subsequently practised as a barrister, but
served during the First World War and was awarded the Military
Cross. Intent on a career in politics, he was finally elected Conservative MP for Lancaster in 1929, and became Parliamentary
Secretary to Lord Halifax, President of the Board of Education,
in 1931. He therefore had earlier experience of this particular
department.

Kenneth Mellanby had now completed a draft of his report on
the incidence of head lice. He noted from the evidence of evacuees
that there seemed to be a serious discrepancy between the official
statistics of the School Medical Service and the observations made
in the Reception Areas. Mellanby concluded that there was a high
degree of infestation with head lice in the cities; girls were more
frequently infested than boys; and the highest rate of infestation
was found in children under 5. Infestation among males decreased
from 40 per cent among 3-year-olds to a low incidence among
young adults, while in females there was no decrease before the age
of 13, and girls over 13 still had a high incidence. Mellanby found
that in his rural areas, which had a low incidence and where examinations by district nurses were more efficient, statistics were more
accurate. In the cities, on the other hand, he found that most of the
affected children had not been detected by medical inspections,

and that as less than a minute was spent on each child this was not surprising. Moreover, he also argued that infestation did not increase in the summer months. Rural areas had lower rates of infestation, as parents considered it 'a disgrace' for their children to have head lice, whereas in the cities less importance was attached to this. In addition, in the countryside one person combined the functions of school nurse, district nurse, and health visitor, and they dealt with smaller numbers of families. Mellanby recommended that efforts should concentrate on older girls, since this would also reduce the incidence among pre-school children; teachers and nurses should cooperate more effectively; and legal changes might be necessary.

Dr J. Alison Glover, the Senior Medical Officer at the Board, wrote on 25 June of the Mellanby survey that 'this is a most illuminating and painstaking report completed in a remarkably short time…I strongly recommend publication even in the paper shortage of the present time'. Glover, at 63, was slightly older than his colleague Cecil Maudslay. Born in 1876, he had been educated at St Paul's School, St John's College, Cambridge, and Guy's Hospital. He had served in the Boer War, and again during the First World War with the Royal Army Medical Corps in Malta and France. Medically trained, but employed as a civil servant, he had also been elected a Fellow of the Royal Society of Medicine.

On 17 May one of Holmes's colleagues had written of clothing and footwear, that 'there can be no doubt that quite a large number of children would suffer if provision were left to the parents'. But it was on the issue of school meals that progress was most marked. Herwald Ramsbotham had told Clement Attlee, Lord Privy Seal from the start of the Coalition Government in May and Chairman of the Food and Home Policy Committees of the War Cabinet, that if communal feeding for children in their schools could become firmly established and popularized it would be an important educational advance. In the Food Policy Committee, Attlee himself argued of school meals, that 'any attempt to discriminate on the grounds of means causes friction, involves expensive machinery and gives to the whole scheme an eleemosynary atmosphere [i.e. one dependent on charity] which will make it repulsive'.

There were also now plans to provide free or cheap milk for expectant and nursing mothers and for pre-school children. The Ministry of Food would bear the cost, but the scheme would be administered on its behalf by local authorities. Income scales for schoolchildren remained more severe than for pre-school children; it was more difficult for them to receive free milk. But civil servants increasingly realized that poverty was closely associated with large families. Incomes that were adequate for small families were inadequate for large ones. In wartime, unemployment, the main cause of poverty, was much reduced, and poverty was due therefore to low wages combined with large families. Therefore, on 19 June, the Ministry of Health announced a national scheme for free and cheap milk to all expectant and nursing mothers and children under 5 years of age. This superseded the arrangements that had been announced in August 1939. Milk would be free if the joint income of parents fell below 40s. per week, plus 6s. for each non-earning dependant. The whole cost, including the administration, would be borne by the Exchequer. Tentative steps were being taken towards a welfare state.

8

Spitfire Summer

In the summer of 1940 the international situation took another turn for the worse. The British Expeditionary Force was stranded in France, and Dunkirk was evacuated on 4 June. Following the criticism of Chamberlain during the Norway debate, Winston Churchill had become Prime Minister. Only about 460,000 children were now away from the urban areas felt to be at risk of bombing, and about half of these had been evacuated as recently as May–July. As the likelihood of air attack and the threat of invasion increased, there was a small flow of population towards the west. Unlike in September 1939, there was no mass evacuation; instead, there was a daily or weekly stream towards areas of relative safety. Those children who had been evacuated in September 1939, and who were still in the Reception Areas, were affected by the war in different ways. The bombing of London began in September, setting off the second major wave of evacuation, the first to take place under battle conditions. This second wave was smaller than the first, and about 1,250,000 people were moved. But September 1940 also brought German air attacks on provincial cities, marking the start of the Blitz.

* * *

It was only on 2 June 1940 that Mary-Rose Benton's school in Broadstairs on the south coast was finally evacuated. Before setting out for Ramsgate the children attended a goodbye service at the local church, Our Lady, Star of the Sea. As they came out, some boys laughed at them because they had seen Mary-Rose's mother crying. None of the children knew it at the time, but it was to be the last day they would spend together as a family. They had already said goodbye to their lodger, Mr Bailey, and had spent the day getting up, going to Mass, and getting on each other's nerves. Mary-Rose recalled of her mother: 'She kissed us all goodbye on 2 June 1940, and parting came, abrupt as death.'

Mary-Rose and her brother Jimmy left the house first, and were told to go and wait at the bus-stop for everyone else. She cried out when they had to let a bus go by—Mary-Rose had a thing about missed buses—but when the conductress heard her cry she stopped the bus and they got on. The children milled about on Ramsgate Station with French soldiers who had left the beaches of Dunkirk, and were now to form the Free French Army under General de Gaulle. They then filled the trains that were leaving. The children each took their own mug, and food for the journey, which they carried in a pillowcase; this was to be used for their beds when they got to their billets. As in September 1939, parents were not told where their children were going nor how long the journey would be. A boy sitting opposite Mary-Rose in the carriage started chatting in a friendly way, and when she took out a bar of chocolate and began eating it he eyed her keenly and said, 'Would you sell me a square of that for a penny?' Since Mary-Rose and her brothers and sister had brought plenty of food with them, she was happy to do so. The boy was delighted; he had probably not had breakfast. This was Mary-Rose's first time on a train. She knew it was going to go very fast, and wondered how they would be able to keep their balance, expecting to be thrown about by the sheer speed. However, this was an adventure, and she loved the motion. Inevitably she became bored with the length of the journey, though, and grew tired after several hours. Some children were lucky enough to be taken off at the first stop.

The children eventually reached the town of Stafford in the Midlands, exhausted and bewildered. They were marched from the station to the Market Place, where they were each given a packet of biscuits and a bottle of milk. There were hundreds of children, many crying and calling for their mothers. The sights and sounds were harrowing; some of the evacuees were not more than 4 years old. Leaving her mother was not a problem for Mary-Rose. At 7, she was ready to face the world, a world in which she had absolute faith and confidence. She later wrote: 'Most of us recognise a time in our lives when we were flung out of Eden. I didn't know it, but this was mine.' The children were taken from the Market Place to a hall, to await distribution to billets. Neither Jimmy nor Mary-Rose were hungry enough for the biscuits and milk, so their brother Billy wisely took them, not knowing when he might eat again.

Jimmy and Billy stayed together, but Mary-Rose was separated from them because of a shortage of bedroom accommodation. Now on her own, she was taken by car to an address in Coton Fields, at first by mistake to 31 Blakiston Street, to an old couple. They seemed baffled by her arrival, but gave her a meal and showed her where she was to sleep. When she woke up the next morning, for the first time without her family around her, she felt somehow that the shine had gone off her adventure. Mary-Rose recalled: 'Just one family member would have been enough, to remind me of the old securities, family strife and all. All this was gone, and an alarming vacuum took its place. My mouth began to go square with dismay. I felt deserted and bleak. In a terrified attempt to stem the tidal wave of grief, I stifled the tears, and busied myself getting dressed, got my small handbag out of the drawer, and went downstairs.' The context had changed, but the experiences of the children evacuated in 1940 were very similar to those of their counterparts who went away in September 1939.

* * *

In Essex, Juliet Norden's family had taped the windows of the house with strips of brown paper, to prevent shattering if they were bombed. They had also put up heavy curtains for the blackout. Juliet was fascinated by the barrage-balloons floating in the sky, and pleasantly surprised to find that there were not men fighting in the streets with guns, which was what she had imagined war would be like. Her mother returned to nursing locally, and became a member of the ARP. By June, France was occupied and a German invasion of England feared, so children on the south coast were to be evacuated as well, as Mary-Rose had already discovered. This included the Norden family. Juliet's mother was still living in Westcliff, but her father had already left for the Midlands, as (being Jewish) he was afraid of being captured by the Germans. Although Juliet did not know it, her parents were never to live together again.

The day of the evacuation was terrifying to a 7-year-old, and very confusing. Juliet would never forget it. The children each had a small rucksack, made by their mothers. Juliet's contained a small book, a favourite toy, a small teddy-bear, an apple and packet of sandwiches, a sponge-bag, change of underclothes, and socks. The children were each given a postcard to send home, as the parents had no idea of their destination. Name-tags were attached to their coats, and they carried their gas-masks. They knew what to do as they had previously had rehearsals at school, but for some time now the school had been closed as it was considered too dangerous for the children to be far from home. Instead, they had been having lessons from their teachers, in small groups, in the homes of different pupils.

Juliet and the other children went to their former school where everyone had gathered and they were shepherded onto buses. The mothers and children were in tears, and the buses drove in a circle so that the children could wave a last farewell, but there was no sign of Juliet's mother, who obviously hadn't realised this was to happen and had gone straight home. Juliet felt frightened—why wasn't she there, where had she gone? The buses took the children to Southend Railway Station, where hundreds more children were waiting, and eventually they were herded onto a train, packed like sardines. The journey seemed endless. At some of the larger stations WVS helpers handed the children drinks and sandwiches, which were welcome as they had eaten their own food soon after setting off. They were also thirsty, as they had not been allowed to take drinks onto the train. Their train kept being shunted into sidings to let scheduled trains through, and this made the journey even longer.

Eventually, hours later, tired, grubby, and dishevelled, the children arrived at Derby Station, where buses were waiting. Juliet's older brother, Bryan, tried to stay with his sisters, but was separated. Juliet was devastated and inconsolable, and wanted to go home. Bryan went on the bus to Hartshorne, near Swadlincote, while Juliet and Myriam were taken to Overseal, near Burton-on-Trent. They were taken to the village hall, where they were to be chosen by foster-parents. As they were viewed, the children felt as if they were in a cattle market. Eventually a childless couple called the Butlers chose Juliet and Myriam. There weren't many children left by then. The first night was dreadful. The children couldn't understand what the Butlers were saying to them; they spoke so differently it was like a foreign language. Juliet was too tired and upset to eat anything, she just wanted a drink; and tripe—which she had never seen before—was put on the table in front of her In the bedroom the light-bulb had been removed, so there was no need for blackout curtains. As Juliet lay crying in the bed she shared with Myriam, she clutched her teddy tightly and sobbed into his soft fur.

The toilet at the Butlers was downstairs, so the children were given a chamber pot in the bedroom. They were told that if they used the toilet or potty, they must not use paper. They couldn't cope with this, so would take toilet paper upstairs, use the potty, and throw the paper out of the window. They weren't to know that there was a water tank on a flat roof outside the bedroom window, and all the paper landed in there. Not surprisingly perhaps, they were called dirty little evacuees. Some of the teachers from the school in Westcliff had been evacuated with the children, and next morning all the pupils and teachers met in the village hall, where the children were asked the names of their foster-parents. Again the different accents of the local people caused confusion.

Mr Butler was a coalminer, and when he got home from work he was black from head to toe. The children had never seen anything like this before, and were fascinated. He would strip off in front of the fire, and wash at the kitchen sink. The Butlers were religious, and the children had to attend chapel with them every Sunday. They all had to look smart, and dress in their best clothes; Mrs Butler bought Juliet a pair of black patent-leather shoes to wear only for chapel. She was proud of them as she had never had posh shoes before, only practical ones. Juliet and Myriam were not allowed to play outside on Sundays. Never having had children, the Butlers did not know how to treat them. They were strict and appeared to resent the children being there. Juliet's mother sent parcels, but these were opened by the Butlers before the children had even seen them. Once, in the box-room, Juliet and Myriam found a toy rabbit and cat intended for them. When Juliet's mother came to visit and saw how unhappy the children were, she had them moved. Juliet had to leave her new shoes behind.

* * *

One day an official letter from the Board of Education arrived at Judith Grunfeld's office in Shefford, saying that His Majesty's Inspector would visit the school on the following Monday to observe the classes during school hours, and that he would require access to all the files and records. The schoolrooms were all dispersed, with each one in a different church or chapel a mile or half-a-mile apart. And as these halls did not really belong to the school, the teachers took no pride in them. They could not exhibit any work on the walls, and could not even leave any drawings on the blackboard. The pupils had learnt to speak English reasonably well, but they could not enter competitions open to the local children, and so they had not received any distinctions, apart from in cross-country races and football matches. Some of the teachers, although qualified on the Continent, were still seen as foreigners, with different accents. What preparations could Judith make? All she could tell the pupils was to make sure they had a good breakfast and to say their prayers well, because this visit might decide much of the school's future. They should all be in time for school and have a good look at their French textbook, which had been compiled and written by the very same inspector.

But when Judith left her house next morning at 8.15 to drive in her little Morris to the Clifton Church Hall 2 miles away, she found that the car would not start. Her baby had not slept well, the housekeeper had overslept, and the grandmother was fussing around her. There was no telephone nearby to ring for a taxi, and the only neighbour, who was normally very helpful, had gone out to work in his car. At that moment a lorry laden with bricks came into sight. Judith waved frantically, the lorry stopped, and she tried to pull herself up to the seat next to the driver; it was so high she had to be hauled up by two strong, dust-covered arms. On arriving in Clifton, she jumped down just in time to see the black-clad figure of a man with a bowler hat and a lady of academic appearance getting out of a shiny black car. Here were the visitors who had come to inspect the school: Mr Collins and Miss Whittaker.

But as soon as Judith saw Mr Collins, a wave of relief went through her. He greeted her with some unassuming remarks aimed to put her at ease from the very first moment. In the little vestibule of the church they sat opposite each other, and he asked Judith many questions about the numbers and ages of the children, school conditions, and timetables. Meanwhile they heard the footsteps of the children who were arriving, subdued noise, and whispers. The two classes taught in this particular church hall were getting ready for assembly, and a prefect came to announce that the school was waiting for the head. They went in. About fifty boys and girls were standing in rows, looking neat and fresh from the country air.

Mr Collins listened to the lessons, examined exercise books, watched the children at work, then went to the other church halls around the district where the other classes were taught. He interviewed the teachers, watched the serving of the food at midday, and saw the supervision of homework after school hours. He saw the welfare room and the pantry, and read the 'White House Regulations' pinned to the wall in the entrance hall. He made his observations, wrote his notes, asked some questions here and there, but made no comments. With Miss Whittaker, he spent two days in and around Shefford. At the end of the second day the two sat in conference in Judith's office for an hour, then at last the door opened and she was invited in. Mr Collins said:

Both my colleague and I are deeply impressed by what we have seen. This is a splendid school—I should say an heroic school. You are doing the

most extraordinary work under the most adverse circumstances. Your
teachers are admirable in their devotion. Your pupils are keen and on the
whole up to standard. Your spirit of loyalty to your educational programme and to your religious tenets is something that has evoked our
whole-hearted admiration. We want to help you and we shall do all we can
for you.

He advised Judith to write to the Board of Education and put in a
request for a better-equipped centre. He suggested that she time
her letter so that it arrived on the same day as his favourable
report.

This visit gave Judith and her colleagues the confidence that
what they were doing was right. Following it, they got a large new
dining-hall, a prefabricated building, and this was put in the middle
of the Olde White House garden. Lunch could now be served in
one shift rather than several, and they had a hall for debates, table-
tennis tournaments, school concerts, and celebrations. On week-
days the children went there after school for tea and homework,
and there was always a teacher on duty to supervise them, help
them with their work, and chat to them. At the end of the first year
after evacuation Judith gave an address to the school. She said that
they had now had one full year's work as a community in Shefford.
The children had grown and matured, and it had been a heroic
period. Judith had been in London the previous week, and had
seen air-raid wardens the same age as the senior boys calmly at
work. In Shefford too, the children had played their part nobly. In
reality there was a fire burning from one end of Europe to the
other, and synagogues had been burnt down. She suggested that
the slogan for the second year should be, 'if you have succeeded
already, keep on trying new methods, new ways and improve-
ments'. The 140 young girls and boys would have to think of ways
to strengthen the community. But the children themselves had

realized they would have to shoulder these responsibilities, and the adults were proud of them.

*   *   *

In Kent, George Prager had moved from Sandown Lodge to the clubhouse at the golf course. He and Norman had such wonderful meals there that they felt they could not do better staying at a first-class hotel. But they were only there for two weeks. Gordon's father had joined the RAF, and with the situation in France fast deteriorating, the boys still in Sandwich were put on a train that was to transport them to South Wales.

George boarded the train with about forty boys and four masters. The train journey took most of the day, travelling along the south coast. George had never travelled so far on a train before, and he and most of the boys considered it a great adventure. They stopped for a short time for refreshments at one station where, on another platform, was a train crowded with battle-weary soldiers. They were being given cups of tea and cigarettes. Later, like Mary-Rose Benton, George realized that these were men who had been evacuated from Dunkirk. By this time many people had dispensed with their gas-masks, either forgetting them or finding that carrying a cardboard box over one shoulder was just a nuisance. Instead, the cardboard boxes and leatherette cases became convenient containers in which to carry lunchtime sandwiches.

George's stay in Whitchurch, a suburb of Cardiff, was very brief; all he could remember was a visit to Llandaff Cathedral. The main school in Gillingham had already been evacuated to the village of Rhymney, at the head of one of the valleys between Merthyr Tydfil and Tredegar, and on 8 June those of the boys still in Cardiff were uprooted once again to join the rest of the school. By the time they arrived most of the billets near the school they were to attend had been taken, and the late arrivals were billeted further away. George's new address was Pen-y-Dre, at the northern end of the village. He had not met Welsh people before, and so was unprepared for their accents and sing-song style of speech, which mixed English words with a selection of Welsh ones. Everyone was friendly, and would call across the road to the evacuees, but sometimes he could not understand the words that they used. One evening a neighbour called out to George and, apparently pointing northwards, said 'North Star'. George looked up in the direction in which he seemed to be pointing, but could see nothing through the clouds. Puzzled, he mentioned the incident to another neighbour, who laughed and said: 'He was only waving to you and wishing you goodnight. The Welsh for goodnight is "Nos Da".'

George's new foster-parents, Mr and Mrs Knight, lived in a council house typical of many built in the 1930s. Mr Knight was a guard on the railway, while Mrs Knight was a housewife. Although they were kind, George felt that the adults could not let the two boys get close to them; they were kept at a distance, and he never discovered their Christian names. Mr and Mrs Knight used only the odd word in Welsh, but a few of the other boys learned some basic Welsh so that they could at least pass the time of day with the local people. The school that they attended was called 'The Lawn', and was situated at the southern end of the village. Again, accommodating the pupils of two schools in premises intended for one proved impossible, so at first each worked a half-shift in the school until extra accommodation was found. The Workmen's Institute, Masonic Hall, and Social Centre were all pressed into use, but until they could be made available games, mountain walks, and swimming at the pool in nearby Tredegar filled up the time. The basement of the Workmen's Institute also contained several full-size snooker tables. Their early days were fraught with danger when the boys ventured south to Pontlottyn, since they were met with a hail of stones, pieces of slate and coal, and bits of brick. But on discovering that the 'Londoners' could give as well as they could take, the local boys called a truce and an end to the conflict was agreed. Friendly relationships were formed between the two groups.

About half of Pen-y-Dre had houses on only one side, with open mountainside on the other, while the other half had houses on both. About 200 yards away on the mountainside, where a metal pipe had been driven in, a spring rose out of the ground from which water could be fetched. The water from the pipe was icy cold, crystal-clear, safe to drink, and constantly flowing. From this spot a well-worn path led over the mountain to the Tredegar Valley. This was to become a favourite walk for George in summer and autumn. Sometimes he saw groups of local men gambling at cards, with look-outs posted so that a warning could be passed on if a policeman appeared on the scene. Exploring Rhymney and the surrounding area was fascinating and full of adventure. The boys found the old ironworks on one side of the road to Rhymney Bridge, and the river on the other. At the site they discovered the remains of an iron furnace, with an old and rusty iron-ore truck still standing on a short section of railway track, and pieces of pig iron lying around. In the rock-pools of the river they were able to fish and catch sticklebacks. At Rhymney Bridge Railway Station it was possible to stand in three counties at once—Glamorganshire, Monmouthshire, and Brecknockshire met on the station platform. From just north of there it was possible to see all the way to the Brecon Beacons. Sheep and ponies could be seen almost anywhere: on the mountains, in the fields, and on the roads.

*   *   *

The Leicestershire village of Groby escaped the bombing but was on the route of German planes making for cities in the Midlands and on the west coast. Maggie Quinn was often roused at night

1. Elizabeth Denby collaborated with the architect Maxwell Fry on Kensal House, Kensington, which was opened in March 1937.

2. Eddy Rowley (4) (second left), Jean Rowley (7), and Joyce Rowley (11), with their parents, North Wales, August 1939.

3. David Hodge (second left) with his brother George, and his mother and father just before the War.

4. Evacuees including Dave Pinchon (capless far left at rear).

5. Dr H. King (later MP and Speaker in the House of Commons) leading Taunton's to Central Station, Southampton, 2 September 1939.

6. Dave Pinchon (right), Bobby Mills, and the Playdons, Bournemouth, September 1939.

7. The suitcase that George Prager took with him to Sandwich, and later to Rhymney.

MEDWAY TOWNS EVACUATION SCHEME

Full Name of Child *George Prager*
BLOCK LETTERS
Home Address *84 Kingswood Rd*
Gillingham

Name of School *County Grammar* Gillingham
School Number *Form IIB*

Group Number

8. George Prager's evacuee label.

9. Judith Grunfeld and the former Shefford evacuees.

10. G. M. Bland leading evacuees from the Castle Station, Lancaster, to find their new homes in the city, 1 September 1939.

11. Evacuees from Seedley School in Salford leaving the Dispersal Centre at Greaves School (Lancaster) to find their new homes, 1 September 1939.

12. Juliet, Bryan, and Myriam Norden, October 1938.

13. Maggie Quinn.

14. Mary-Rose Benton.

15. Carl Coates, his sister June, and their father on the only visit that Carl's parents made to Easton.

16. Carl Coates with Tom Browett holding the horse used for pulling the trap for bread and groceries.

17. Sir Maurice Holmes.

18. The Branksome Dene Hotel,
Bournemouth, as Zetland Court (1983).

19. Frank Walsh and his grandson Liam on their return to the Clarkson Green
Farm, Catforth, August 1999.

and spent many hours under the table in the living-room, which was deemed to be the safest place to shelter. The family listened intently for the sound of the planes' engines, distinguishing easily the repetitive 'drum-drum' of the German bombers from the single note of the British planes. It was an anxious time, as they could see from the red glow in the sky where the bombs had been dropped, so could identify cities such as Birmingham and Coventry from the direction. Of course Maggie also worried about her own mother and father, and her brothers and sister. She later wrote: 'To this day I cannot bear low-flying aircraft at night and give an inward sigh of relief when they have passed over safely.' There were stories of enemy planes flying low and firing at people, and the children were taught at school to throw themselves flat on the ground any time they were aware of a low-flying plane. Maggie did that herself more than once.

Double summertime had been introduced to help the farmers. Many of the men in the village came home from work, and then went to help in the fields, often until after ten at night if the weather was dry. Maggie and the other children had great fun riding on the empty carts from the farm to the fields, and then walking back for another ride. On Chapel Hill one horse was insufficient to pull a loaded cart, and a second would be hitched in front to get the cart up the steep, rough lane to the farm. A huge black shire-horse called Spider was used for this job. He was enormous, and Mark Burdett said to keep well away from him as he had a nasty temper. Maggie thought Spider was just still young and a bit spirited, and she loved and admired him because he was so beautiful. The corn was stacked in the farmyards, and later a steam-driven threshing machine arrived and went from farm to farm. Everyone joined in to get the job done as quickly as possible, and Mr Burdett helped out again— hard work when every sheaf had to be moved by pitchfork.

Mr Biggs, a nearby farmer, turned his hay dressed in a cream linen blazer and a broad-brimmed hat—every inch the gentleman farmer.

* * *

But farms could also be dangerous places for children. While playing in a stable on the farm in Balmungo with George, Peter, and local children, David Hodge had a bad accident. They were climbing a ladder onto an open-ended hayloft, then jumping from the edge of the loft on to a huge pile of hay. It was great fun, but there was a queue at the jumping-off point. David became impatient, moved along a few feet, and jumped. On the way down he came into contact with a harness hook which ripped a one-and-a-half-inch tear in his cheek, just below his right eye. It bled heavily, and when David saw all the blood he panicked and started to yell his head off.

Hendry Ballantyne heard the commotion and came running. He managed to staunch the flow of blood, and calmed David down a bit. As Hendry was the chauffeur, he kept the car in the garage opposite his house. There was a phone-line from his house to the 'big house', as the Nish residence was known, but no outside line. Hendry phoned the big house and asked permission to use the car to take David to hospital in St Andrews. The answer was 'No'. Hendry then asked Mr Murray, the farmer, if he could borrow his car, whereupon Murray said he would drive David to the hospital himself.

Mr Murray put David in his car, and they set off. By the time they had arrived at hospital the wound under David's eye had stopped bleeding. The farmer decided that it was no longer necessary to go to the hospital, so he drove back to the farm and dropped David at Hendry's door. Hendry was astounded, and immediately phoned his doctor from a neighbour's house. The doctor drove to

Balmungo from St Andrews and stitched up the wound by the light of a Tilley-lamp. He did a first-class job: the wound healed, and left no scar.

* * *

In Lancashire, Frank Walsh, and Ronnie, the Cornalls' grandson, had discovered that in the village of Catforth there was a large poultry farm. To make some extra pocket money, he and Ronnie went over to give a hand with the chores. The different enclosures with cockerels, hens, geese, turkeys, and all manner of fowl were all in orderly rows, with a wide path down the middle of the open pens. Frank and Ronnie stood with two shovels in the rear of an open-backed lorry loaded with feed. One of the farmhands drove slowly along the line of pens on both sides while the boys shovelled the chicken-feed over the top of the pens, left and right, until the lorry was empty. Then it was back again to load up and finish off all the other rows.

In the barn there were two huge incubators that held large wooden trays with holes in the base ready to be filled with eggs. A powerful hand-lamp would then be passed underneath each tray of eggs to show the outline of the yolk. This revealed all the fertile eggs by revealing a number of dark spots. Those eggs without spots were put to one side. When the trays were full up with fertile eggs, they all went into the incubator, which had a rotating centre wheel. The incubation period lasted a few days, until the eggs began to hatch out. When the time was up, Frank, Ronnie, and the farm-hand looked through the windows of the incubators, watching the trays rotating inside the heated compartment and waiting for the hatching to begin. First one chick would break through its shell, followed by another, then suddenly all the eggs began breaking open, with the chicks walking about inside the ridged trays. The incubator was stopped, the big doors opened, and the trays taken out one at a time. On long tables there were large cardboard boxes stacked up, with air-holes in the side. Each tray was then placed onto the table ready for sorting. The hens went to the right and the cocks to the left. Eventually all the trays were empty and all the chicks neatly ensconced in the cardboard containers. The boxes were then stacked into a waiting van that took them to the railway station. Frank's job was to clear the trays of eggshells and wash them in water and disinfectant, leaving them to dry and then be made ready for the next batch of eggs to be processed. The two incubators operated in sequence, so that as one finished the other one was halfway through the hatching process.

Another of the jobs was holding a bowl of 'Izal' disinfectant and a handful of cotton wool after a large litter of piglets had been born. The farmhands took small wooden stools into the sty and sat on them, while Frank caught the squealing piglets one by one and passed them to the farmhands. The piglets were each castrated with a razor-blade, and it was Frank's job to apply the disinfectant to the wound with the cotton wool.

The one thing that Frank's family had in Hulme that the farm did not was a flush toilet. On the farm there was a plank of wood with a hole in the middle. (A second toilet, never used while Frank was there, had two holes in the plank.) A large bucket stood underneath the plank, and removing a large slate from the back of the building allowed this to be emptied. Frank and Ronnie used to wait until Frank's sister Marjorie was inside, then Ronnie would give a signal from the corner, whereupon Frank removed the slate and thrust up a handful of nettles. On one occasion Ronnie gave the signal, Frank removed the slate, and pushed up the nettles, only to find to his alarm that the farmhand was sitting there. This custom stopped immediately, and Frank's backside was sore and stinging for quite a while, but not from any nettles.

In July all this came to an end when Frank returned home to Hulme, just in time to experience the first bombs falling on Manchester. One dropped only 40 yards from his family's news-agents on City Road, where it ignited a gas main. Now the green fields of the Catforth farm seemed very far away. Frank found it hard going back to Manchester. His family lived in a two-up, two-down, and everything seemed smaller and dirtier. The house seemed to have shrunk. Frank had only been on the farm at Catforth for ten months, but the Cornalls had been very good to the evacuees, and had treated him like one of the family. Living on the farm had taught him a lot, widened his experience of life, and in many ways assisted his passage into adulthood. Frank later wrote that, 'coming from a city where the only green grass was in local parks, this was something else—an entirely different world'.

* * *

When Juliet Norden and her sister Myriam moved from the Butlers, they went to stay with Mr and Mrs Eyre, who lived on the outskirts of the village of Overseal, overlooking open fields. They had a daughter called Dorothy aged 18, and a son, Frank, aged 14. Dorothy went out to work, and Frank had just left school. He was a butcher's delivery boy, and had a bicycle with a large basket on the front; the bicycle often tipped over and the meat fell out. Mr and Mrs Eyre were kind and, being older, were almost like grandparents to the girls. Once, after doing some sewing, Juliet left a needle on a chair, and Mr Eyre got it stuck in his bottom. He had to suffer the indignity of having it removed by his wife, but the couple weren't even cross. On the way home from school Juliet used to run through mounds of lime, piled up in the fields. But she was never told off. Occasionally Mrs Eyre took the children on the bus to do some shopping in Burton-on-Trent. The smell of the malt from the city's breweries was a lasting memory.

On 6 August Juliet had her eighth birthday. Her mother couldn't be there because of the air battles overhead, but her father came, Myriam was there, and Bryan cycled over from Hartshorne. The four sat in a field in brilliant sunshine, just talking. It was then that Juliet's father made the children promise never to tell anyone that he was German and Jewish; the children were instructed to say that he was Dutch. Later Juliet was to break that promise. Bryan cycled over to see Myriam and Juliet whenever he could, and told them that in his village the local boys lay in wait for the evacuees, chasing them with sticks and calling them names, such as 'horrid little vaccies'. Things became worse for Bryan after their father visited. Local children noticed his German accent, and as he tended to sit in the middle of a field during the day on his own, writing while waiting for Bryan to come out of school, the boys even thought he might be a German spy.

Before they had left home the children's parents had applied to send them on the Overseas Evacuation Scheme, and they had been selected to go to Canada. They even got as far as having a medical examination in Derby. But when *The City of Benares* passenger liner was sunk in September 1940 en route to Canada, the Overseas Evacuation Scheme was stopped. Instead, Juliet and Myriam sat at night in Dorothy's bedroom, watching the air-raids over Derby when they were supposed to be sheltering under the table. Juliet found it exciting, but she was apprehensive too. They could see the searchlights with aeroplanes caught in the beams, hear the anti-aircraft guns, the sound of the bombs exploding, and, most frightening of all, the drone of German planes.

*   *   *

A few weeks after war was declared in September 1939, when the expected invasion had not happened, the schools had reopened in Birmingham, and Eddy Rowley had been able to start as one of the infants. It was only in August 1940 that the bombing of the city began. Most nights, Eddy and her family heard the sound of the sirens and went outside to the Anderson Shelter which her father had erected in the garden. It got worse as the weeks went by. Birmingham was heavily targeted because of the war work carried out in the local factories. Moreover, the family lived in Sparkbrook, which was a particularly hard-hit part of the city. The BSA (Birmingham Small Arms) factory was a short walk away (it was later destroyed by a direct hit), and there were lots of other, smaller factories. There was a huge railway marshalling yard at the bottom of Grace Road. The family was in the middle of a prime target area, and experienced heavy bombing.

* * *

By the summer of 1940 the Board of Education was coming under fire for having failed to provide direction and planning during the evacuation of September 1939. In Whitehall, Sir Maurice and his colleagues were unsure what to do about the Mellanby report on head lice. Sir Arthur MacNalty, the Chief Medical Officer, argued that the report should not be published, partly because of the paper shortage, and instead should be summarized in the next annual *Health of the School Child* report. Other civil servants agreed that this was not the right moment to publish; it was pointless ridding children of head lice if they were immediately reinfected, and there was far too little emphasis on the homes that the children came from. But Dr Alison Glover thought that it was unlikely that publication of the report would discredit the School Medical Service, the school system, or the Board of Education. On the contrary, it would exonerate the School Medical Service in showing that the problem lay outside its reach; it would suggest that more attention should be given to pre-school children; and publication would indicate a frankness and willingness to acknowledge criticism.

Sir Maurice wrote to Herwald Ramsbotham, the President of the Board, on 15 August that the Mellanby report showed a state of affairs that was 'a disgrace to a civilised country', and that the remedy lay not in circulars or papers, but 'in bringing home to the public the fact that lousiness is a disgusting state and that it can be cured by simple measures'. For this reason, the report should not only be published but should be the subject of a press conference to ensure that it received the widest possible publicity. As far as head lice were concerned, it was apparent that routine school medical inspections were too short, and the solution was in fewer and more thorough inspections. But head lice were prevalent in pre-school children, the Ministry of Health was complacent, and the powers of local authorities were neither wide enough nor properly used. Holmes suggested that Ramsbotham should discuss the issue with Malcolm Macdonald, the Minister for Health; the issue was so serious it merited an independent conference attended by both ministers.

A House of Lords debate on 9 July had highlighted that the evacuees' footwear and clothing continued to pose problems. The Earl of Malmesbury, for example, claimed that one Evacuation Area had sent a large number of children to a Reception Area, where they had arrived in a disgraceful condition: 'their boots were very bad and their clothing was very bad; everything they had wanted mending or replacing.' The Earl of Radnor said he knew that many householders had been upset by the frequent visits of parents, and these people should be expected to pay more towards the upkeep of their children. Organizations such as the Association of Municipal Corporations passed resolutions that LEAs should have the power to provide footwear and clothing for children who were unable to attend school or take full advantage of the education provided for them. Civil servants admitted that their position was based on the principle that providing clothing and footwear was the responsibility of the parents, and it was only when the parent failed that the state should step in. In particular, the Treasury would oppose any scheme whereby clothing was provided for evacuees without recovering the cost from parents. Meanwhile, officials from the LCC asked for another £5,000 for the coming winter. They argued that the prospect of raising funds in London, bearing in mind other appeals and the general situation, was bleak. Progress on school meals was more marked than on footwear and clothing.

* * *

One study, by Magdalen Vernon of the Cambridge Psychological Laboratory, and funded by the Medical Research Council, investigated the effects of evacuation on the leisure habits, working habits, social relationships, and attitudes to careers of girls aged 14–17. It was published in June 1940. In fact, these were predominantly middle-class girls, who were scornful of the habits and customs of the people with whom they were billeted and whom they considered to be socially inferior. Vernon concluded that it was not possible to distinguish between the influence of evacuation on such issues as attitudes to careers and that of war conditions in general. The most common point made about evacuation was that 'it was quite an interesting experience, but now I want to go home'.

Some writers took a more conservative position, arguing, for instance, that bedwetting was primarily the fault of mothers and that this was endemic among an inter-generational underclass of socially inadequate people. Over 14,000 children had been evacuated from London and Croydon to Brighton, for instance, and 200 cases of bed-wetting had been referred to the local Guardianship Society. Its Secretary, Samuel Gill, suggested that in terms of the financial and social position of families, the majority of those of bedwetting children were 'below average'. Out of seventy-nine children, in nineteen cases the financial position of parents was 'good', in twenty-two cases 'average', and in thirty eight 'poor'. Gill suggested from the records for eighty-eight children that, with regard to social status, in thirty-one cases it was 'good' and in fifty-seven cases 'poor'. Instead he blamed 'faulty home training', writing that 'there is a deplorably low standard of cleanliness and social behaviour in a considerable number of families living in overcrowded districts in London and Croydon, but not necessarily in overcrowded houses or tenements'.

Gill alleged that many mothers did not seem to mind their children's bedwetting; some were even annoyed with the foster-parents for objecting to the extra washing entailed, and some had taken their children home for that reason. There did not seem to be any connection between housing conditions, the employment of fathers, or other general issues. Rather, the common factor in most cases was that the children had inherited the 'low social standards' of the parents. Gill wrote that: 'It seems quite likely that the late acquirement [*sic*] of clean habits by children coming from these overcrowded areas of our large towns is an inherited condition and an expression of a low social standard which has for generations existed there. Lice and pilfering are other expressions of the same low standard.' What Gill termed 'this want of cleanliness' was associated with severe neglect of the children, either because the mother was at work all day or because one or both parents were more interested in drink or amusement.

* * *

These children were Londoners, and in the capital the work of Elizabeth Denby and her colleagues continued into the summer. The Women's Group on Problems Arising from Evacuation was renamed the Women's Group on Public Welfare on 2 July, and the

Hygiene Sub-Committee met again on 17 July. In discussing the issue of 'character', Elizabeth Denby drew on the work that she had done earlier on Vienna and some Italian cities. In Vienna, for example, new dwellings had been let only to those tenants likely to keep them in good order. Families with a 'low' standard of cleanliness or behaviour were housed in reconditioned properties. Through the First World War and inter-war years *Kindergarten* had been set up for children deemed to be poor, ill, or unhappy, and parents' associations had also raised standards of behaviour in slum homes. In slum-clearance schemes, families thought to be 'unsatisfactory' for new dwellings were offered cheap accommodation in municipal 'hotels'. The rents were nominal, but the attendance of mothers at Infant Welfare Centres and of the children under 4 at nursery schools was compulsory. These nursery schools were of attractive colour and design. In summary, Elizabeth wrote that:

The authorities have found that a rough and dirty woman of independent spirit will rarely take outside advice on the running of her home, but if her own children want and expect cleanliness, order, higher standards of living, she will exert herself to comply, and so protect herself from criticism. They claim, and with considerable evidence, that they are cutting the slum mind off at its root at the lowest expenditure of time, money and energy.

At the same meeting, Letty Harford said that the reform of housing and sanitary conditions had to be a priority for state investment after the war. In her view, the main causes of the lack of personal hygiene and sanitary habits in the evacuees were: a lack of discipline among parents; indifference to low standards; and bad conditions in housing and sanitation. The remedies were to raise the school-leaving age and allow more time for the teaching of hygiene; to provide better housing and sanitation; to reduce economic insecurity;

to provide information on how to furnish and maintain a new home or flat; to organize family clubs and community centres; to set up holiday camps; and to employ housing managers, health visitors, and volunteer visitors. In contrast, Fabian Brackenbury favoured a narrower approach to health education, concentrating on the obstacles posed by school buildings, children's homes, and the question of scholarship versus education.

The Group met again only a week later, on 24 July. Elizabeth set out policies for both the short and the long term. In the short term, nursery schools should be established immediately in every slum area, along with parents' clubs. The sanitation and appearance of all schools should be overhauled. There should be sufficient hot water for washing, with towels and soap. Excellent meals should be cooked and served. New homes should be offered in the first instance to those poor families who kept their homes clean and tidy. She said, 'it is psychologically bad to pass over the good house-wife in favour of her sluttish neighbour when new houses are being allocated'. Clubs should be run for men and women. In the long term, co-educational schooling should be available to all, with all classes being taught side by side.

Irene Barclay, on the other hand, discussed the link between housing conditions and the lack of hygiene and character training evident in some children. She argued that the evidence given to the Group had revealed, more than anything else, 'a lack of training and self-control among a section of the children coming from poor homes in large towns'. The remedy, in her view, was to be found in cultivating a natural vitality, 'the desire for friendship and fun, and for a fuller and more varied life'. Similarly, Amy Sayle argued that no single remedy for low standards in child-care and training was more effective than the education of mothers (in their own homes) by health visitors. It was critical to overcome the opposition or indifference of the father to 'higher' standards. Sayle noted that 'the smell of urine which clings to the beds of the poorest of the health visitors' "problem" families may well be due to the drinking habits of the father'.

In the discussion, attention turned again to health education, and to the obstacles to a child preparing itself for adult life. Fabian Brackenbury argued that, 'with a healthy environment, a happy co-operation and an adjusted sense of values established, then, and then only can teachers claim to be agents in that process by which each child is helped to prepare itself for adult life'. The Group thought that in the light of these debates it was advisable to produce two final reports, one short and popular, and the other longer and suitable for serious discussion. Dora Ibberson agreed to write them. A statement by her on clothing, one by Cicely McCall on 'Town and Country', and one by Amy Sayle on 'Dirt Diseases' were to be circulated to the Group. McCall, for example, argued that many village women no longer had an inferiority complex; rather, it had been replaced by a contempt for the town mother who turned to the nearest Welfare Centre when her baby needed medicine, who lived on tinned food, and who didn't know how to mend her children's clothes. While there was no love lost between the town mother and the country mother, among the younger generation there was a friendliness and understanding that had never existed before. In the future, rural and urban children would know much more about how their counterparts lived in the towns and the countryside. By early August the Hygiene Sub-Committee reported that it had almost completed its work. Moreover, the renaming of the organization to include 'welfare' was a significant change.

9
Victims or Vandals?

The bombing of London began in earnest in September 1940, setting off the second major wave of evacuation, the first to take place under battle conditions. The second wave was smaller than the first, and about 1,250,000 people were moved. But September also brought German attacks on provincial cities, marking the start of the Blitz. Many of the evacuees who had been away from home for a year were now bored, and minor crime and misbehaviour had become major problems. More general studies were published, such as Celia St Loe Strachey's book *Borrowed Children*, a study of the reception of evacuees in the South West, and this was extensively reviewed. Apart from academic studies, there were novels that featured evacuees, including Richmal Crompton's *William and the Evacuees*, part of the popular 'William' series, and Joyce Cary's *Charley is My Darling*.

* * *

The articles published in this period were more on the psychological effects of both evacuation and bombing rather than the physical welfare of the children. Writers on both refugee children and the evacuees, such as Evelyn Fox of the Central Association for Mental Welfare, increasingly advocated hostels for those children who could not go to ordinary billets. These were generally children with aggressive or delinquent behaviour, or those who had been identified as bedwetters. One report concluded that hostels for 'difficult' children had to be adequately staffed and small enough for each child to be known as an individual; special cases should have individual psychological treatment; ideas on organization and equipment should be pooled; and schemes for retaining special billets should be considered. It was increasingly realized that there would be a role for these hostels after the war ended.

There were studies by staff of the Psychological Laboratory, University College London, which itself had been evacuated to Bangor in North Wales. A second study by Cyril Burt's colleagues was based on 100 children evacuated to Wales. This examined the factors that made for successful or unsuccessful billeting, and relations between children and foster-parents. In particular, the study explored the adjustment of children and its relationship with sex, age, change of billets, parents' visits, the presence of other children in the foster-home, the size and financial status of families, and intelligence. It also examined neurotic symptoms. The authors found, for instance, that there was no relationship between the children's adjustment to their new homes and the financial status of their parents; children from very poor homes adapted as successfully as the well-to-do.

There were other studies of the factors which made for successful billeting, and of the relations between children and foster-parents. A University of Liverpool survey, for example, carried out house-to-house interviews in Liverpool and in two Reception Areas in Wales. Of the 685 children, 426 (62 per cent) were still evacuated, and 259 (38 per cent) had returned home; the aim was to find out if evacuation had succeeded or failed. The survey found that 9 per cent of children were suffering from bedwetting, boys more than girls, and the younger children more than the older ones. While 90 per cent of the bedwetting cases mentioned other emotional disturbances, 72 per cent had head lice, dirty clothes, or were badly washed. This raised the question of whether bedwetting was a neurotic symptom or the result of poor training. The survey noted that children who were neglected suffered not only physically but also psychologically, and neurosis (caused in part by overcrowding) was much more common among them than other children. The report found that 17 per cent of the children arrived with head lice, and of these 11 per cent also had 'dirty' bodies and clothes. It did not accept the excuse that the children only had head lice because they were at the end of five weeks summer holiday. Hosts spoke well of parents.

Overall, the University of Liverpool survey concluded that half the hosts said that they had enough money for food, but not for extras such as clothes; the strong desire to clothe the children properly meant that they were unable to manage on the billeting allowance. One Billeting Officer had said of the evacuation scheme that, 'less respectable mothers drank, were lazy and dirty, and sooner or later tried to introduce strange men into the house'. But Tom Simey, Professor of Social Science at Liverpool, suggested that the conclusions were reassuring; it was the administrative machinery that had been at fault, and there were not fundamental weaknesses in social ties, or an absence of public spirit, in the adults or the children. Nevertheless, general standards of cleanliness and hygiene left much to be desired, and much could be done on health education through a strengthening of the School Medical Service.

One of the most interesting social surveys was edited by Richard Padley and Margaret Cole for the Fabian Society. They reviewed the way that the evacuation had been planned, arguing that the limit of £1 per 200 children for expenditure on equipment could 'hardly be regarded as other than derisory, while its application as a flat rate over areas with widely differing incidences of poverty seems hardly well considered'. The report was sympathetic to the return home of evacuated mothers, and noted that the enforced mixing of social classes 'had enforced also a realisation of the immense differences between different social strata'. The report was sympathetic, too, to the cultural differences of working-class children; they were likely to feel cold and lonely in a middle-class home, while their hosts would find the children a nuisance. One of the contributors, Dr Leslie Haden-Guest, Labour MP for Islington, had been a member of the Anderson Committee in 1938. Haden-Guest argued that the 10.8 per cent of children found at school medical inspections to have 'slightly subnormal' nutrition remained 'as a pointer to economic, social and individual conditions of deprivation and insufficiency at the base of the social pyramid'. School meals and milk should be supplied irrespective of the financial circumstances of parents; to discriminate in this way was expensive and 'socially and psychologically disastrous'.

* * *

On the outbreak of war, Carl Coates's sister June had been evacuated to Cornwall. But Carl himself had no memory of how he got from his home in London to the village of Easton-on-the-Hill in Lincolnshire. His first recollection was of being with a group of children in what he was to come to know as the bake-house. The room was pitch black and full of shadows cast by candles. People kept coming and going, with children being taken away until there were just two left: a 6-year-old girl called Betty, and Carl. It was because Betty was Jewish and Carl was the youngest, that they were the last two to be chosen. It was decided that Betty and Carl should spend the night with Minnie and Tom Browett, and a decision about them would be made in the morning. Although she was only 6, Betty declared that she would not sleep with someone who was not Jewish; she went across the road to a Mrs Brittain, while Carl, who was now 5 years and one month old, stayed with the Browetts, in a double bed. In October 1940 about seventy mothers and children had arrived in the village.

Next morning the arrangements were unchanged. The Browetts had no children of their own, and were well established in the village since they owned the main village store. Minnie and Tom worked very hard. The shop sold groceries, bread baked on the premises, cigarettes, haberdashery, bran, coal, cooking oil, paraffin, and the weekly newspaper, the *Lincoln, Rutland, and Stamford Mercury*. In the grocery store many of the items such as sugar, cheese, and butter had to be pre-weighed. Treacle came in medium-size containers fitted with a tap, sugar in large sacks that had to be weighed out into pound and half-pound bags provided by the company, and cheese in large, complete round moulds; it was placed on a cheese-board and cut to order with a wire. On the counter there were different scales to weigh different types of produce. In place of fridges there were cold slabs in the chilly, dark areas of the storeroom. Although there was no electricity in the house and shop, the Browetts did sell light-bulbs. It was not unusual for items to be sold 'on the slate'; all written work was done by hand in pen and ink. On Wednesday, which was half-day closing, Tom would 'do his books'.

In the main, goods were brought from Wherry's wholesale merchants, based in Bourne. Whenever there was a delivery, it was all hands on deck to unload the vehicle while Minnie checked the goods against the delivery note. All the cardboard boxes were saved in preparation for home deliveries in the village once a week. The weekly orders would start to be made up on a Thursday evening, and finished on Friday for delivery some time that day. Some were delivered with the bread by pony and trap. Orders for shorter distances were delivered in a four-wheel handcart. Every night, shutters were placed over the shop windows, and locked with a metal bar.

Carl tended to think of the Browetts' house in terms of the different rooms. The bake-house doubled for many activities other than baking bread. It was a large area with its own entrance separate from the shop, and was the regular entry-point to the house for all deliveries. But unsurprisingly, the main activity was the baking of bread, which was principally white loaves, large and small. There were other types, such as plaited and cottage loaves, that were baked on a regular basis, and special ornate loaves were made for harvest festivals. Along one part of the wall were regular mixing bins, and continuing along the rest of the wall was the tabletop storage area for the bread bins, prior to their being placed in the oven. The same area was used to empty the tins once the bread was baked and taken out of the oven. Tom Browett always got up early on a baking morning, to mix the dough in the tins. The dough was then covered with empty flour-sacks, and the lids put on to allow it to rise over a period of several hours.

Once the dough was ready, the lids were lifted off in turn and the dough hauled, again by hand, to adjacent lids. Tom cut the dough and weighed it, often very accurately, and dropped the bundles onto the lightly floured surface. Meanwhile, Minnie pummelled, folded, and kneaded it into bread shape, then dropped the finished dough into pre-greased rectangular pound or half-pound baking tins. While this was taking place the fire would have been started in the furnace along the side and length of the huge oven. Suspended from the ceiling in 'U'-shaped holders were the long-handled 'peels', ready for use when the tins of dough had to be put into the oven. As well as their long handles, the peels had flat sections at one end, where the bread tins were placed. People sometimes brought large joints of meat on a Saturday to have them cooked in the oven, and on Christmas morning many turkeys were roasted inside.

All the baking activity was on one side of the bake-house, apart from the oven and fire which was right across the far end. There was a door in the right-hand wall at that end, and another door halfway along the opposite wall to the baking tins, which gave access to behind the counters or into the main body of the shop. A window between these two doors allowed people in the sitting-cum-dining room to see who had come into the bake-house. Opposite the regular baking tins there was a large table where all inward goods were stacked if not on the floor. The weighing-up also took place on the table, and the sorting of the rounds for the *Lincoln, Rutland, and Stamford Mercury* on a Friday. Along the wall and behind the table there were more bins, but these were used for bran. Any working after dark would be done either by candlelight or the light of oil lamps.

*   *   *

By November 1940 Sparkbrook was a very dangerous place to be, so Montgomery Street School was closed and the parents were given the opportunity to send their children out of Birmingham, to be evacuated to the countryside. Those who did not want to go had to be transferred to other schools. Eddy Rowley's parents chose evacuation. Her sister Joyce was now 12 and at Conway Road Senior Girls' School, Jean was 8, and Eddy not quite 6. Eddy's parents insisted that the children must be billeted together as Eddy was so young.

The children met at the school, and were excited as they walked in twos down the road and up the hill to Small Heath Station. They each had a luggage label pinned to their coats with their name and school written on it. Jean hung on tightly to Eddy's hand, as their mother had said that she must not let go of her sister and they had to stay together. They each carried a small bag containing a change of clothes and one toy. Eddy had chosen a small doll that had been given to her by Father Christmas when she was 2. The children also had their gas-masks. The other children carried them in cardboard boxes, but the Rowleys' were in specially made metal containers. Their father was a sheet-metal worker and made items like kettles and saucepans in his shed at the bottom of the garden, so he had made each of them a gas-mask holder. The mothers were very quiet, grimly holding on to their emotions, and not knowing where their children were going, who they would be living with, or when they would see them again. The children got on the train, waved until they couldn't see the platform from the windows, and settled down. Before the war Eddy's family had gone on holiday by train to seaside towns in North Wales, and she loved paddling and playing in the sand. So she was enjoying herself. Travelling on a train was an adventure to her.

The train took the children to Pershore in Worcestershire, where they had a meal at a girls' school. Then they travelled by bus to the village of Drakes Broughton, 3 or 4 miles away. On arrival, the children went into the village school. There were a lot of children, but it seemed tiny compared to their school in Birmingham. The children assembled in its one large room. Eddy's cousin Ken, who lived two doors away, was with them. At 10, he was one of the oldest there; he and his friends were big, strong boys. Some adults came into the room and started looking around. A woman in a WVS uniform was in charge, and as children went off with adults she made notes on a pad. A large man made straight for Ken and his friend, and they went with him. Gradually the room emptied, and Eddy and Jean were the only ones left. By then, the children were very tired and it had stopped being an adventure. No other adults came in, and they wondered what was going to happen to them. It was very frightening. Then the WVS woman said that the children were going to stay with her. What a relief. She took them home in her car. Her husband also had a car. The children couldn't believe it; two cars in one family. Even though their father worked in the car industry in Birmingham, he didn't have one. They only knew a single family in their part of the city who owned a car.

The children found they were to stay on the largest fruit farm in the area. The house was double-fronted, big, standing in its own grounds. There were stables for the two shire-horses which pulled all the farm equipment on the acres and acres of land owned by the family. Many of the people who worked on the land lived in houses dotted around the farm. There was an Airedale dog that Eddy fell in love with on sight. She was to spend many happy hours playing with him. At night, the horses were let out in the paddock behind the house, and the children could see them from their bedroom window—galloping around, rolling on their backs, and kicking their hooves in the air.

* * *

In Stafford, the mix-up in the addresses had been sorted out. Mary-Rose Benton met her brothers Billy and Jimmy at school, and they compared billets. Some children envied those who were staying with better-off families, while others were disappointed and found their billet was not as well furnished, or as clean, as the home they had come from. Jimmy later recalled that: 'As evacuees in Stafford my brothers, sisters, and I knew we were unwelcome. We came from Margate and our southern accents marked us as strangers. I remember seeing "Vaccies Go Home" scrawled on the side of a static water tank. I added, "We Want To!"' Nevertheless, Jimmy had made friends with a local boy, Leslie Hughes, and it was Leslie who told him, when Jimmy eventually left Stafford: 'The best of luck, Jim, and don't be frit [reluctant] to come and see us when you can.'

After school, Mary-Rose was taken to 36 Blakiston Street, where the Newbolds lived. There was the mother, Jessie, her husband

Frank, his own father, and the couple's children, Doreen, who was 12, and David, at 6 a year younger than Mary-Rose. The house was at the end of a terrace. There was no front parlour, but a main living-room and kitchen. The indoor passageway had the kitchen on one side, and on the other the pantry, bathroom, and lavatory. There were the usual three bedrooms. The garden, long and narrow, ran down to the backs, a broad footpath between streets with the gardens backing on to it.

Mary-Rose was allowed Doreen's doll's house to play with, as an introduction. While she self-consciously moved the pieces of toy furniture about, the family sat and stared at her, watching and assessing what she did. They had heard stories of evacuees and their strange habits. Mary-Rose was to hear these stories often. How the city children were dirty, verminous, and out of control. How they slept in their boots because they were afraid the rats would bite their toes. In short, that they were ignorant, stupid, and little more than savages. Later on, having seen that Mary-Rose's manners were disappointingly civilized, the adults and children gave up staring and went about their usual family routine. They relaxed, and Mary-Rose played with David.

Too polite to comment, and too immature to judge, Mary-Rose tried to fall in with the family's ways. She became confident enough to take part in the everyday badinage that the children engaged in with their mother. Meanwhile, she had to learn the patois. 'Do you want a piece?', Mrs Newbold asked her. Mary-Rose stared at her. What the hell was a piece. A piece of what? She asked her again, louder. Mary-Rose looked puzzled and said nothing, not liking to ask Mrs Newbold what she meant. 'She's an idiot, she doesn't even know what a piece is.' Mary-Rose had to figure out for herself that a piece was a slice of bread-and-butter. David also thought that the way Mary-Rose spoke was comical. She read to him, and he

laughed when she pronounced the word 'grass' with a long 'a'.
'She talks like the man on the wireless', he said. David was a good
playmate, but his mother treated him like a baby. Until he was 8
she took him on her lap.

Mary-Rose subsequently had a child's altercation with David.
As they played in the inner passageway, he took a necklace from
her which her mother had given her and teased her with it. Not
one to wear jewellery, the trinket was a talisman nevertheless, and
when David refused to let her have it back it seemed as if the last
link with home was gone. Mary-Rose recollected: 'At first the new
life had felt like a dream, from which I would wake and return to
normality. Now it was the old life that was the dream. It was a
million years and a million miles away, and as he twirled the gaudy
beads round his head, I was suddenly overwhelmed with hysterical
grief.' By coincidence, the others were listening to a radio broadcast about the sinking of *The City of Benares*. Mrs Newbold pretended
that this was what Mary-Rose was crying about, that she feared she
was being taken away from her. Mary-Rose would later learn that
Jessie was not only a liar, but an ingenious opportunist.

Aware that Mary-Rose had not lived up to the reputation of the
evacuees, Mrs Newbold put about a few lies about her. She said
that the old couple had said Mary-Rose licked the plate. Moreover,
she took her Disney mug from her and said it was David's. Any
money Mary-Rose had left after getting her sweets ration she told
her to put on the sideboard. She knew Mrs Newbold would take it
back each time, but there was nothing the girl could do. Jessie
disapproved of her being called Mary-Rose. 'Who do you think
you are, with a silly posh name like that? You're Mary, so don't you
forget it.' She kept her from school to help with the housework and
the shopping. The only time when she did not bully her was when
they were out in town, as she looked furtively around for school

inspectors. A nun from the school called to see why Mary-Rose had been absent. She told Mrs Newbold to send the girl to school.

Jessie took reprisal, determined to enjoy giving the girl a sound thrashing. She was very violent, and kept hitting and hitting. Mary-Rose wondered when she was going to stop. But Mrs Newbold inflamed herself the harder she hit, growing quite uncontrolled in her language, of the kind Mary-Rose had heard only in the school playground but this time more shocking to her by its association with violence and anger and its being used by an adult. From being merely rude words used by little boys, the words took on a sinister meaning. Mary-Rose's mother's swearing had been only lavatorial or blasphemous, never sexual. Fortunately Jessie tired of beating the girl, and poked her up the stairs with a clothes prop. By now, Mary-Rose was crying uncontrollably. She had never before met with such crudity from an adult, such mocking derision, as she was jabbed with the prop. Mary-Rose recalled: 'As I went higher up the stairs, I descended further into Hell.'

* * *

In Leicestershire, Maggie Quinn was finding that everyone worked very hard, and nothing was wasted. Even though Mark Burdett was retired, he had a daily routine. First, he made up the food for the hens every morning by boiling up the 'pig potatoes', which were too small to eat but still carefully gathered and stored. To this was added all the household scraps and a kind of ground cereal powder which people could apply for if they gave up their egg ration. Then he would go off to the allotments, from which he fed the entire family and other people with fruit and vegetables. Everyone helped with the cultivation, and when they took on a new plot covered with weeds, Maggie earned pocket money by pulling them up, seven-eighths of a penny per dozen. She spent hours there, sitting on top of the bank of the quarry side, watching the small figures of the quarrymen and the stone trucks going up and down the incline. Cyril Burdett worked in the quarry, as did Mark Burdett's brother-in-law, Tom Spencer.

While she lived at Groby, Maggie learnt all the domestic skills from Sarah Ann Burdett and Amy Sedgley. They were both good cooks and housewives, so everything was kept spotless, and there was always lots to do. Maggie's keenness to sneak away and read was much frowned upon; the chores had to come first. In spite of the food shortages, the family always ate well, albeit plainly. There were potatoes cooked in the ashes of the fire, and toast made with a fork. The family followed the old-fashioned style of eating their pudding first, before the main course, in which there was very little meat. An ice-cream van came round the village from time to time, and when it stopped outside Maggie's house they took out a cup or a basin according to how much they wanted to buy. There were no fridges at that time, but ice-cream would stay frozen for a while if it was kept on the 'thrawl', a thick slate shelf in the pantry. Everything needing to be kept cool was stored there, but even so, in the summer the thick, creamy milk would sometimes go sour. Sarah Ann Burdett would then put it in muslin and hang it over a basin to drain out the liquid. The resulting cream cheese, well seasoned with pepper and salt, was delicious.

Fruit and tomatoes were bottled, and fruit vinegars, pickled onions and beetroots, jam using home-grown fruits, chutneys, piccalilli, and many other preserves were all made, to see everyone through the winter. Blackberrying was an enjoyable occupation, and the resulting fruit used in pies, puddings, and jams. Hazelnuts were also gathered and buried in a tin in the garden to mature; they were dug up just before Christmas. Apples were placed on newspaper under the beds. Coal, too, was rationed, so it was eked out with deadwood from the trees and hedges.

More generally, Maggie recalled of growing up in the 1940s that clothing and textiles were only available on coupons, so everything was made to last as long as possible. Worn sheets were turned side to middle, then into pillowcases, handkerchiefs, and finally dusters and cleaning-cloths. She remembered, as her feet grew, pushing out the backs of her shoes. No new shoes unfortunately, just a trip to the village cobbler to have a piece of leather sewn in to reinforce them. 'Best clothes' were kept for Sundays and special occasions, as they also had to last as long as possible.

* * *

Towards the end of 1940 there was a heavy snowfall in Wales, and George Prager decided to photograph some sunlit snowscapes. The glare from the snow was painful to his eyes, and after about half-an-hour he developed a splitting headache and felt very sick. He took three or four pictures, then made his way back to the house as quickly as possible. He sat quietly in an armchair for about two hours before feeling better. Mrs Knight insisted on his being checked over by the local doctor. The doctor thought George had suffered a mild form of snow blindness. Mrs Knight wrote to George's grandmother in November:

He has had a bad cold, but is quite well again, and is taking some malt I have in the house. I bought it for Mr Knight but he did not like it, so George is taking it. We will soon have Christmas with us, it won't seem like it, for a good many, will Mr Coleman be working? I think most people everywhere will be working. This War is looking bad, it will be nice to see it all over, and everything back to normal again but I am afraid it's going to be a long time before that happens, and we must all live in hopes of better times to come.

In the same month a British aircraft crashed on the mountain above Pen-y-Dre. It happened during the night at about 2.30, and the noise of the crash woke most of the residents nearby. It seemed that the plane had attempted to land on the mountainside, but it had been too low coming in over the summit, where it lost its undercarriage and then slid down the mountain on its fuselage. The wheels and legs had been left behind nearer the top. People from the neighbourhood were very soon on the scene, and the first official to arrive was a special police constable from Rhymney Police Station. The crew were taken to the local cottage hospital, where their injuries were treated; one crew member died, but the rest survived. A few souvenirs (small fragments of aluminium) disappeared from the crashed aircraft, but the RAF salvage team arrived very quickly, soon after dawn, and recovered the plane. The bombs that it had been carrying were removed, and exploded on the mountainside. Otherwise, the salvage team left nothing but a furrow in the ground.

* * *

In Scotland, David Hodge found (like Juliet Norden and Mary-Rose Benton) that sometimes the war impinged on the lives of himself and his friends. At one point, for example, it was decided by the authorities that the children should all be taught to swim. Evacuees from Britain had been sent to Canada, and it was thought that children evacuated within Scotland might be sent there as well. But it was the sinking of *The City of Benares* liner in mid-Atlantic that led to the crash course in swimming. The children were given lessons at the Step Rock swimming-pool on the waterfront. This was covered at high tide, and as the tide receded, it left behind seaweed, small fish, and other forms of sea life. The children did not mind the fish, but it was bitterly cold, and very unpleasant.

David found that weekends at Balmungo were unique. On Saturday afternoon the boys got all spruced up and took the bus into St Andrews. Occasionally they went to see a film, but not many films were deemed suitable for the children, so this did not happen very often. Whether they went to a cinema or not, they always ended up at the house of Mrs Ballantyne's sister, which was in the centre of St Andrews. The boys had tea there, and after the table was cleared the adults played cards while David, George, and Peter played board games. Later they would leave to catch the last bus back to Balmungo.

On Sundays the boys had to wear their best clothes, and they were forbidden to play. They were allowed to read or go for walks, provided they kept within certain boundaries. Now and then they went to church, but the church did not open every week; many ministers had been called up, and one had to cover several churches. These mornings and afternoons were boring, but the boys knew that the evening would not be, as Jim Ridley and his wife had by far the biggest living-room of all the houses owned by the estate workers and every Sunday evening all the relations of the Ballantyne and Ridley families would arrive there. All the women were good at baking, and everyone brought something. The huge table was set, and they all sat down to tea. There were usually between ten and twelve people. Tea was followed by cards and other games, including Ludo. On these occasions the atmosphere in the room was marvellous. The laughter and enjoyment everyone created was amazing, but none of the merriment was fuelled by alcohol. David did not see as much as a bottle of beer the whole time he was there.

* * *

In Lancaster the WVS had published advice in October for both housewives and visiting mothers. For the housewife, they advised: 'Remember your guest is probably unused to country life. Tell her about local arrangements and about how best to do her shopping. You may also be able to help by introducing her to the local church and to a Child Welfare Centre or Women's Institute which may help her to feel less of a stranger in her new home.' As the winter approached, the previous year's problems over footwear and clothing began to re-emerge. One householder wrote to G. M. Bland in December that two children, Dorothy Quick and Sheila Leonard, had each been measured for a dress and a coat in July, but had still not received them. Their foster-parents were very anxious that they should each be provided with the replacement clothes. Bland noted of these people that 'they themselves have done a great deal for the children whose own parents are, I understand, very poor'.

Bland was dealing with individual evacuees, and there certainly were some unusual cases. A boy called Leslie Welsh, for example, from Seedley Boys' School in Liverpool Street, Salford, had been evacuated to Lancaster, and he had an artificial eye. In September he had lost it while doing recycling work on waste paper with the Scouts. An old spare eye had to be sent to be re-polished, at a cost of 17s. 6d. The cost was recovered from donations from the Scouts, in the form of a postal order which was handed to Leslie's parents. The parents wrote to Bland: 'we wish to thank you for the trouble you have taken on our behalf & also the money to which we are greatly indebted to you.'

* * *

In Bournemouth, Dave Pinchon had left the Brocks in July, and that autumn moved to stay with Mr and Mrs Croucher. Mr Croucher was a chimney-sweep, and when not sweeping he chopped and bundled firewood for kindling. It was at this billet that Dave joined up with John Richman, who was to be Dave's close friend during the war years. What probably would have been a pleasant stay was brought to an abrupt end at 3.30 a.m. on 16 November. Dave recalled that:

I think John Richman and I were probably sharing a bed. We were obviously awoken by the explosion and the ensuing clatter of glass breaking, tiles coming off roofs and the sound of timber and brickwork being torn apart. Both of us have a distinct memory of a large picture which hung above the headboard crashing onto our pillows just above our heads. When we collected ourselves, the ceilings were down, windows blown in, and doors blown off. The bedroom door lock had been blown off and had embedded itself in the wardrobe door on the other side of the room. We collected ourselves and made our way downstairs covered in debris.

Six parachute mines had been dropped on Bournemouth, including in the area of St Leonards and Malmesbury Park Roads. Even at the time, this was regarded as a severe raid. In total, 53 civilians were killed, around 120 were injured, and 2,321 properties were damaged, including Alma Road School.

There were several possible reasons for the raid. The Germans may have been aware that hotels on the seafront were being used by the RAF for the intake and initial training of aircrew. Or bombers that had been inland had failed to reach their targets, and jettisoned their payload on the way home. Whatever the cause, Mr Croucher lost an eye and Mrs Croucher had a damaged arm. Dave's last recollection was of getting down the stairs. He had no idea how the Crouchers got out, or of who helped them. Mr Croucher was in obvious need of medical attention, but how or where he got it, Dave simply did not know. What happened to Dave and John was also a mystery. Dave had no recall of where they went, where they got cleaned up, or what happened after things settled down. He could only think that his parents must have driven down from Southampton and taken the boys home until a new billet was found for them. Somehow or other they must have recovered their clothes, books, and other possessions.

* * *

Although they did not know it, Sir Maurice Holmes and Dave Pinchon were now in the same town, for also in Bournemouth were civil servants from the Board of Education. The Government

had requisitioned the Branksome Dene Hotel in 1940. In November
the officials had themselves been evacuated to the hotel, and were
now separated from their political leaders. The President, Sir
Robert Wood, and the Private Office Secretariat remained at the
Board's offices at Alexandra House, in Kingsway, London. The
hotel had an interesting history. It had been designed by the well-
known architect Edward Buckton Lamb, and enjoyed a cliff-top
position in three acres of land. The foundation-stone for the
substantial property had been laid in August 1860, and in 1880
Lord Wimborne had purchased the house as a 'seaside villa', and
added a considerable number of extensions. During the 1890s
Winston Churchill and his family had been in temporary residence,
Lady Cornelia Wimbourne being a sister of Winston's father
Randolph. Sir Ernest Cassel, the publisher and banker, purchased
the house in 1903 and further enlarged it in 1913. On the death of
Sir Ernest in 1921, his granddaughter Edwina (later to become
Lady Edwina Mountbatten) inherited the property, and she, in
turn, offered it for sale in 1925. In 1927 Arthur Dunn, of hat and
clothier fame, had purchased the property, acquired more adjacent
land to be developed for building, and had converted it into a residential hotel, the Branksome Dene Hotel, which became known as
the first reform and vegetarian hotel in Bournemouth.

The Ministry of Health had issued a circular on footwear and
clothing on 2 October. This announced that a lakh of rupees
(£7,500) had been received from the Maharajah of Gondal, in
Gujarat in India, to meet the needs of evacuated children in the
countryside. This was to be distributed in the Evacuation Areas as
contributions to boot and clothing funds. But the circular also
continued to encourage voluntary effort. It said that children could
get assistance from gifts collected and sent to Reception Areas by
the Evacuation Areas; from the County Clothing Depots of the

WVS; from the products of local make-and-mend parties; from clothes collected by voluntary agencies; and from purchases made by the Evacuation Areas. There was some progress. In November the London Clothing Scheme was set up, along with clothing depots run by the WVS in the Reception Areas. These were stocked with 'official' and 'gift' materials, especially from the American Red Cross. Clothing was now issued from the depots according to the means of the parents, and the LCC was issued with special coupons once clothes began to be rationed. On the other hand, some argued that the circular was inadequate. The Mayor of Barnstaple in Devon, for example, argued that while it was desirable to force parents to meet their responsibilities when they were in a position to do so, it was also essential that the children should not suffer in the process. At the Board, civil servants admitted that the circular was unworkable. In practice, the damage would be avoided where the requirements of the circular were ignored. However, they conceded that many children 'will suffer where a conscientious effort is made to stick to the circular'.

There were signs that some of Sir Maurice's colleagues were now willing to admit that the statistics on nutrition generated by school medical inspections were useless. Dr Alison Glover wrote that it was not the difference between the number of children found to be 'subnormal' by a visiting Medical Officer of the Board and those returned annually by the local School Medical Officer which was most surprising. These disagreements were to be expected. Rather, it was that in so many cases school doctors would continue, after having been visited, to return 'such improbable figures'. This tended to destroy the hope that time and effort would eventually make the statistics reasonably comparable and reliable. Looking at the figures for 1938 and 1939, for instance, it now seemed that about half were plausible; more than a quarter had at least one serious

error; and less than a quarter were obviously implausible or classified in a way entirely different to that intended by the Board. Glover
couldn't deny that a large proportion of the figures were 'valueless
for any purpose'. His colleague Cecil Maudslay suggested that the
current system of assessing nutrition could continue, and that the
number of 'improbable' returns could be reduced by more frequent
investigations by Medical Officers. However, Glover wrote in the
margins of Maudslay's memo that 'hope springs eternal'.

The scepticism about statistics was accompanied by an expan-
sion in school meals. There were now plans for communal feeding
in school canteens. The Ministry of Food might take over 300
feeding centres managed by the billeting authorities, and no cost
would fall on the LEAs. Maudslay admitted that new proposals for
school meals highlighted the fact that the gap between the best and
the worst LEAs was very wide. But Sir Maurice had other problems to contend with. The report on the effect of evacuation on the
height and weight of schoolchildren, based on 1,119 children from
the LCC, had found that, in fact, a period of evacuation did not
cause any significant difference in their rate of growth. Moreover,
one of his colleagues now argued that the Mellanby report on head
lice should be published. What he called 'this ostrich policy' was, in
his view, deplorable, and might land the Government in serious
difficulty. A lot of people knew that Mellanby had written the
report, and nothing would be easier than to ask awkward questions
in the House of Commons about its non-publication.

The outbreak of war in September 1939, along with the
upheaval associated with evacuation, had meant an end to the
reforms that had been planned in the late 1930s, such as the raising
of the school-leaving age. But pressures for reform increased as the
war began to impinge more upon the lives of individuals. By the
summer of 1940 the Board was being criticized for having failed to

provide greater direction and planning during the evacuation of September 1939. Therefore the civil servants themselves began to consider the place of education in post-war reconstruction. In November, what was called the Committee of Senior Officials on Postwar Educational Reconstruction was formed. Sir Maurice wrote on 2 November that:

I find that some of my colleagues, besides myself, have been considering whether we should not, now that we are working without constant inter-ruptions be bending our minds to a study of the educational problems which will arise when the war is over. It is clear from references in the Press that other persons and bodies have ideas on postwar educational recon-struction, and I think this is a matter in which the Board should lead rather than follow…

In some respects, this was a reversion to the approach adopted in the earlier years of the century by Sir Robert Morant. The Committee was not a formal body, but a group for informal discus-sion including most of the senior civil servants at the Board. It worked through memoranda, and included both traditionalists and those who saw an opportunity for more radical change. For example, Sir Maurice wrote of a deputation from the Workers' Educational Association that the Government could not listen to every group that had a grievance to air or an axe to grind. He was going to tell his colleagues 'to go full speed ahead on the post-war problems. Half-baked ideas and individual brainwaves are as dangerous as they are useless.'

One Year On

Throughout the winter and spring of 1941 the Blitz continued, with heavy German raids on cities such as Glasgow and Belfast. A feeling of disorder, confusion, and indeed panic filled some accounts of the later waves of evacuation. In Belfast in Northern Ireland, for instance, the planned evacuation of September 1939 had been something of a non-event, and most children were not evacuated until after heavy air-raids, in April 1941. Moreover, while there was an equivalent to the official evacuation scheme that had operated on the mainland, the evacuation in Northern Ireland was largely a private one, organized by individual families themselves. In this respect it more closely resembled what has been called the 'trek-king' movement, when families moved out of the cities, often for quite short periods, as a means of allaying their anxiety about the raids. Moya Woodside, a surgeon's wife living in South Belfast, who was a diarist for Mass Observation, recorded that on 16 April 1941 she watched: 'An exodus on foot, trams, lorries, trailers, cattle floats, bicycles, delivery vans, anything that would move was utilised. Private cars streamed past...all sorts of paraphernalia roped on behind. Hundreds were waiting at bus-stops. Anxiety on every face...where they are going and what they will find when they get there, nobody knows.' A few days later, on 19 April, she described the forecourt of the Great Northern Railway Station in Belfast:

I have never seen anything like it…thousands of people crowding in cars, buses, carts, lorries, bathchairs, women pushing prams and go-carts with anything up to six children trailing behind, belongings in blankets, pillow-boxes, baskets and boxes. [Later, at 5 o'clock that afternoon] the station doors had been shut. Crowds were waiting outside on the pavement all around, a constant stream of people arriving on foot or on buses, many looking exhausted. It was a heartbreaking sight.

* * *

These mothers and children ended up in small towns, such as Downpatrick in County Down. Elsewhere on the mainland the evacuees watched bombing from the safety of the countryside; those who went home searched for shrapnel. Apart from the Mellanby report on head lice, which had been published in February, there was a Ministry of Health report on the Reception Areas, and a report on 'war strain' in children. In Huntingdonshire, for example, a Child Guidance Officer was appointed to counter the mental strain imposed on children by separation from their normal surroundings. A study based on children evacuated there in September 1940 found 420 cases reported as needing Child Guidance treatment. The most common problems were bedwetting, anxiety, depression, incontinence, epileptic fits, and sleep-walking. Some children who had been bombed were unable to concentrate and do their schoolwork. It was estimated that in 80 per cent of these cases the strain could be traced directly to the war. The main issues in 'war strain' were depression because of separation from home, insecurity in a new environment, transferred adult strain, and the direct experience of air-raids. The author concluded that while separation from mothers was clearly established as a cause of bedwetting, those children where the main disturbance was due to a physical agency, such as bombing, were more likely to respond with unruly behaviour. Following the Blitz of 1940, commentators were able to compare the influence on children of evacuation with the effects of heavy bombing.

The best-known of the social surveys of evacuation appeared in 1941, by the educational psychologist and psychoanalyst Susan Isaacs, on children evacuated to Cambridge from London. Issacs was perhaps the leading English-born child psychologist of her generation. She had earlier done outstanding work on the intellectual and social development of young children at the Malting House School, Cambridge. At this school children were given great freedom for their intellectual and emotional development, supported by loving firmness rather than punishment. The child was seen as a research worker, the teacher an observer and provider of the material and equipment required. This work had great influence on the education of children under 7, establishing play as central for a child's means of living and for understanding life. A member of the British Psycho-Analytic Society from 1923, Isaacs had set up the Department of Child Development at the Institute of Education, University of London, and was appointed its head in 1933. Moving to Cambridge in 1939, she went on to conduct this Cambridge Evacuation Survey on the effects of evacuation on children.

In September 1939 about 3,000 children had been evacuated to Cambridge from London. The survey was based on 300 unaccompanied schoolchildren from the London boroughs of Tottenham and Islington, and on a questionnaire, interviews, and essays written by them. The survey was amplified by a questionnaire to the London teachers, a special study of recreation, and analysis from the local Child Guidance Clinic. The Research Committee chaired by Isaacs included social workers, psychologists, sociologists, teachers, and psychotherapists from Cambridge and from other educational institutions evacuated from London, such as the

London School of Economics, Bedford College, and the Institute of Education. It included such well-known figures as the penal reformer Hester Adrian, then a Cambridge magistrate, and a Billeting Officer for the WVS involved in organizing accommodation for evacuees. Other members were the psychiatrist John Bowlby and the psychoanalyst Melanie Klein, who had been the first analyst to work therapeutically with young children and whose play technique strongly influenced all child psychotherapists and child analysts. A Consultative Committee included such figures as the sociologist and academic administrator Alexander Carr-Saunders, earlier much involved in the Eugenics Society, the sociologist and philosopher Morris Ginsberg, and the philosopher Gilbert Ryle.

Cambridge itself provided a case-study of evacuation in practice. Following earlier surveys of accommodation, the plan had been to place 16,000 evacuees in approximately 8,000 households. However, in the event the number of evacuees received in September 1939 was about 6,700, half of whom were unaccompanied schoolchildren and the remainder mothers, babies, teachers, and helpers. During the first month about 2,500 returned to London, and by the end of October at least a further 800 had returned. It was the WVS, along with the LEA, that was involved in billeting the children, but undergraduates, the churches, and the Scouts and Guides were all involved; the students organized a club for the evacuees at Newnham College. Isaacs noted that there were real grievances: 'a Greek head-waiter's wife was given a bed inferior to that of an under-waiter's wife. Greeks and Turks found it difficult to live under the same roof.' Nevertheless, she also wrote that irresponsible mothers were isolated cases, 'due to a chronically low economic level and to poor mental endowment, aggravated by depression in the face of the overwhelmingly new situations that had to be faced'. A census taken on 11 November 1939 had indicated that 3,128 children and

522 adults remained, while by 14 July 1940 only 1,371 children and 253 adults were left in Cambridge.

While the Research Committee stressed that it was aware of the limitations of the research, generally the survey was very carefully planned and conducted. A preliminary report had been published in the *British Journal of Educational Psychology*. In the survey itself, Isaacs acknowledged that evacuation had led to friction, writing that, 'from every quarter came rumours and reports of distress and disillusion. The town was ill at ease in the country. The country was shocked at the manners and morals of the town.' Nevertheless, she also argued that evacuation had shown the strength of family ties, writing that: 'among the simple and the poor, where there is no wealth, no pride of status or of possessions, love for the members of one's own family and joy in their bodily presence alone make life worth living. So deeply rooted is this need that it has defied even the law of self-preservation, as well as urgent public appeals and the wishes of authority.'

The Cambridge survey was particularly interested in the consequences of evacuation, especially those affecting the children themselves. Only 25 of the 304 Tottenham children and 29 of the 352 Islington children were found to have an unsatisfactory relationship with their foster-parents. Billeting difficulties were greatest for the adolescent children. However, the presence of other children helped adjustment. Moreover, differences in economic and social status between the child's own home and the foster-home did not seem to make any difference in determining whether adjustment was satisfactory. Overall, the survey concluded that 'the quality of individual affection and care is of greater importance for the child than the more easily defined differences of material circumstance and characteristic manners and customs'.

* * *

Perhaps the most interesting aspect of the survey was the attempt to find out what the children themselves thought, through essays. The set topics were 'What I like in Cambridge' and 'What I Miss in Cambridge'. The lists of the most frequently mentioned subjects were closely similar for boys and girls. What boys liked in Cambridge were the rivers and fens, the colleges, their schools and foster-parents, and the parks. For girls, they were the parks, their foster-parents, the colleges, play centres and clubs, and their schools. What boys missed in Cambridge were their parents and relatives, the friends who had not been evacuated, home activities, their schools, and ice hockey. For girls, it was these things along with their pets. But the essays themselves were wide-ranging, with themes that included such diverse topics as appreciation of beauty, Cambridge children and people, church, cinema, country, cyclists and traffic, family, food, foster-parents, freedom, friends, hobbies, houses, open spaces, public baths, reading, schools and teachers, shops, and social activities.

One boy aged 14, for example, wrote that: 'I like to look at the Colleges which are beautiful. The free swimming pool is very handy in the summer to have a swim especially as we have no mother to get threepence off, to go, if the baths were not free. The river's for fishing in the summer not very far to walk or ride to where ever you like in Cambridge. There are also plenty of places to ride on a cycle to, not very far away.' Another boy, aged 13, wrote that 'I like the town because we don't have to go far and we are in the country. I like the school here because it has a better gym than what we have got in London. The town has not got any factories in it and it is not very dirty, as London.' Food was frequently commented upon. A girl aged 13 wrote that 'we have very nice food such as venison, pheasant, hare and other luxury which we cannot afford at home'.

But more poignant was what the children missed most. A boy aged 13 wrote that:

the things I miss most in Cambridge is my Father and Mother and family. I miss my dog and cat and I miss going to the Pictures on a Friday Saturday and Monday. I miss going errans [errands] here and I miss the People who live near me my friends. I miss going to see Ice Hockey Played at Harringay Areama [Arena]. I miss Playing on my skates with a hockey stick. I miss my sister saying 'Come for a Ride on your bike'. I also miss playing football in Playground at school. I miss going swimming at Tottenham Baths.

A girl of 13 wrote:

I miss my home in Tottenham and I would rather be there than where I am. I cannot find much to do down here. I miss my sister and my friends. I haven't any of my friends living in Newnham where I live and I never know where to go on Saturday and Sunday as I have no one to go with. At home I can stop in on Saturday if it is cold, but I have to take my brother out because the lady in this house goes to work and sometimes it is too cold to go any-where. I miss my cup of tea which I always have at home after dinner. I miss my mother's cooking because the lady does not cook very well.

A girl aged 15 wrote that 'I also miss my fish and chip suppers and my peas-pudding and saveloy suppers'. One boy aged 13 wrote that 'I miss the buses and the heavy lorries which go passed [past] my house at home'. A girl aged 15 wrote that: 'Over the week-ends when I feel as if I'd like to stay in by the fireside the lady I'm billeted with generally expects us to go for a walk, and as it is almost wintry it is not very nice. I miss my relations, parents and friends who are in Tottenham. And often wish our foster mother wasn't so particular although she does that for our good, as she says.'

Cambridge did not necessarily lead to an improvement in the housing situation of the children, as one boy of 14 indicated: 'I live in a small four room house with no bath no hot water laid on only gas light where at home I lived in a nine room house bath hot water electric and all convenience should be in a house two of us have to sleep in a small single bed where at home I had a big one to myself there is only one lavatory to two houses where at home we had two in one house only a very small back yard instead of a big garden.' Nor were schools necessarily better, as one 14-year-old girl suggested: 'I do not like this school it is cold and draughty and it does not come up to our good old Downhills Central School. I miss our teacher Miss...very much. I miss my dancing on a Saturday night.' Interestingly, very few children referred in their essays to the risks of war. One boy aged 12 wrote: 'All the surroundings are new and I feel very strange, though I am happy here and feel safer I am rather homesick.' Perhaps the most poignant essays were those by the younger children. One boy aged 8 wrote in response to being asked what he liked in Cambridge: 'I like my dog I like my cat I like my Granny dog to it is dead my Granny did not cry I made the grave the other dog run and run he nock [knock] the grave down.' In response to what he missed in Cambridge, he wrote: 'I miss my tortoise in lanDon [London] he is Robert taylor he bit me once he bit me. And I tol [told] him he wac [was] a note [naughty] boy and I fod [fed] him a los [lots] of tam [times].' A 7-year-old girl wrote: 'I miss dolls Pram and mummy and Daddy and granna and bathing her at night and putting her to bed and put cums [crumbs] down her throat and bits of fish and dressing her in the morning and put her plats [plaits] in and cloming [combing] her hair and nursing her.'

Apart from the essays, additional information was gained through interviews with the children. An examination of the records of children rated as unsatisfactory in their foster-homes had shown that the causes of 'maladjustment' between the child and the foster-parent were due either to the child, the foster-parents, or the child and the foster-parents. The Cambridge survey was interested in understanding the child's part in foster-home relationships, and the small number of children that had an unsatisfactory relationship

with their foster-home were interviewed and tested by an educational psychologist: forty evacuees and forty controls. The children
were classified according to six types of 'difficult' children proposed
by John Bowlby. It was suggested of the delinquent children, those
of an 'affectionless, anti-social character', that this was the result of
'a deep-lying, fundamental lack of emotional life, perhaps due to
certain special circumstances in the child's early years. The only
possible cure lies in the very difficult task of reviving the human
affection which has somehow failed to live.' In general, the difficulties of behaviour that reduced the chances of success of billeting
were anxiety, aggressiveness, and delinquency, and it was anxiety
that was the most common.

                                    *   *   *

In Stafford, Mary-Rose Benton was discovering that the more severe
abuse is, the less likely it is that a child will tell anyone about it. She
told her brothers Billy and Jimmy only about the petty theft of the
Disney mug. Their own landlady, Mrs Gibbs, considered Mrs
Newbold vulgar, and kept away from her. But all Mary-Rose's terrified crying at the pain of being struck and humiliated occurred
unheard and unseen by her brothers, sister, or the outer world,
behind the walls of 36 Blakiston Street. David and Mary-Rose often
played happily enough, but Jessie got bored in the evening, and
would set the children on her guest; as many of the evacuated children found to their cost, they were only too welcome as unpaid
servants and scapegoats, as were their money and ration books. One
evening David and Dorothy both took turns in slapping Mary-Rose's
face. Sometimes there were too many witnesses for Mrs Newbold to
beat her; for her it was a solitary pleasure. Mary-Rose later recalled:
'Intellect was lacking in Mrs Newbold, and she knew it. Her only
recourse was to bring me down to what she could cope with. She
told people I was backward. She would "speak for me", as one does

for a pet dog, but without the affection; making up dialogue to put in my mouth, adopting a gormless tone of voice. I didn't know how to pre-empt this; she was always one step ahead.'

Mary-Rose began to realize that much worse could be done to the powerless than what she was being put through. She had begun by thinking that she had reached the bottom, but she now suspected that, in matters of child abuse, there is no bottom. Frank Newbold made no effort to protect her, and put forward only the slightest protest. On most occasions he was absent, but even when he was there, he was too weak to intervene, or there may have been a pact between the two of them. Either way, Mrs Newbold had absolute power over Mary-Rose, and it corrupted her absolutely. At some point she began to starve the girl. Mary-Rose would be given one slice of bread for breakfast, or nothing at all; her food was set on the plate separately, always a smaller portion than for the others. She was a naturally thin child and did not need to eat much, a fact of which Mrs Newbold took full advantage. It was not because of rationing; the other children had enough.

Mary-Rose imagined shouting for her mother, loud enough to carry to her home in Broadstairs in Kent, and have her come and collect her. Running away was out of the question; she was too intimidated, even if she had known which direction to go. Billy and Jimmy, bored with Stafford, had made their way south out of the town, but had been picked up at the city boundary. Mary-Rose began to get painful cramps in her stomach, went to bed hungry, and began to scavenge for food. She took cabbage leaves through the allotment fence, ate berries and leaves, and picked up discarded sweets and chewing-gum. Once, at school, she was given an apple by the teacher for keeping her eyes shut during prayers. On other occasions she stole crusts of bread from the pantry.

* * *

In Lincolnshire, Carl Coates found that the haberdashery shop at Minnie and Tom's could be approached by a door behind the counter, or from under the stairs. It was a broad internal doorway, and originally it was also an entrance from the road outside. Customers could no longer wander in there from the road and browse, and the range of stock was not very great. The main items were wool, shirts, blouses, underwear, needles, pins, and stockings of the lisle or cotton-yarn variety. The area was also an overflow stockroom, in particular for biscuits. They tended to arrive in large tins, then had to be weighed out in the quantities that were required by the customer. On the outside and inside of the shop were all sorts of metal display signs advertising a variety of goods—Bovril, Woodbines, and Brooke Bond Tea—and there were also mobiles hanging from the ceiling.

The house itself was on two floors. Downstairs was the main sitting- and dining-room. There was a wall-to-ceiling corner cupboard, and next to the cupboard a window. The chest of drawers next to the corner cupboard had oil lamps on the top for evening use, and a grandfather clock was in the room along with a table and four chairs, one of which was always referred to as 'Uncle' Tom's. There was a black-leaded grate fireplace with an oven on one side, and a hot-water boiler on the other, along with a fender and set of fire-tongs. The grate had to be cleaned every day, and the oven blackened after use. One morning, when Minnie was cleaning the grate and Carl was having his breakfast, he got down from the table and, as she remained kneeling in front of the grate, said 'Auntie Minnie I will always love you'.

On most Friday evenings in summer, Carl and his sister were bathed in a zinc bath; there was the added advantage of a warm fire from the grate during the winter. On one side of the alcove a large, free-standing cupboard held all the food in use and the crockery. The cutlery was in a drawer built into the dining-table, which also doubled for other activities such as Tom doing his books, writing letters, board games, and so on. In the other alcove there was shelving, covered by a curtain. On the wall above the curtain was Tom's pipe-rack, since he was a regular smoker despite having only one lung. Close to his chair, a container held his hand-made spills. He cut long, thin lengths of wood then reached into the fire with them, enabling him to light his pipe. Tom sat in what Carl later discovered was a Queen Anne chair. Minnie always sat on a stool close to the fire, and as a result her legs were heavily mottled. Along the wall, under the window that looked out on the large yard and outhouse, was a horsehair chaise longue which extended behind Tom's chair. To the right, where Tom sat when relaxing, was a small table with a radio on. It was not operated by mains electricity, and one of Carl's jobs was from time to time to take the 'accumulator' to a small shop in somebody's house and get it refilled. This glass container was filled with a liquid that stored electricity. It had two screw points, negative and positive, and when connected to two corresponding points from the wireless produced a current that enabled the radio to work.

There were three doors from the living-room, one leading to the lobby or passage and the bake-house, another into the shop, and the third down some steps to a storage area under the stairs and a door into the haberdashery shop. At the end of this area was a large, dark, narrow pantry with cold slabs, small windows to the outside, and fly-covers to protect milk, cheese, meats, and other foods. Flies were always a problem, particularly in summer, so fly-swats and fly-papers were useful. The stairs led to the first floor, with its four bedrooms, a large, beautifully furnished lounge, and a washroom with a table, large bowl, and jug. This room was never properly used and also doubled as a storage room. At the far end of the long corridor more steps led into a first-floor storage area used mainly for the flour. This could also be approached from the yard by a series of steps that the deliverymen had to climb up with heavy bags of flour on their backs. Behind the door from the dining-room to the lobby passage stood eight water-buckets, and there was an alcove for the paraffin-burning cookers and a sink but no running water. There were storage cupboards and the enclosed paraffin oven sat on top. The water had to be collected as required about 300 yards from the house, from a central tap for which the Browetts had a key. All the buckets had hand-made wooden covers to keep the dust from settling on them. At the end of the lobby a door led into a large, dark storage area with two small windows looking onto the yard at the back. All the windows in the building were taped, to protect people in the event of one being shattered by a blast.

Double wooden doors led into the yard from the lobby, which the family could use to get to the lavatory tucked away round the back. The collection from the toilet was by a horse-drawn large metal tank, balanced between two large cartwheels. This was emptied on a field owned by a local farmer, and at some point the contents were ploughed into the soil. Outside the back door was a rock garden, with another small garden on the left-hand side, going towards the double gates. There was a third, border-type garden, not very wide, but alongside the path that ran parallel to the wall that went to the toilet.

Lorries drove into the yard through the large double gates from West Street. Coal was tipped in a large heap out in the open, then had to be shovelled under cover. There were openroof-covered sheds where the paraffin was stored in large tanks with drain taps. People brought their own containers to the shop to be filled.

Deliveries to people's houses were often arranged, including coal delivered in handcarts, some with two wheels and some with four. As Carl got older, this was often one of his jobs. Inside the sheds the 'traps' were stored, used for delivering bread and boxed grocery orders. At haymaking time grass was cut by hand by the village road-sweeper with his long-handled scythe. It was gathered up from the roadside verges, spread out around the yard, and turned in the sunshine to make hay. There was a barn on the site, where the hay was stored in the dry. There was a chaff machine in the barn, for turning the hay into horse-feed. There was a stable for the horse, and a tack room where the horse-collar and various pieces of harness were stored.

There was usually a pig in the sty, but Carl only saw a pig killed once. He recalled: 'I clearly remember seeing the live pig hauled up by its front legs on a pulley system. When it was off the ground and still alive it was cut the full length of its underbelly and bled to death with loud screaming noises. Later in the week various items of pork were brought to our house, like brawn, faggots, pork meat, and pies.' One large covered and boarded area, well protected against foxes, was for the chickens that roamed around the yard during the day. They were fed corn from time to time, but since this must have been either in short supply or expensive, in the summer Minnie and Carl went gleaning. She got permission from a farmer to go onto his cornfield after he had cut the crop, then they picked up all the heads of corn that lay around and put them into bags for the chickens.

Monday was washday, when activity was centred on the lean-to shed specially constructed against a wall of the house in the yard for the 'wash day blues'. In one corner was a brick-built boiler with a copper lining. This was filled with water, and the fuse lit in the tunnel below to set the fire going. Water had to be brought from the nearby village tap or, if it was clean, from the rainwater tubs in the yard, since it was much softer. There was also a large mangle, 'dolly tub', and 'dolly peg' to stir the clothes. Large tongs were used to remove the clothes from the boiler, and there was also a bath supplied with hot water, scrubbing-board, and brush to get stains removed. Monday washday was an all-day event, since it required a great deal of time and energy to get clothes clean. As Maggie Quinn had discovered in Leicestershire, Monday lunches were always simple: cold meat, boiled cabbage, and potatoes, or for a change they might have beetroot instead of cabbage, or sausage instead of cold meat.

* * *

While at home in Essex, Juliet Norden's brother Bryan had passed the scholarship exam for Southend High School. The whole of this school had been evacuated to Mansfield, in Nottinghamshire, and her father thought that Bryan should go there. He also felt it was vital that the three children should stay together, so it was decided they should all go to Mansfield. The children's happiness with life in the countryside and with the Eyre family thus came to an abrupt end. For Juliet, this was the beginning of a nightmare.

Mansfield was very different to the rural life in Overseal. Juliet and Myriam went to the homes of two brothers called Greaves who lived next door to each other; their wives did not get on, and went for long periods without speaking. In the house where Juliet was billeted there was a daughter called Elsie, about the same age as Juliet; an older boy, Basil, was away, serving in the Navy. In the other house with Myriam were a small girl called Pat, aged 5 or 6, and a boy of about 9 called Malcolm. Myriam had to sleep with Pat, who wet the bed most nights. The children also went to the local school. One day Juliet saw something crawling on her neighbour's shoulders. The following day her foster-mother noticed things crawling in her hair: Juliet had head lice. Mrs Greaves was angry with her, making her use her own pocket money to buy stuff to treat it at the chemist's. Juliet was very unpopular, or rather more so than usual.

It wasn't a happy household, and Juliet's being there strained things even further. Juliet's parents had now separated, and were fighting in court for custody of the three children. Mrs Greaves was told by Juliet's mother that under no circumstances was she to allow their father to see them. When in bed one evening Juliet heard shouting and recognized her father's voice. Then the door slammed and she heard him going down the road, sobbing loudly and saying 'My chillern, my chillern', in his German way. Those anguished cries haunted her ever afterwards. Around this time, her father took Bryan to live with him elsewhere in Nottinghamshire. But Juliet's mother and Mrs Greaves managed to find and remove him, then hid him away. It was decided that, for the time being, Juliet and Myriam should also be removed from their billet to a place of safety. They were taken to a vicarage at Edwinstowe, in Sherwood Forest. They were pleased to be in the countryside again.

The children did nevertheless have some good holidays during their time as evacuees. They went to see their grandparents in Surrey, and stayed with their aunt in Coventry, travelling there by train. The children were shocked to see the bomb damage: the cathedral was just a shell, and there were houses with rooms open to the elements. The town centre was all but destroyed, but Woolworths continued to trade from its cellar. Fireweed was sprouting everywhere among the debris on the bomb sites. The children slept on a mattress on the floor, as their aunt didn't have a spare bedroom. She had to keep the mattress under the stairs, and it was always damp, even though she tried to dry it in front of the electric fire. The children also went to stay with their relatives in Norfolk, on a farm. The farm was a whole new experience, and one that the children revelled in. With the dew still on the grass, they got up early to go mushrooming, and brought the mushrooms to their aunt, who cooked them for breakfast. Juliet learnt to drive the tractor and to milk the cows by hand. The most thrilling thing for her was to ride home from the fields, at the end of the day, on the back of one of the massive shire-horses.

Juliet's mother was now practising midwifery, and moved around the country working at different locations. Whenever possible she had the children to stay with her in the area for an occasional break. Sometimes all three siblings went together, at other times it was Juliet and Myriam, or they went separately. Juliet tried hard not to get too excited when it was her turn to go, because it seemed that if she did something always went wrong. The desperation she felt if her trip had to be cancelled was unbelievable. One of the happiest holidays was spent at Bridlington, partly because, unlike in Southend, they were allowed on the beach. Another place that they stayed at was a village called Gate Burton, near Gainsborough in Lincolnshire. Juliet's mother was nursing at Gate Burton Hall, a stately home which had been taken over. The children were allowed to go to the Hall with their mother, and felt overawed by the splendour of the place and the size of the rooms. On one occasion there was a dance at the Hall, which provided a memorable break from the drabness of wartime.

* * *

In Shefford, Judith Grunfeld realized that although the school was there 'for the duration', they did not know how long this would be. They often assembled the children and told them what to do when the sirens for air-raid warnings sounded. They had staff meetings when they organized duties in case of emergency and if casualties occurred. In this way they passed into the years of rationing of food and clothing, scarcity, blackouts, and air-raids. Judith's husband Isidor was serving as a judge at the London *beth din*, the Jewish ecclesiastical court. One night, when she collected him at Shefford Railway Station, he emerged from the train badly shaken, wounded, and shocked. The premises of the court in Mulberry Street, off Commercial Road in East London, had been bombed during the day. There had been casualties and some people had been killed. Judith's husband had escaped with shock and minor injuries, but the Proceedings Book in which he had been making entries had been pierced by shrapnel from cover to cover.

In other bombings in London the parents of some of the evacuated children had lost their lives. At the time of the heavy attacks people came and begged Judith and her colleagues to let them sleep on the floors of their classrooms, or offered their services free in some domestic capacity, such as in the canteen. The staff helped as much as they could. But soon every spare room was accommodating teachers, helpers, children, and friends. Some friends assisted in the sewing room, mending the children's garments and darning their socks. Others taught them gardening and handicrafts with bits of material and leather. Some taught the children new songs, or how to play chess. Some of the women who helped with the preparation and serving of meals had up until then lived in comfortable homes, and the work they were doing had been done for them by their maids. They were well educated and cultured, and the talk over the scrubbing of large pots and pans was very different from the chatter usually heard in such situations. The girls and boys on kitchen duty benefited, and did not realize they were receiving an education while they were working.

* * *

Following the raid on the night of 16 November 1940, Dave
Pinchon and John Richman moved yet again, to stay with Mr and
Mrs Bingham in Charminster Avenue. This was a nice house, and
a middle-aged couple. Mr Bingham was the ex-manager of a furniture shop, who had retired early on the grounds of ill health. One
of his favourite tricks was to ask Dave to go to the corner shop for
a pint of pigeon's milk. Even at this age Dave knew that milk didn't
come from pigeons, so he duly returned with a pint of milk
explaining that they didn't have any pigeon's milk, but would cow's
milk be all right? This routine was followed quite regularly, and
obviously gave Mr Bingham some enjoyment. The Binghams had
other boarders, including Mr and Mrs Wragg, a young soldier and
his wife. Dave assumed that Mr Wragg was stationed nearby, as
they came from Matlock in Derbyshire. After they left they were
replaced by a young Christadelphian lady, who may have shared
the religious views of the Binghams. But these religious views were
never forced on Dave and John.

While they were there they witnessed another bombing incident, on 12 March 1941, about 100 yards away. Two high-explosive
bombs had been dropped on Portland, Murley, and Ripon Roads.
One woman was killed, one man seriously injured who subsequently died, another woman was seriously injured and fifteen
other adults and children were slightly hurt. Altogether, 723 properties were damaged and the water-main burst. Two friends of the
Binghams were bombed out, and stayed with the family for a few
days. But apart from some damage to the front door, the Bingham
household was unscathed. Dave and John were quite happy at
Charminster Avenue, and in retrospect Dave was unsure why they
had to leave. He thought it may have been more financially
rewarding for them to take in older lodgers.

*   *   *

Eddy Rowley's mother came to see the children every other Saturday, travelling by Midland Red bus from Birmingham city centre. She brought with her their sweet ration, as there was more choice in Birmingham—Harvo loaves (malt bread, originally made by Harvo Ltd.) which Eddy's foster-parents could no longer get in the country, cream cakes, and other items impossible to find in a small village. In turn, she went home laden with freshly picked fruit and vegetables. Eddy's mother never missed a visit. The girl remembered one very snowy Saturday when her foster-mother gently tried to warn the children that their mother might not be able to come, but Eddy insisted on digging a little path from the farm up the country road to the bus-stop for her mother to walk along. Her faith was rewarded—the little path was used. On the other hand, Eddy's father came only very occasionally on Sundays. He was working long hours, six days a week on war work. There were some Italian prisoners of war living in a camp in the area and labouring on the land. Eddy's father would go and talk to them; he had been a soldier in the First World War so knew how they felt. Somehow they made conversation, and there was lots of laughter.

* * *

In Leicestershire, Maggie Quinn was finding that, for many people in the 1940s, their lives were governed by the seasons and the land, whether it was farming or gardening. Great importance was attached to the storage of potatoes, one of their staple foods, to see the family through the winter. First of all, Mark Burdett dug a circular pit and lined it with straw. Into this he placed the potatoes in a wooden box. Over the top of this went some wood or planks, to be covered liberally with straw, and finally soil was heaped up over the whole structure to make a cone-shaped 'camp'. When the time came to open the pit up it was already covered with grass and weeds, anchoring the soil in place. The potatoes kept perfectly in these conditions, and the only thing to be feared was whether any rats or mice had managed to get in. Baked slowly in the ashes under the fire, with some salt and a little butter or margarine, these potatoes were delicious.

From Mark Burdett, Maggie learned how to build hedges and ditches. He shared all his knowledge with her, and his sayings about the weather and the seasons were very often true. For example, 'As the days lengthen, so the cold strengthens', and 'If the sun shines at noon on Christmas days it will be a good fruit season'. As well as hens, the family kept rabbits for food and never went out without a bag to gather clover, groundsel, dandelions, and cow parsley. Mark collected every bit of horse-muck he came across for the garden. He had a little truck on four wheels which accompanied him almost everywhere, and on top of this sat their dog Peggy, a black mongrel terrier and a hunter, the terror of the local rabbit population. She was a great fighter, losing half an ear in one battle.

Maggie remembered many places in and around the village— Shaw Wood, where they used to admire the bluebells and go black-berrying and nutting in the late summer and autumn, and the Wharf with the sheds for the engines that hauled the stone trucks up from the quarry to the crushing mill which stood back from the Markfield Road. The train ran alongside Ratby Lane, on its way to the junction with the main line. There was a little brook at the bottom of the hill in Newton Lane, thick with celandines in the spring, known as Fever Brook, posted with strict warnings to keep away. In the old pit adjacent to it, used as a rifle-range, there was a pool which was reckoned to be bottomless.

Maggie attended the Congregational Chapel twice every Sunday. The main feature was the seemingly huge pulpit; at anniversary times scaffolding was erected on either side and over the top to form a gallery of seats. The older children sat on the top row, with the younger ones ranged below. The children practised special hymns for hours, and Maggie often got to recite poems, as she had a good memory. The children all had something new to wear for the anniversary; Maggie had a dress of pink satin trimmed with coffee-coloured lace. It had been made up by the village dressmaker, who lived by the chapel, and was purchased using Amy Sedgley's clothing coupons. The Sunday School Superintendent lived in Anstey, and cycled up every week to work in the chapel. On Sundays from spring onwards the family would set off after tea and walk to Bradgate, Markfield, Pymm Lees, Desford, Anstey, and Copt Oak.

For all the attractions of country life, Maggie found that health services were still primitive. In this part of Leicestershire folk cures were still much in use. There was goose grease, saved from the Christmas goose and potted to be used for coughs and colds. With a weak chest, Maggie had brown paper smeared with castor oil fixed to her back and chest to protect her from the winter chills. Each spring the children all had a dose of 'Brimstone and Sulphur', a mixture of Golden Syrup and sulphur powder. This was supposed to be a tonic after the sluggishness of winter. Chilblains, which were a common condition, were said to be cured by soaking your feet in your own urine. The doctor's surgery was in Anstey, but there were few cars and even less petrol, so a trip there meant a bus, if there was one available, or a long walk. The doctor dispensed all his own medicines, and it was customary to take an empty medicine bottle along in case it was needed. This made the waiting time quite long, since people not only had to wait their turn, but in between each patient the doctor had to make up and record his last patient's particular medicine. However, the doctor also made regular house calls, and if medicine was required then someone had to go to Anstey to collect it from the evening surgery. Maggie's one dark memory of Groby was of the dentist. He visited often, setting up his surgery in the front room of a private house in Ratby Lane. To have a tooth extracted meant going into the front room, having a painful injection, then being left to wait until the gum was numb. The dentist would come back in time to test it, but in the meantime would have a little conversation with other people. Maggie found the whole experience very frightening.

*   *   *

In Lancaster, there was an on-going correspondence between the Town Clerks of Lancaster and Salford about the condition of the Salford children. H. H. Tomson, the Town Clerk of Salford, wrote to his counterpart in February 1941 that the primary responsibility for clothing a child rested with the parents, and although an Evacuation Area had certain powers to assist, a child did not become an evacuee until he or she had arrived in a Reception Area. In light of the experience of September 1939, every Salford child who might be evacuated was now required to have a completed medical-inspection card. Head teachers were instructed to arrange for a member of staff to be at the examination, and to be responsible for the cards. These were to be given to pupils on the morning of evacuation, fastened to their coats so the Medical Officer at the station where they arrived could see them. Children who did not satisfy the Medical Officer, or who did not present themselves for medical examination, were not to be included in the evacuation party.

By March there were around 1,090 Salford children on the school rolls in Lancaster; there was a slight increase in April. However, G. M. Bland was finding his workload excessive, and asked his Town Clerk for a full-time Assistant Billeting Officer. The clothing problem had become very acute, and as far as unaccompanied children were concerned, Salford, like other local authorities, had handed responsibility for this over to the WVS. Locally, the WVS was doing its best, but there were long periods of delay before the clothing was to hand. Consequently, because of the poor condition of their clothing and footwear, householders were reluctant to have in their homes, or to take out with them, children of whom they were ashamed. There were individual complaints. The foster-mother of a boy called John Rothwell, for example, had complained that he needed boots, shirts, another suit, slippers, and other items. The boy's father had a regular job in the Parks Department at Salford Corporation, but made no effort to send clothes, apart from things which were worn out. His foster-mother was tired of having her various appeals ignored. Moreover, the boy's sister was in the same position.

On the other hand, there were plans for a children's Christmas party, to be held on 30 December 1941 in the Ashton Hall for around 750–800 children. A similar party had been held the previous year. Many individuals and organizations responded to appeals to help with this. For example, the patients of the Royal Albert, an institution for people deemed to be 'mentally defective', had given £6 9s. out of their own pockets, for the benefit of the city's evacuees.

* * *

Sir Maurice Holmes and his colleagues in their Bournemouth hotel had become concerned that evacuees, both mothers and children, were growing bored in the countryside. The secretary of one club for evacuated mothers, for instance, had written to Malcolm MacDonald, the Minister for Health, that 'I am convinced that boredom is the worst enemy that evacuees must fight, and they can only do this by outside help'. There had been attempts to set up welfare centres for evacuees. And MacDonald himself acknowledged that the boredom of the evacuees was understandable, in a radio broadcast on 15 December 1940:

You London mothers find the country almost as strange as a foreign land. It is quiet and lonely. There is plenty of activity there, but it is not the activity that is the breath of life to you. The slow growth of the hedges and the flowers and the trees is too imperceptible and too silent. You want the roar of traffic; you want the chatter of crowds; you want a hard pavement under your feet, and all the sights and sounds and smell of town. London is a magnet which draws you like steel. But I say to you simply; don't be foolish. You will enjoy those things when it is safe to return. It isn't safe now.

MacDonald claimed that a mutual sympathy was growing and deep friendships were being formed between town and country, forming a new comradeship which would make for a nation firmly united in facing the future. The real aim was to keep the evacuees in the countryside and away from the danger they would face in the cities.

On 15 November 1940 the Ministry of Health had appointed a committee to inquire into the welfare of evacuated and homeless people in the Reception Areas, to examine the provision made for their comfort and contentment, and to see how the burden on the householders receiving them might be eased. The team comprised Geoffrey Shakespeare, Parliamentary Under-Secretary for the Dominions and Chairman of the Children's Overseas Reception Board, Alice Johnston of the WVS, and the Town Clerk of Bedford.

Shakespeare had been born in 1893, the second son of John Shakespeare, minister of St Mary's Baptist Church, in Norwich, and his wife Amy. He had attended Highgate School and Emmanuel College, Cambridge, where his education had been disrupted by the outbreak of war in 1914. After serving as a captain in Gallipoli and Egypt, he returned to Cambridge in 1919, where he was President of the Union. Shakespeare had intended to pursue a legal career, but became an MP in November 1922, winning the seat of Wellingborough, Northamptonshire. However, he lost his seat in December 1923, even before making his maiden speech, then for the next six years had a successful career on the *Daily Chronicle* and *Financial News*. In the General Election of 1929 he had been returned as a Liberal for Norwich, became Junior Lord of the Treasury in November 1931, then Parliamentary Secretary at the Ministry of Health, where he was involved in the campaign for slum clearance. It was largely because of his role as Chairman of the Children's Overseas Reception Board that he had been chosen as Chairman of the committee to review arrangements in the Reception Areas.

Shakespeare himself recalled of his tour of the Reception Areas that:

It was not to be expected that the invasion of the country-woman's home by the London mother would be achieved without friction. I can see in my mind's eye now, during our visit to a town in Cornwall, fourteen perambulators parked outside the public house in which the London mothers were drinking their morning glass of stout. The country women complained that their children were being corrupted by the unruly children from London, and the London mothers bitterly complained of the hostile reception they received.

The team spent seventeen days in the Reception Areas in four regions, and produced three interim reports, with a final report published on 2 January 1941. The Committee reported that there was a wide gulf between the outlook of town- and country-people. The London woman was gregarious, and the city's crowded streets, shops, cinemas, and other diversions formed the background of her life; she was not overburdened by domesticity, was partial to tinned foods, and readily resorted to fish-and-chip shops. The report concluded that evacuation had been successful. What was needed was a frank recognition of the remaining difficulties inherent in the scheme, and the adoption of practical measures to overcome them. These included adequate arrangements for reception, including billeting and welfare, medical treatment, water supply, and clothing.

Meanwhile, following the concerns that mothers and children were bored, which had prompted the radio broadcast by Malcolm MacDonald in December, reports were landing on the desk of Sir Maurice Holmes about mothers in the Reception Areas. Welfare workers in Leicester and Leicestershire, for example, had reported that it was difficult to arouse much interest in any form of activity among the evacuated mothers. They did not want classes, but preferred to spend their time shopping, visiting cinemas, or simply walking around. Suggestions for talks on the care of clothing, First Aid, and crafts had aroused no enthusiasm. One observer wrote of Leicester that, 'in nearly every case the women who come to the Centres appear content to sit and talk to each other. This apathy...'

Similarly in County Durham, it was reported that the women from the towns wanted to congregate and talk to each other like they did at home. Those evacuated to Aycliffe returned quickly to Newcastle and Sunderland, because they could not live together side by side in a street as they had before. A meeting place such as a club was essential for the women if they were to stay in their new surroundings. There had been misunderstandings about billeting allowances. When the householders took the allowances the mothers felt cheated. One allegedly said, 'what the hell's good of coming if we can't get nowt out of it'. With no sense of the countryside and no place of their own, the women felt lost. Civil servants wrote that without the high walls and buildings, paved alleys and passages, they seemed stripped of their possessions, and 'felt naked in the open country'. There was often hilly ground to be covered when out for a walk, a hardship to feet accustomed to level pavements. The report concluded that, 'on the whole the women were representative of the bottom layers of town society. Dutiful wives and thoughtful mothers sent the children away but stayed behind themselves to look after husband and homes.'

Apart from the mothers, the other issues were as before— footwear and clothing, and school meals. Civil servants maintained that it was an essential part of the policy on boots and clothing that local effort should be drawn upon to the fullest extent, especially in the Evacuation Areas. Sir Maurice wrote on 21 April, with regard to pressure from the Association of Education Committees, that 'Percival Sharp's attempt to father the President with the responsibility for an adequate supply of boots and shoes for schoolchildren is grotesque. He is no more responsible for the condition of their footwear than for the condition of their homes.' There was little doubt that voluntary funds and clothing collections had played a significant role during the winter in meeting the needs of evacuated children. The Board accepted the LCC request for £20,000 for the bulk purchase of boots and clothing; this was to be distributed through the WVS depots. Overall, the civil servants felt that the clothing situation in the winter of 1941 had been better than during the winter of 1940. But with the arrival of American clothing supplies, they felt that the time had arrived when greater use should be made of the gift clothing without enquiring too closely whether the parents could afford to pay. Although this seemed revolutionary, and might loosen parental responsibility, the main purpose of any scheme should be to ensure that the children received the necessary clothing.

The other issue was school meals. There was no doubt that a recent circular had given an impetus to the provision of meals and milk; forty new school canteens had been approved by the Board, and proposals for a further sixty were being considered. The aim was that every child should receive a school meal as a permanent feature of the education system. Furthermore, following Dr Alison

Glover's report on the nutrition statistics, one civil servant wrote that, 'the figures themselves are so obviously inconsistent and unreliable that I think it is not merely misleading but unwise to publish them, since they could be readily attacked'. In early 1941 there were cuts in the meat supply, and Sir Maurice was concerned about the impact of this on school meals. He wrote on 24 May that, 'if the facts of the inadequacy of midday meals of school canteens were known to the public, the Government would be subjected to severe and perhaps not unmerited criticism'. He recommended a direct approach by the President of the Board of Education to the Minister for Food.

The Long Haul

In the summer of 1941 Moya Woodside described for her Mass Observation diary the frenetic atmosphere of a County Donegal hotel, writing that it was:

...almost the last place in Europe where the lights are still alight...Last year it was only half-full and those wearing evening dress were in a minority. This year it is crowded out mainly with Belfast's wealthier citizens and about 75 per cent are in evening wear. In fact the display of jewellery and furs is terrific. I am amused to note that a man's economic status is indicated by the number and size of the precious stones which adorn his wife's person and by the comparative length of her silver fur and mink shoulder cape.

On the mainland and the Home Front there were some tentative signs of the movement for post-war reconstruction. In Whitehall, for example, as we shall see later in this chapter, Herwald Ramsbotham was succeeded as President of the Board of Education by Rab Butler. There were major shifts on welfare provision, with the acceptance of the argument that all children should receive school meals; in the late 1930s these had been available only to a minority. Articles in medical journals by SMOs such as Edgar Wilkins, from Birmingham, increasingly reflected more radical arguments.

There were further studies on the psychological effects of evacuation. Cyril Burt, for instance, wrote of billeting that children had adapted themselves to new people and environments more readily than expected. There had been only a small increase in delinquency and nervous disorder, although 'a greater risk arises from the passion, perhaps quite harmless in itself, that many of the older emotional girls acquire for men in uniform'. He recommended that children should be placed in homes that, as far as possible, resembled their own, and that those from large cities should be sent, not to country districts, but to small towns. In each Reception Area social workers with training in child psychology should be available to examine cases of 'maladjustment' and to give other assistance. The drafting of the *Our Towns* report, by Elizabeth Denby and her colleagues, was proceeding. However, at the local level, as there seemed no end in sight to the war, the evacuees themselves were increasingly homesick and unhappy.

* * *

In Stafford, Mary-Rose Benton found that, to her great relief, her sister Ruby came to stay at the Newbolds; she was later convinced it was this that saved her life. At first Mrs Newbold was glad to get another girl—they were popular with landladies who wanted unpaid servants—but she soon began to feel the restriction on her sadistic games. She still kept a sharp eye on Mary-Rose, eagerly looking for faults. When the teachers got the child to write a letter home, for example, Mrs Newbold keenly took it from Mary-Rose, and scanned it for clues as to what she was telling her mother before putting a stamp on the envelope. She censored and policed the child's every move. But although she kept both children short of food, and continued to take every opportunity to humiliate Mary-Rose, the edge was taken off the situation and the girl began to cope. Mary-Rose decided that even if the big things were missing in her life—a supportive family, good food, and the confidence to make friends—she could still be the mistress of small things—practicalities like mending a shoelace, or collecting safety-pins. She was determined now not to be a victim.

By this time Mary-Rose's mother had left Broadstairs, to look for work in Birmingham. When she took time off to go and see the children her daughter could say nothing to her about the way she was being treated. Once, they all went for the day to Stafford Castle, but to try and talk about Mrs Newbold's behaviour would have been to 'try to describe a nightmare in broad daylight'. Everything looked too normal. In any case, Mary-Rose's mother was taken in by Mrs Newbold's rough-and-ready air—'the rough diamond with a heart of gold'. As the two women sat talking together, each impressed the other and found common ground. But after her mother left, Mrs Newbold reverted to her previous treatment. One night, when Mary-Rose and her sister could not sleep for hunger, they crept out of bed and took some sweets from an old toy sweetshop belonging to Doreen. It dated from before the war, but the sweets were still edible.

Sometimes life achieved a degree of normality. Frank Newbold's father taught Mary-Rose how to play dominoes, and how to take snuff. She played at the recreation ground, and joined in the boys' games of dare, taking her turn on the long swing while it was pushed by two boys, one on each end. The children had to get into the middle seat, and keep their heads well down, to avoid striking them on the overhead bars at each end, while the boys swung the ride up to its limit. As Mary-Rose later recalled, 'it was something achieved, something overcome; a minor victory totted up'. The children had been put in the top half of Tenterbanks Road School. At playtime they used the park across the road, playing on the swings, much to the annoyance of the local children, who grumbled that the evacuees got the best of everything. They also used the air-raid shelter there. Sheep were driven along Tenterbanks

Road to the market, bleating loudly and alarmed at the hard, unfamiliar tarmac under their feet after the soft meadow and field. The drovers and dogs had a hard job to do, as they hustled the sheep on to their doom. The children were no better; they ran down the steep slope of the playground to the railings and called out, mocking the sheep.

Mary-Rose always enjoyed playing with the other children, the more the better. She preferred the outside community to 'home', and found safety in large numbers. She enjoyed street games. There was Tag, which was called 'Tig' in the Midlands but 'It' in the South East; according to Enid Blyton, middle-class children called it 'He'. The Sargeants, next door, raised pigeons. Mr Sargeant often presented Mrs Newbold with a couple, their necks already wrung, but she couldn't bring herself to pluck, behead, and cook them. Mary-Rose went shopping with their elder daughter, a good-natured girl of about 14. She made her laugh at her antics with an old rag doll. Frank Newbold worked at Bagnall's. At Christmas the workers' children were given a party, and the evacuees were invited. They had several treats, including a film show at the Community Hall, where they showed the Charlie Chaplin comedy *The Ice Rink*. Mary-Rose found it more exciting to watch the film in this hut than in a proper cinema. It seemed out of place, exotic. At the party the Mayor of Stafford presented each of the children with a small gift, they had music and games, and were entertained by the adults. Then they sat down to a feast, and Mary-Rose ate well for the first time in months.

One day Mary-Rose found that her sister Ruby and brother Jack had been taken to Tamworth, to separate billets. So, apart from Billy and Jimmy, the children were all split up. The two younger boys stayed with Frank and Florence Gibbs, a middle-aged couple who lived at 2 Izaak Walton Street. Jack had been taken to the garden of a pub, and the local families were invited to go along and choose their evacuees; he was the last to be taken. He went to 24 Dormer Avenue, Boleshall, on a council estate. The following October he joined Billy and Jimmy at the Gibbs'. They were very tolerant, according to Billy. When the boy next door had the idea of giving a concert party to raise money for the Red Cross, the children all got together to find performers. The show that Mary-Rose saw in a hut in Izaak Walton Street—piano, accordion, songs, sketches, monologues, conjuring tricks, and recitals—was the kind of thing that delighted them all, and was as good as what passed for entertainment on the wireless or in British comedy films. The children found the topical jokes about gas-masks and the blackout far funnier than any George Formby film. Jack was amused to see his name in the local press, printed as 'Jackie Benton'; for one of his temperament, it seemed a bit junior for him. The Gibbs could not have foreseen what a blow it would be for Jack to be told by them on a Friday evening in 1942 that he would be leaving the following day. They were taken aback by the effect it had on him. He had come to regard them not as landlady and husband, but as friends and foster-parents. He was sent to live, for the next two years, with a family in Oxford Gardens.

At school, Mary-Rose and the other children were given some clothes from a charity. She got a pair of shoes, which she was glad to have. She was malnourished, and got impetigo, as did many other children. This acted as a counter-irritant to the head lice in her hair, which drove her frantic. They were treated with undiluted vinegar and Derbac soap. Lack of Vitamin C made the skin on her knees split in the cold, tiny streaks of blood radiating across her kneecaps. Vitamin deficiency affected most of the children that Mary-Rose knew. The corners of Billy's mouth bled, and when the oranges came that were to make good the deficiency, the citric acid got into

the open wounds around his mouth. Transatlantic supply ships were
being torpedoed, which meant that bananas didn't arrive; nor did
dairy foods, now that Denmark was occupied. At one point, the
cheese ration for a fortnight would have gone on a round of toast.

The clothes the children wore were impractical. Girls wore
frocks and skirts in the coldest weather. Young boys had to wear
short trousers; long trousers on small boys were disapproved of
among the working class. In the same way, the humble headscarf
was considered common. Warm tights would have been ideal, but
they were only worn on stage. Mary-Rose had a liberty bodice.
This was a lightly quilted, sleeveless garment, to keep the chest
warm. It either buttoned up or slipped over the head, and was
worn over the vest and under a jumper. Eventually she acquired a
pixie-hood, but before that she went bare-headed in all weathers.
Her mother bought each of the boys a leather helmet, modelled on
those worn by RAF pilots. After this they were regarded by their
schoolfellows as the elite—keeping your head warm seemed to be
considered an upper-class thing.

* * *

Juliet Norden had moved from Mansfield to the vicarage at Edwinstowe, in Sherwood Forest. The children loved the area, and found
it great fun to explore the forest and go inside Robin Hood's enormous oak tree. The vicar, the Revd Haslar, and his wife were kind,
and they had a daughter, Mary, who was a schoolteacher. The
vicarage was an enormous rambling place, ideal for playing hide
and seek, with two staircases and long corridors. The Haslars never
seemed to get angry with the children or reprimand them; they
were very patient. The children attended the local school and
revelled in village life.

However, the happy period at the vicarage was not to last. After
a few months Juliet's mother got custody of all three children,

and it was decided that they should return to Mansfield. Juliet and Myriam went to a couple called the Bentleys, who had a small daughter aged about 3. Every evening Myriam had to stay with the girl until she went to sleep. Whenever she tried to get out of the room the girl would wake up and cry; it took Myriam ages to settle her. The dinners were put in the oven on a plate at midday, until the children got home from school at teatime. As with the Butlers in Overseal, the Bentleys also kept the parcels that Juliet's mother sent to them. But when Juliet's mother came to visit the children she saw how unhappy they were, went to see the Billeting Officer, and had them moved. Their next home was with a young widow, Mrs Kirkwood, a hairdresser, who made it very plain from the start that she did not want the children. She had a boyfriend who spent a lot of time at the house, and Juliet and Myriam had to stay outside, whatever the weather, while she entertained him. Juliet once went downstairs late at night for a glass of water, and saw them canoodling; she was in real trouble then. Mrs Kirkwood gave her boyfriend the children's food rations and they were always hungry, so their mother complained to the authorities about her behaviour. Soon after this they came back from a weekend away to find all their belongings thrown outside in the rain.

By now there were many evacuees in the area, and billets were in short supply. Myriam returned to the Greaves', and stayed with them for the remainder of the war. She wasn't happy there, and was often given bread and jam for tea while the rest of the family enjoyed pilchards on toast. Juliet's next home was in a deprived area of Mansfield. Her foster-mother lived on her own, was very fat, and was quite kind. There was only one bedroom, and Juliet had to share the bed with her. Juliet began to get terrible pains in her legs, and had to wear thick, black stockings. When Juliet's mother heard that her foster-mother had had tuberculosis, it became imperative that she be moved immediately.

* * *

The war occasionally intruded on the life of Carl Coates in Lincolnshire. When he worked in Minnie's shop he found that rationing and the black market were not subjects that he fully understood. Rationing was in place, with many goods unobtainable, and there were weight restrictions which meant that many essential items were only available in exchange for coupons. On one occasion Carl made a terrible mistake when somebody asked for a particular item and was told there was none in stock, whereupon Carl informed all and sundry there was one under the counter. While the war was not on Easton's doorstep in the form of nightly bombing, searchlights, and perpetual air-raid warnings, the sound of aircraft at night was nevertheless fairly constant. There were many airfields in and around Lincolnshire, and as Carl lay in his bed he could hear the drone of Lancaster bombers. He sometimes saw them during the day, flying in formation.

While Carl and the Browetts never went hungry, though the food was always plain, there were sometimes special treats such as 'Canary' pudding, a large sponge eaten with treacle, and Yorkshire pudding, either covered in gravy or with raspberry vinegar. Minnie's brother Harry had a very good allotment, and always had fresh vegetables to pick when in season. He lived with his wife Nellie but always grew more than the pair of them needed; root vegetables like carrots, along with lettuce, cucumbers, radishes, onions, and tomatoes. Most gardens had apple, pear, and plum trees, with other fruits such as red- and blackcurrants, raspberries, and gooseberries. The fields around were also a source of food, with blackberries in the hedgerows, mushrooms in some fields, and wild crab-apple trees. To supplement their meat ration, there were plenty of rabbits. Carl and the Browetts had rabbit stew from time to time, with potatoes and dumplings in gravy.

While eggs were usually available, a large boiled egg with freshly made bread, cut into 'soldiers' with real butter, was always a treat. Chickens were killed for their meat after they had finished laying, and most families kept them for table use. There was always plenty of tea and chicory-flavoured Camp coffee, and different-coloured fizzy drinks in large bottles. Tom kept a couple of these by the side of the dresser. Bread-and-treacle was a treat, and home-made jams were available when people could get hold of sugar. Condensed milk and sugar were used on bread, while dripping was always saved from the Sunday roast. In winter the family toasted bread on forks in front of the fire, sometimes with cheese if it was available. There was always a swivel-plate fixed to the front of the fire-grate with a kettle with hot water on it, on the go for a cup of tea. In summer they did not have toast, since the fires were not lit, and kettles had to be boiled on the paraffin stoves.

Tom Browett worked long hours in order to make the business a success, and he was not physically fit. For years he got up early on baking mornings to prepare the dough and wait for it to rise. Tom and Minnie also sold coal in small quantities; this had to be shovelled into bags, weighed, then taken by handcart to whoever had ordered it. Sometimes this was Carl's job. On one delivery he was lifting a lump of coal out of the cart but forgot he was in between the shafts, tripped himself up, and went headlong to the floor, landing heavily on his chin. This meant a screaming run back home, and a debate about whether he should go to the hospital in Stamford for stitches. The decision was, 'No, it will heal.'

The stock required lifting and stacking whenever there was a major delivery. There were the chickens, horse, and pig to look after, along with preparing the feed. Whether it was connected with his limited lung function or not, Carl noticed that Tom had a problem with a runny nose. It was not uncommon for him to have a little liquid blob at the end, which seemed to stay there forever—his affectionate nickname was 'Dew Drop'. All the time Carl knew him he smoked a pipe, but not excessively; it seemed more for relaxation than a habit. He never smoked in the shop, and Minnie never smoked either. Tom suffered from gout, but there was no alcohol in the house and Tom was not a regular pub-goer.

Carl found there were a variety of things to do when he was not at school. When he was younger he did things around the house, like collecting eggs from the chicken-house, changing the candles when they had burnt down, fetching goods from the shelves when Tom or Minnie were making up orders, and going to get the accumulators refilled. Carl and his sister June got into trouble from time to time, but being threatened with being taken away by the rag-and-bone man or having a visit from the village policeman usually calmed things down. In the evening Minnie gave Carl spelling tests, and he had to write down the answers in chalk on a metal notice-board that they used in the shop to record what was available that week in exchange for coupons. There was also a little money to be made, since at the right time of year rose-hips to be made into syrup were collected from the hedges and weighed by the stone.

Carl had a friend, Teddy Smitheringale, who lived on a farm, run by his mother and father, almost opposite the shop. Mr Smitheringale was a huge man and very strong, and although a farmer, he also built farm-carts of varying sizes and types; he had built most of his own, and others he sold. Carl and Teddy often went and got the family's only cow for milking, and kept the water-trough filled for the two shire-horses and the cow. The water had to be pumped, and in the early days it took the two of them to work the handle. Carl later realized that Teddy had learning and behavioural difficulties. Throughout his evacuation in Easton Teddy relied on Carl, and they spent a lot of time together. Once, when they went to get the cow and Carl was wearing his Sunday best, he returned covered in manure from head to toe and had to be stripped and washed down in a bathtub in the yard. The Smitheringales had a large rocking-horse, which was great to ride. On one of his visits to the farm Carl saw the real meaning of the term 'headless chicken': Mr Smitheringale had cut the head off a hen, and Carl saw it run and run until it dropped dead.

Cow parsley was good for making pea-shooters, by cutting the hollow stem to a usable length. Although they were called pea-shooters, the children used grains of corn instead of peas because of the size; with a powerful-enough blow the corn would sting if it landed on skin. Catapults were another popular item with the boys, but they were banned in school. Nearly all boys had pocket knives as a matter of course; Carl had been told to carry one, along with a length of string, and a sixpence in case of emergencies. The children also had spinning-tops, marbles, and hoops that they raced around by hitting them with sticks. They also played hopscotch, jacks, and 'tig'. It was during one of these games that, racing to touch base, Carl fell and hit his head on the door surround. There was blood everywhere, and screaming. Carl was taken indoors and cleaned up to see how deep the wound was. As before, there was a discussion as to whether he should be taken to the hospital in Stamford, two-and-a-half miles away. Again it was decided not to, and the wound was not stitched. So Carl now had two scars, one on his forehead and one under his chin.

Scrumping fruit was another popular activity, since there were so many orchards and fruit trees around, but after being chased on a scrumping raid it was not one of Carl's favourites. The children had to go to Sunday School every week, and during the summer they would often go on walks after lunch on Sunday afternoon. Sometimes the Browetts took a picnic down towards Tinwell, where there was a river and the children could swim and paddle. Often, on a summer's evening, they visited the Meadows where there were woods, and collected kindling for the fires in the house and the copper boiler.

*   *   *

In Shefford, the adults and children were determined to fight the boredom which, isolated from the rest of the world in a remote village, could easily have got the better of them. They made sure that communal life should not become set in its routine, and stale. Boys and girls of 14, 15, and 16 organized debates, concerts, sports events, competitions, and musical evenings. There were prefects' meetings at blackout time, and group leaders' discussions on how to improve Jewish studies. Sometimes a teacher was invited to a meeting by the pupils, and this was considered a great honour. The 'White House Army' was the name for the team of pupils recruited to clean the rooms, tend the garden, and generally keep everything neat and tidy. Judith and the teachers had no domestic staff, and all the cleaning was carried out by the pupils. As in a real army, there were different ranks, promotions, and the awarding of stripes, badges, and diplomas. On the meadow, military-style parades were held.

There were births and marriages, bar-mitzvah festivities, and some deaths. Some children lost their parents, two of them in a bombing raid. One day five of the best teachers were called away to be interned. They were given half-a-day to pack their belongings and follow the police, then were taken to an internment camp on the Isle of Man. There was no choice. They were technically considered aliens, as they came from an enemy country, even though that country had forced them to leave. They did not have British nationality, and so were considered a risk and put under guard. The members of staff who were left had, in addition to their own work, to fill the gap. It was a year before these teachers were allowed to return.

But there were also the special days of the Jewish calendar, including the Ninth of Av, a day of mourning for the destruction of the Temple. The villagers gradually became acquainted with the calendar and its demands. The ways of the staff and children grew familiar to them, a part of their landscape, social life, friendly gossip, and a welcome distraction in their comparatively uneventful and quiet country life. They became attached to, and even proud of, the children. They listened to them singing in the choir, watched them playing football and cricket, and took an interest in their success in examinations. Important visitors included the celebrated conductor Sir Adrian Boult, who lectured to the children in the school hall. They listened spellbound, and had eager questions for him after the talk.

* * *

In the spring of 1941 one warm sunny day, George Prager and a friend had each borrowed a bicycle for an excursion. They decided that they would ride south, possibly to Cardiff. However, they did not realize how far that was. Neither of them had a watch, nor did they have any idea of how far they might be capable of riding in a day. Since they did not ride regularly, they were out of practice. They set off at a leisurely pace, enjoying the sunshine and the sense of freedom, there being next to no traffic on the roads. The few sandwiches and bottle of lemonade that they had taken with them were consumed after about three hours, sitting on a grassy bank at the side of the road. They resumed their ride and eventually arrived in Caerphilly, about halfway on their intended journey.

By now they were feeling rather tired, and suddenly became concerned about the time. They realized it was early evening and they had no lights on their bicycles, nor did they have more than a few coppers in their pockets. There was no telephone at their billet, and very few telephones in ordinary houses at that time. Quite by chance they discovered that they were not far from the train station, and it seemed that the railway might be their salvation. Mr Knight, George's foster-father, was a guard, and they might be able to put their bicycles on the train. So they made their way to the station and fortunately found a sympathetic porter to whom they recounted their sorry tale. By this time it was almost dark. When the next train for Rhymney arrived, the porter escorted the boys to the guard's van at the rear and explained their predicament. To their great surprise and relief, the guard was indeed Mr Knight. All he said was, 'Put those bikes in the van, get yourselves in and stay put.' However they received a lecture all the way home.

At the end of the spring term some boys returned to Gillingham, creating vacancies in the billets near the school. Being at some distance from the school in Pen-y-Dre, George was selected as one who could be moved. He went to a small house barely more than 100 yards from 'The Lawn' (the local school) and in the High Street. The house had previously been a butcher's shop, and was a two-up, two-down. The garden was a small dirt area with a fence dividing it from next door. The man of the house, Tom Pritchard, was the special constable who had been the first official on the scene of the plane crash. He lived there with his wife Jennie and their son Douglas, who was about five years younger than George. The police station was about 200 yards away. The people at this end of Rhymney had an 'open door' policy, and at first George found this hard to get used to, as it was very different to his life in Gillingham with his grandparents. In Rhymney relations, friends, and neighbours were allowed to walk into the house without knocking, for the front and back doors were never locked except at night or when the house was unoccupied. They said 'hello' as they walked into the back room, and sat down at the table or in any convenient chair as if they owned the place. The kettle was always on the range for tea, and instantly they engaged the members of the household in discussion and debate, usually at the tops of their voices. After a good session, they just stood up and walked out of the back door.

This back room, in which the Pritchards and George had their meals, took baths in front of the range, read the paper, did home-work, and listened to the wireless, was lit after dark by a gas-lamp hung from the ceiling directly over the centre of the table that stood in the middle of the room. Listening to the wireless was common, hoping for good news on one of the battlefronts; bad news was censored or made light of. The radio programmes of William Joyce, 'Lord Haw-Haw' (a fascist and propagandist, who became Germany's main English-language broadcaster), with his exaggerated claims of German successes, provided endless amuse-ment. Very few took his pronouncements seriously. On Thursdays the whole nation came to a standstill to listen to Tommy Handley on the comedy show *ITMA* (or *It's That Man Again*). George enjoyed the 'Jane' cartoon strip in the *Daily Mirror*, along with comics like the *Beano*, *Dandy*, and *Hotspur*.

A short distance along the High Street was a grocer's shop where George worked after school on Fridays and Saturdays to earn some pocket money. The owner was Abel Evans. George became quite proficient at weighing out flour, sugar, tea, rice, washing soda, and so on. All of these items, and others like butter, margarine, and bacon, were supplied to the shop in bulk, and had to be made up according to each customer's ration or allowance.

As Carl Coates had found in Lincolnshire, biscuits were also supplied to the shop in bulk, and broken biscuits became so popular that the quantity allowed to each customer had to be restricted. Items like tea, sugar, flour, and rice were weighed and packaged in different-sized cones of blue paper.

If the customer lived nearby, George delivered the order on foot. But on Friday evenings and Saturday mornings Abel Evans and George also drove to Pontlottyn, Abertysswg, Tredegar, Rhymney Bridge, then back to Rhymney, with the orders securely packed on the back seat of Abel's car, an Austin Ruby of 1935 vintage, chocolate brown, with black wings and running-boards. Although petrol was rationed, Abel was allowed extra because he had customers living at a distance from the shop. After some lessons George was allowed to drive the car out of the garage at the start of the trip, and back in again at the end. Once Abel accidentally drove over George's foot; fortunately his toe was only bruised. George also helped on a milk-round on Saturday mornings in a nearby area, in return for a small sum. But the daily milk at the house on the High Street was delivered by a milkman with a horse and cart. The milk was carried in churns, then dispensed from the churn to a jug using a long-handled galvanized steel measure. This milk was much creamier than that delivered in bottles. Frequently the milkman stopped to enjoy a cup of tea at the house, while the horse contentedly munched hay from a nosebag.

Sunday was chapel day, and afterwards a large number of young people paraded in their best clothes up and down High Street and Church Street. If the weather was good this could continue all day, until dusk in summer, with a lull perhaps during evening service. Much courting went on during these walks. Pubs were closed on Sundays, as were most of the shops. George spent school holidays roaming in the local countryside, usually with friends from school.

The boys took a snack, often Welshcakes, supplemented with the wimberries that grew wild on the grassy parts of the mountains. During their excursions, the boys discovered the 'Bent Iron' situated on top of the mountain to the east of the Rhymney Valley. This was an iron girder stuck in the ground, originally upright but now bent and twisted into a strange shape. They often set out with the iron as a target—the most direct route up to it was the most difficult climb, and they enjoyed the challenge. It involved climbing on loose scree, and many of them ended up with small fragments embedded in their knees.

After the Battle of Britain there had been a gradual return of boys to Gillingham, and at the end of the summer term in 1941 the majority of those still in Rhymney returned to Kent, leaving behind just one master with about thirty boys. The intention was to stay on for just one more year. George's grandmother had died in April, and his grandfather preferred that he should stay in Wales, partly because he would have had difficulty in looking after him while working long hours in the Chatham Dockyard. So George was to stay in Rhymney, and the other boys that remained were integrated with the pupils of Lawn School. It was only fifty-five years later that George found out his grandmother had taken her own life. She had become depressed because George was so far from home and the rest of the family had left the area to go and work in Scotland. At the inquest, the coroner recorded a verdict of suicide while the balance of her mind was disturbed. Annie Coleman was 56, and had hanged herself in the kitchen of her house in Kingswood Road.

* * *

In Worcestershire, Eddy Rowley did not go to the village school, as there was no room for the children. A teacher had come with them and was also billeted in the village. They had the use of one upstairs room in a chapel building, and the teacher taught all of them, from the top juniors right down to Eddy and one other boy who were still infants. The teacher must have been very good—when Eddy went home she was at the standard of first-year juniors, could write stories legibly using pen and ink, and was able to work to a high standard in maths. In summer the children helped with the harvest. There were very few men in the village as all the young men were in the forces, so everyone helped. The women who lived in and around the village and their children showed the evacuees the best way to pick fruit. Eddy became quite good at picking strawberries, raspberries, black- and redcurrants, loganberries, apples, pears, plums, and vegetables. The children also helped their foster-mother to preserve fruit by bottling it or making jam. It was fun, as well as being useful. They did it because they wanted to, and enjoyed being in a crowd of lovely, friendly people.

But Eddy's cousin Ken later told her that he and his friend were badly treated by the farmer who had chosen them. They were woken early every morning, and had to work on the farm until it was time to go to school. After school they worked again until it was too dark to see. Ken was desperately unhappy and tried to run away, but had no idea how to get home. Fortunately for both of the boys, they had entered the examination for King Edward's Grammar School before they left home, and in the summer of 1941 they heard that both had passed. So they left the village at the beginning of the summer holiday.

* * *

In Scotland, it was eventually realized that Glasgow was the main target for the German planes, and Edinburgh was reasonably safe. Parents started to bring their children home. David Hodge's mother was a bit of a snob, and had been alarmed on one of her visits to find that David, George, and Peter were turning into country yokels. The boys had picked up the local accent, and she found this offensive. In any case, Mrs Ballantyne was finding keeping three boys in her home increasingly stressful. The boys had become troublesome, and had taken to stealing fruit from the walled garden. Hendry Ballantyne and Jim Ridley had found their footprints around some gooseberry bushes, and were nervous at the prospect of their being seen by a member of the Nish family. The boys promised never to repeat this crime. Neither Mrs Ballantyne nor Mrs Ridley had any children of their own, so they were lacking in experience when it came to dealing with disobedient boys. A few days after stealing the gooseberries, David, George, and Peter went into the coal-shed and used the dust to create war-paint on their foreheads and cheeks. They got carried away, and finished up blackening their faces totally. When Mrs Ballantyne saw them she burst into tears, and was still crying hours later. That was the last straw—David's mother was contacted immediately. She arrived a few days later, and the boys were taken home to Edinburgh.

When David and George returned home, in June 1941, they found that their mother had moved house, from Pilton to St Stephen Street in Stockbridge. It was a much smaller house, but more central, and only 30 yards away from their air-raid shelter which they fled to when the warning sirens sounded. The period David had spent at the Burgh School under Miss Buckip had been really the only time in his life when he was happy to go to school. He didn't recall Miss Buckip once losing her temper. She was a far cry from the draconian, unhappy bunch of teachers David encountered on his return to Edinburgh. Most of the young teachers were either in the forces or doing work for the Government. The gap was filled by bringing retired teachers back to work. Most of them did not want to be there, and the children suffered accordingly.

There was a total blackout in the city, no street-lighting at all with all windows and doorways screened or shuttered, and wardens patrolling the streets to check that no light was being shown. There were very few policemen who were not elderly, as all the young men had been called up. This provided an ideal opportunity for criminals, and there was a ready market for almost anything in the way of stolen goods. All factories had been converted to produce supplies for the war effort. Ordinary, everyday items were no longer made in any quantity, and those that did find their way to the shops were stamped 'Utility'. It soon became recognized that 'utility' items were of very poor quality. The Black Market was very lively in Edinburgh; clothes and all food other than vegetables were rationed, but anything could be bought on the Black Market, at an inflated price. Everything sold on the Black Market was stolen, but David personally never knew of anyone who refused goods when offered them. People deluded themselves that it had merely bypassed the retailer.

On their return, David and George very quickly became quite independent. They were both capable of cooking a basic meal, getting themselves ready to go to school, and, if necessary, making their evening meal. They usually had a quick snack, and went out again, not coming home until about 9 o'clock at night. The boys had almost unlimited freedom to do whatever they wanted, and went through a delinquent period which was tremendously enjoyable. David managed to get hold of a powerful air-rifle, and he and George started to thin out the pigeon population on some of the local buildings. Meat was so scarce that they could sell all the birds they shot. They found a way into a warehouse that was full of sacks of shelled peanuts. They stole about two hundredweight, carrying them home in a crate with rope handles, making several trips in the blackout. They sold them in little bags they made up in the school playground. Fruit was in short supply—no apples, oranges, grapes, or bananas were being imported. Occasionally one could buy cooking-apples, but even these went quickly. The local boys had always known which houses within a mile radius had nice apples, but it was a case of diving over a wall or fence, then grab a few and run. David and George felt this was amateurish, and started going at night with large bags. It was so much easier, and there was big demand for the apples in the playground.

David's uncle, who they were staying with, was in the RAF. He failed to respond to a guard's challenge once, and came close to being shot. He was found to be quite deaf, and discharged from the RAF, so they had to move again. David's mother got a house in the New Town. She was to be the caretaker in a large building owned by the Unionist Association. The house was at street level, with a basement underneath. The family lived in the basement and various meetings took place in the rooms above, a bridge club or union meeting once a week but it was quite quiet most of the time. It was a massive house with large rooms that meant they could have friends staying overnight if they wished. David and George loved staying there.

* * *

Stimulated in part by the evacuees, the more progressive school doctors were beginning to appreciate the wider dimensions to the work of the School Medical Service. Some, such as Dr Edgar Wilkins, Assistant SMO in Birmingham, now placed their work in a wider context of poverty and housing. Wilkins had earlier been Director of School Hygiene in New Zealand, and this meant he had a different perspective to his British colleagues. In May 1941, for example, he provided a sympathetic account of the links between poverty and malnutrition, commenting that, 'compared with the well-off, the poor have less money to misspend, and at the

lowest levels sheer necessity compels the most economical spending'.
The income scales at or below which children were granted free
school meals were too low, while the amount of food regarded as
sufficient was about half what was required for good nutrition.
Wilkins agreed with the civil servants at the Board of Education
that routine school medical inspections did not assess nutrition reli-
ably. The growth rates of the poorer children were three-quarters
of those attending private schools, and those of the poorest were
much less. Environment was the key factor for health, and the
housing and standard of living of a large section of the population
required substantial improvement.

Wilkins argued that the 'degenerate few' were a small minority,
and to a great extent were the product of poverty. Evacuation had
led to a 'reshuffling' of the population, and had enabled middle-
class families to get a close-up view of working-class children from
the cities. It was clear that on issues such as head lice official standards were too low, and the remedy was not medical, but sociological and economic. Wilkins wrote that the prescription was not a
bottle of medicine or a course of injections, but a way of life, and
people had to have the means to live it. He said that what were
needed were: 'Better houses, and bigger houses, in well-planned
areas, houses with well-designed interiors, and at the same time
greater, not less, ability to buy better food, better clothing, better
household equipment, and maintain a standard of cleanliness and
decency that would wipe out lice, scabies, old-clothes markets, and
all that these sordid things stand for.' Poverty meant that much of
the work done by the School Medical Service was wasted, and
medical inspections should be more searching and more educational; they were a 'series of wasted opportunities'.

In a further article in July, Wilkins argued that foot problems
were common, and were bound up with well-being and the standard

of living rather than medical treatment; the remedy lay with economics and not with medicine. People could be sorted into the different social classes according to the state of their feet, so that 'bad feet' were typically an attribute of poverty, and a result of poor-quality footwear. School medical inspections revealed the poor state of children's footwear, showing that the children of the poor rarely bought new shoes, but wore the cast-offs of their older brothers and sisters or second-hand shoes bought cheaply at street markets. Wilkins found from a survey of 4,000 children that the proportion of children with foot 'ailments' rose from 20 per cent at the age of 5 to 45 per cent for those aged 5 to 10, and to 70 per cent for children aged 11 to 15. But medical inspections did not examine children's bare feet, and the efforts of voluntary organizations had been inadequate. The problem would not be solved by an extension of medical treatment, but by improved nutrition and a rise in living standards.

Moreover, Wilkins argued that, apart from bare feet, medical inspections should include general posture, ears, teeth, the state of the gums, and skin. He noted that superficial and careless inspection, done at high speed, had little value and contributed to the low status of the School Medical Service within the medical profession. Medical inspections required a quiet place, with privacy, and suitable furniture, along with adequate lighting while avoiding direct sunlight from a window. He claimed the unannounced medical inspections carried out in Evacuation Areas had given much more accurate results than the customary pre-arranged routine inspections. In addition, Wilkins argued that there were few medically defined standards for health and hygiene, and SMOs tended to accept as inevitable the impaired growth and height that were attributable to poverty, poor housing, and poor environment. As in many official spheres, medicine was characterized by watertight compartments; Wilkins wrote that 'the job requires less of the prescription-writing type of medicine and more sociology, more humanity'. He argued that poverty was contributing to illness and interfering with the attainment of maximum health; he wrote that, 'for any substantial improvement in the health of children a generally raised standard of living is necessary'.

* * *

Letty Harford later wrote of the women on the Hygiene Sub-Committee of the Women's Group on Public Welfare that, 'more than once they met during an air raid, when they sat, amongst a storm of typewriters, in our basement shelter'. There were innumerable drafts of sections of the survey which the members revised again and again. But finally Elizabeth Denby and her colleagues had completed a complete first draft of their report. They agreed that the 150-page manuscript, entitled 'The Conditions of English Town Life as Disclosed by War-Time Evacuation', should be shown to Margaret Bondfield before any further action was taken. The women asked members to volunteer to read the complete draft and send in their comments. They passed a resolution that the report had been prepared with three aims in mind—for the information of the Women's Group on Public Welfare; for consideration by government departments and local authorities; and for the information and rousing of the general public to a sense of responsibility to solve problems. Those passages relevant to central and local government (the sections on cleanliness and hygiene in schools, feeding, clothing, bad sleeping habits, and education) were to be summarized and presented to them. The women further recommended that a shorter, more popular form of the report should be published for the general public, in a sixpenny edition.

Elizabeth now dropped out of these activities for a time. Instead, she became involved with G. D. H. Cole, working on a different social survey. In 1940 Cole had been asked by William Beveridge at the Ministry of Labour to draw up a plan for the effective use of manpower during the war, and in 1941 he had been appointed sub-warden of Nuffield College, Oxford. He combined these two roles in creating the Nuffield College Social Reconstruction Survey, which aimed to collate an enormous range of demographic, social, and economic data, and to use it to argue for an extensive programme of social reform. Elizabeth and Cole were in touch from June 1941, when she said that she was interested in the survey that he was undertaking as a preliminary to reconstruction. His committee need not fear that she would expect to be associated with the college after the war. She wrote: 'I am hoping to be actively engaged in the work of Reconstruction. It is because of that that I should value the opportunity of helping in the preliminary exploration under your direction.' Subsequently Elizabeth was involved in the reports on Shropshire, Herefordshire, and South Worcestershire. In Worcestershire, for example, she was asked to cover everything west of the Severn and south of a line passing through Droitwich. Travelling by bus, she visited these areas gathering information. She wrote in September that, 'my plethora of information was partly because every job I've ever had was short of facts, so I've had to invent a technique for doing what's called "research" in double quick time'. The job was so 'laughably impossible' that she had tried to do it 'as a kind of bet'. For weeks, Elizabeth worked from seven in the morning to eleven at night. But by early September her draft reports on the three areas were complete.

* * *

The Board of Education civil servants were still ensconced in their Bournemouth hotel. Sir Maurice Holmes did not draft papers or intervene in the initial discussions of the Committee of Senior Officials on Postwar Educational Reconstruction, but he did intervene decisively later on. By May 1941 the civil servants had reached their conclusions about the contents of educational legislation. It was agreed that schools would be divided into primary and secondary; that the break would be at the age of 11; that there would be three types of schools; that the leaving age would not be raised beyond 15; and that some selective schools would continue to be financed from a direct grant from the Board. All of these were a continuation of policies laid down in the Hadow report of 1926.

On 13 May Holmes had handed in the final drafts of two important chapters of what was now called the Green Book, *Education After the War*, to the President of the Board of Education, Herwald Ramsbotham. Holmes wrote that the work was now complete, and that:

The Memorandum does not commit the Board in the slightest degree. It represents nothing more than the views of some officers of the Board and was prepared by them simply to serve as a basis for discussion with the other interests concerned. I do not, therefore, ask you to endorse all or any of the provisional conclusions which we have reached. The time for Ministerial determination of post-war policy will not arise until those interests have had the opportunity of considering the Memorandum, discussing it with us, and formulating their own views.

Later the same day he had sought permission to print and circulate, confidentially, the views of the officials as expressed in the Green Book. Ramsbotham now declared publicly that the Green Book offered a suitable basis for action at the end of the war. He wrote that: 'There do not seem to be any major suggestions on policy with which I disagree, and I should like the document to be printed as soon as possible and circulated...I feel sure that this document will be of inestimable value in settling a definite post-war programme.' He congratulated the civil servants 'upon its breadth of vision, the clarity of its contents and the method of their presentation'.

Yet this public support was the main reason behind Ramsbotham's removal from the Board and his elevation to the peerage in July 1941. He was succeeded as President by R. A. ('Rab') Butler. Butler, the son of an administrator in the Indian Civil Service, was still only 38. He was educated in England at Marlborough and Pembroke College, Cambridge, where his father later became the Master. His wife Sydney was the daughter of the industrialist Samuel Courtauld, and this financial independence had enabled Butler to settle on a parliamentary career. Elected MP for the safe Conservative seat of Saffron Walden, he was appointed Parliamentary Private Secretary to Sir Samuel Hoare, India Secretary, in 1931. Butler went to the Foreign Office in February 1938, and stayed there until he became President of the Board of Education.

When Butler was interviewed by Churchill in Downing Street, the Prime Minister said:

'You have been in the House fifteen years it is time you were promoted... You have been in the government for the best part of that time and I now want you to go to the Board of Education. I think you can leave your mark there. You will be independent. Besides... you will be in the war. You will move poor children from here to here'; and he lifted up and evacuated imaginary children from one side of his blotting pad to the other; 'this will be very difficult'.

Education had seen no major reform since 1902, and the post of President carried little weight with other members of the Government. Occupants had usually been keen to move on to something more prestigious—there had been six Presidents between August 1931 and July 1941. But Butler had wanted to go to Education, as he knew war was a productive time for educational planning and advance, and much talent was wasted in the existing system. As we have seen, even before Butler's appointment to the Board civil servants had drawn up tentative plans for reconstruction, and he found intense activity and infectious enthusiasm when he arrived there. Churchill was reluctant, saying that he could not contemplate a new Education Bill in wartime; he saw Butler's main task as being to get the schools working as well as possible. Moreover, Butler recalled that Sir Maurice Holmes was 'disappointingly compliant'. Nevertheless, the new President decided to disregard Churchill, and push ahead with the proposals made in the Green Book.

12

Reconstruction

The opportunity offered by the evacuation was seized upon by some professional groups. The Child Guidance Council, for example, had argued in 1941 that there was great scope for more preventive work, by educating adults in ways of looking after children more efficiently and training teachers to recognize what children's reactions meant. Psychiatric social workers, after they had been thrown out of their clinics into the Reception Areas, also found there was much work to be done, through close contact with Billeting Officers, in dealing with homes for difficult children, children in bombed areas, and in terms of the whole issue of evacuation. The Council claimed that psychiatric social workers had taken child guidance 'out to the people'. It stated that: 'If the War has necessitated vast evacuation of children and families—uprooting and transportation, it must help us to study social and psychological phenomena as they have never been studied before. It is from such studies that we will draw wisdom for a future mental hygiene plan.' It was a chance to study children living with foster-parents, or in hostels with their families, or in families divided by the war, as well as children under 6 who were still 'unformed psychologically'. More generally, on the Home Front, there were gradual moves towards reconstruction, which in part reflected the debate about the evacuees. The Beveridge report was published in

December 1942, and there was an important House of Commons debate about it in February 1943.

* * *

In Stafford, Mrs Newbold was still trying to hit Mary-Rose on the sly, when she thought Ruby was not looking. But the girl's sister caught her at it. When Mary-Rose's mother moved up to Birmingham she first took a job at Wright's Ropes, then settled for one with the Midland Red bus company. She wanted to drive, but Digbeth Garage was the only garage that did not allow women drivers. Still, Mary-Rose's mother was at last getting a wage that she could live on. She came to love the smell of the place: it meant work, and money coming in. Mary-Rose could not remember the day in 1942 that she left the Newbolds. There was no dramatic rescue; the abuse simply stopped. Mary-Rose noticed a sudden improvement in Mrs Newbold's behaviour. Thinking it was a change of heart, she began to feel she would not mind staying there. In reality, Ruby had told their mother some of what had been going on. Around this time, Mary-Rose was given some clothes that had belonged to a child who had died. A friend of her's made a face and said, 'Ooh, she's wearing a dead girl's clothes.' But her display of distaste didn't bother Mary-Rose; they were just clothes, which she needed.

The summer of 1942 was hot, and in the holidays the children rambled over the Staffordshire countryside, getting brown and coming home with armfuls of bluebells. They played out until 10 o'clock, and as they came off the recreation ground at night and the last of the children were going indoors, some still in the swimming costumes they had worn all day, their mothers chatted contentedly about how cheap it was to clothe the children in summer. The children made their way back, the sweat cooling and sticky on their skin. Mary-Rose now considered that she was happy.

* * *

George Prager later admitted that he did not write home from Wales as often as he might have done; there were too many other things to do. Very often the Pritchards would write on his behalf, informing those at home in Gillingham of any news regarding his health, progress at school, behaviour, and activities. George later discovered that the school had also sent reports to his home at the end of every term, and that these were filed away by his grandfather. Having an arts bias in the subjects that he studied at school, and having both a liking and an aptitude for art itself, he often spent time on winter evenings making Christmas and birthday cards, painting them in watercolours and sending them home. Often, too, he would draw something on a postcard, such as a Spitfire or Hurricane, or a ship that was in the news, colour it in, and send it home with a message like: 'Dear Dad, I am well and everything is fine. George.'

Usually, though, he had to be reminded to send some real news home. Life was for living, and most of the time there were not enough hours in the day to fit in all he wanted to do. George's stepbrother Ronald had been evacuated to Resolven, in South Wales, and George realized that it was near enough for him to visit. Having saved some of the money he earned by running errands and helping in the shop, he decided to make the journey by bus. This meant taking the local bus between Rhymney and Tredegar, then boarding the coach that passed through Resolven on its way to Swansea. George's impression was of a journey that seemed to be much too fast on narrow country roads. But he spent a very pleasant day with Ronald, exploring the locality while recalling the times they had spent together in and around the Medway towns before the war.

Tom Pritchard had obtained a small film projector, and with it a single short black-and-white cartoon film. The illumination was from a low-wattage lamp, and the film had to be cranked through the projector by hand. The characters in the little comedy were a horse and a wasp. The wasp annoyed the horse by buzzing ever closer, and the horse tried to retaliate by swishing its tail. It ended with the wasp stinging the horse on its hindquarters, which caused the horse to jump right out of the picture. George got a lot of pleasure showing this sixty-second film over and over again. From the local wireless-repair man he bought a table microphone and small speaker, and spent much time experimenting with them. There were two real cinemas as well, both only minutes away—the Scala, opposite the police station, and the Victoria Hall, which was just around the corner. Many of the evacuees went to one or the other about once a fortnight. George found another source of amusement when he acquired a punchball and a pair of boxing gloves.

George learned First Aid from a manual that had been issued to Tom; soon he could name the bones in the human skeleton and tie the basic bandages for various injuries. From Jennie he also learned knitting, sewing, and cooking. Most of the older houses in the valley had a coal-fired range for cooking and heating. Coal was delivered by lorry, normally in a half- or full load, dumped unceremoniously outside the front door. The whole family would then fill buckets, tin baths, sacks, and any other suitable containers, and carry the coal through the house to wherever the coal store happened to be. The coal was usually ungraded, and consisted of lumps ranging in size from a pea to a piece weighing half-a-hundredweight. The huge lumps were soon reduced to a manageable size with a hammer.

During the autumn of 1942 George was invited to help in the Rating Department of the local council. He spent several Saturday mornings transcribing rate payments from carbon copies into the main ledgers. He was provided with a high stool at a long bench with a sloping top on which the ledgers rested. They were larger than any books George had ever seen, and in order not to damage a page when turning it he had to get off the stool and step sideways with it. In the same building, on the ground floor, was the Civil Defence Headquarters. This was the control room, and was connected to other wardens' posts by telephone. From here, the warning siren would be sounded in the event of a raid, and messages from the police and other control points in the area could be received. At the end of January 1943, since George was now 16, it was agreed that he could assist in the control room on Friday and Saturday nights, and be a messenger if telephones were out of action. In fact most nights were very quiet, and George spent them sleeping or jogging around the tennis courts across the road.

* * *

From late 1941 Dave Pinchon had been living at 5 Court Road, where he was billeted with the Wright family. This was his sixth billet in Bournemouth. Mr Wright was a bus driver, with rugged features and large ears, while Mrs Wright was a thin, grey woman. They had a pleasant grown-up son called Ron, who lived away from home, and Gordon, who was younger. He was spoiled, irritating, and a nasty piece of work; even Dave's friend John Richman, who was normally very placid, lost his temper with him once, when Dave and John thought that their jam ration had been tampered with. In his spare time Mr Wright was an entertainer, assisted by Gordon. The opening of the act was based on a play of words between father and son. It started with Mr Wright stabbing a finger at Gordon's chest and asking 'What is that under there?' Gordon replied, 'Underwear'. Mr Wright asked, 'Under there'. Gordon replied, 'Underwear', and so on. The routine was practised endlessly and was wheeled out at any opportunity.

Mr Wright was a competent gardener, and grew some of his own vegetables. He also kept three or four chickens to provide a few eggs. Fresh eggs were scarce at the time, and had largely been replaced by National Dried Egg. Mr Wright introduced Dave to organic gardening. Making manure water required filling a cotton bag with manure, lowering it into a bucket of water, then squeezing the bag until the water took on the colour of strong tea. To a young town boy from a fairly sheltered background this aspect of organic gardening left slightly stained hands and a lasting impression. Food was not plentiful during this period, and Dave's diet was supplemented by the occasional bread pudding cooked by his mother. Made in an old roasting tin, it consisted mainly of stale bread, dried fruit, sugar, spices, and lard. It kept well, and Dave rationed himself to one slice at a time. One day, fuelled by the pudding's calories, he and John were kicking a tennis-ball about in the road outside the billet when he kicked it through the window of the house opposite. As it was broad daylight Dave was sure his crime had been witnessed, so was left with no alternative but to knock on the door and confess. Unfortunately the owners were out. He called back later to apologize and offer to pay for the damage. The owner said, 'I will ask you to pay only half of the repair cost because of your honesty, and do you want your ball back?' On this occasion, his honesty was rewarded.

In early 1943 Dave and John moved to stay with Mrs Hawthorn at 53 Fortesque Road. She was shortish, quiet, and motherly, up to a point. She was in her fifties, and her life had not been easy. If there was a Mr Hawthorn, he was never mentioned. Mrs Hawthorn's legs were permanently lagged with crêpe bandages, and walking was difficult. Dave did not know whether the problem was ulcers or varicose veins. The real tragedy in her life was that she lost her only daughter to tuberculosis while Dave and John were there. They had never met the girl, as she was in a sanatorium, but they did send her some chocolate, and received a nice letter back. She was about 19 or 20 when she died. Dave didn't remember the funeral, and she may have passed away while the boys were on holiday. Mrs Hawthorn had been a cook and housekeeper to either Gilbert or Sullivan, of 'Gilbert and Sullivan' fame. She told Dave how she used to spin sugar into a basket shape, and fill the basket with coloured marzipan miniature fruits.

Like George Prager in his Welsh village, Dave listened to Tommy Handley's *It's That Man Again* on the radio. Very often, just before the Nine O'Clock News, they heard, 'Here are some personal messages, *ici Londres, ici Londres*.' This would be followed by several rather short, obscure sentences in French, which were always repeated. They were clearly coded messages, intended for the Resistance in France and Holland. They were sentences like 'The owl will hoot twice tomorrow night' or 'The apple tree is in bloom again'. At the time Dave didn't know what their purpose was, nor that they were directed across the Channel. He now wonders what happened to the intended recipients.

* * *

Juliet Norden's ninth billet was with an old lady, Mrs Tallon. Juliet slept in an enormous, sparsely furnished bedroom at the front of the house, right next to the road. When buses went by at night the whole room lit up. It was a terraced house, and Mrs Tallon's son and his family lived next door. They had a daughter, Muriel, about the same age as Juliet, and the two became great friends. At Christmas in 1943 Muriel gave Juliet an illustrated book, *Rumanian Fairy Tales*. Next to Mrs Tallon's son lived her daughter. Myriam told Juliet she had a recurring dream that she had found her way back to their bungalow in Westcliff. In the dream, the children were all in the kitchen, the smell of baking filled the room, their mother was quietly ironing, and everything was back to normal. It was the children's way of keeping their memories alive and their hope for the future.

But Mrs Tallon had applied for a one-bedroom bungalow, which was now available. Juliet's brother Bryan had been living in various billets in Mansfield, and now lived with a couple called the Sages and their son Barry. Juliet had often been to visit Bryan there, so knew the family well. Bryan offered to move to a hostel for difficult children so that she could go and live at the Sages. Mrs Sage was kind but quite strict, and not very motherly; she always seemed to be ill. Mr Sage worked for the Co-Op as a baker's roundsman, using a horse-drawn cart. He was a jolly man, fairly plump with a smiling face. When he came home in the late afternoon he was always in a jovial mood; it was only later that Mrs Sage told Juliet he had been drinking. Barry was about Bryan's age, three years older than Juliet. He made holes in Juliet's photograph of her mother in her nurse's uniform, which was one of her most treasured possessions.

Mrs Sage was a good dressmaker, and Juliet loved to watch her at work, especially when she was making wedding and bridesmaid dresses. She made two dresses for Juliet, one blue with white spots, the other red with white. She also used to cut her hair. Juliet and the Sages all moved house, just a short distance away, and found a greenhouse in the new garden, full of ripe tomatoes. They had tomatoes for every meal, day after day. Juliet had never eaten so many in her life. Her stomach objected and one night she had a severe bilious attack and was sick all over the bed. Not wanting to disturb anybody, she just got in the other end. The next morning there was a horrible dried-up mess, and Mrs Sage was not pleased.

She said that she would rather have dealt with it at the time—'What was Juliet thinking of?' The highlight of her time with the Sages was the outings that they had to their relatives in the country. There was a long bus journey, then they had to walk down a lane before arriving at the cottage. The appetizing smell of dinner would greet them as they walked through the door. Juliet always saved some of her meagre sweet ration to spend at the village shop.

* * *

By January 1942 the number of Salford children on school rolls in Lancaster was down to about 563. At the same time, planning for future evacuations had improved. Two types of examination were to be held before any new evacuation: a medical inspection and a check of equipment. It was recommended that children should have a comb, soap, facecloth, toothbrush, and handkerchiefs, and that these should be packed in a rucksack or case, with all property marked with the child's name. Other equipment to be taken included ration books, identity cards, and gas-masks. Meanwhile, some of the Evacuation Areas had become better organized. Information sent by the LCC to G. M. Bland in Lancaster, for instance, included: what to do if a child needed clothes; how to get money for a child's boot repairs; and how to fill in forms. While parents were still held responsible for supplying their children's clothes, by March 1943 there were forty-eight Clothing Depots in the Reception Areas, forty-six of which were run by the WVS. Mothers were now told that, in future, both adults and children registered for evacuation would be medically examined before leaving the Evacuation Area. Only those who attended the examination would be allowed to travel.

* * *

Many of the evacuees recalled stealing apples and so on, and juvenile delinquency was a popular area for research. There was, of course, an existing secondary literature on this problem. In his study of crime in inter-war England, for example, Hermann Mannheim, then Lecturer in Criminology at the London School of Economics, had listed some fifty-three possible causes of juvenile delinquency, based on an investigation of the records of 1,017 boys and girls at a Borstal institution. Mannheim left out poverty, owing to a lack of data, although he conceded that it might be the real cause of ill-health and educational failure, family quarrels, the premature death of parents, poor housing, and unemployment. Overall, he argued that both social factors, and physical and mental factors, were causes of juvenile delinquency. He claimed that unemployment was a direct cause, especially when it coincided with 'unfavourable home conditions', but he was reluctant to go further, since there were no control groups in his study. In November 1942 Richard Titmuss commented that 'faulty parental training is a factor in the causation of delinquency but Mannheim's work does not show it to be the most important agent'. He argued that 'overcrowding and bad housing conditions produce social misfits, frustration, petty delinquencies and so on'. It remained unclear how much could be blamed on parents and how much on wider social factors.

In an expanded version of lectures given in Cambridge and London in early 1940, Mannheim had also considered the relationship between war and crime, and between group and individual phenomena. Juvenile delinquency did seem to have increased in wartime. Relevant factors included the disruption of family life, the absence of fathers, the war work of mothers, a lack of supervision, and the curtailment of social and educational influences. Added to these were a general atmosphere of restlessness and excitement, and practical issues such as lighting restrictions. During the First World War, Germany had seen a decrease in juvenile delinquency in 1914 but a great increase by 1918. Mannheim also explored the relationship between evacuation and juvenile delinquency, suggesting that there was a strong chance that crime would increase even more than it had done during the First World War, along with the need for Approved Schools and Child Guidance Clinics.

By 1941 there were newspaper reports that juvenile delinquency was increasing and that play centres were needed; some commentators argued that state aid had diminished a sense of parental responsibility. A report from a Child Guidance Clinic in Bristol, for instance, noted that the number of juvenile offenders referred to the clinic by magistrates and probation officers had increased from 68 in 1939/40 to 100 in 1940/1. The authors argued that economic deprivation was not as great an aggravating factor as lack of consistent parental control. Families moved in slum-clearance schemes to large housing estates, for instance, had found that the estates were too large to have any sense of social cohesion, while opportunities for group activities and recreation were fewer than in the neighbourhoods they had moved from. Moreover, parental discipline was absent because of war conditions, and the opportunities for adventure had multiplied in the bombed areas. Children needed more supervision than was available in weekly interviews with probation officers, and the same children were continually being brought before the courts. Those children categorized as 'dull' and 'defective' required more provision, including in residential schools.

* * *

There were further studies of evacuees from the autumn of 1941: on juvenile delinquency in Bristol; on the effects of evacuation and air-raids on children; and on bedwetting. Following the London Blitz in 1940, psychologists and psychiatrists were particularly interested in comparing the effects of evacuation with those of bombing. University College London's Psychological Laboratory had been evacuated to Bangor, North Wales, and one study was of 100 pre-school children evacuated there, 90 per cent of whom had experienced severe air-raids just before evacuation. Of these, fifty-six had settled down satisfactorily and forty-four had not. The author, Enid John, claimed that, even after three to six months in a quiet area, children who had experienced air-raids were apt to show nervous after-effects. This was not due to their having experienced a raid, the severity of the raid, or the length of the raid, but to the amount of fear that the child had experienced at the time of the raid. What was key here was not the noise or the proximity of the raid, but the amount of fear that the child's mother had expressed when the child was close to her. This made it much more difficult for the children to settle down after evacuation.

The general thrust of these studies was to argue that the effects of evacuation were worse than bombing. Another study, of seventy-three children attending the Manchester Child Guidance Clinic, by Mary Burbury, suggested that in terms of their mental health, six were better because of evacuation; seventeen were worse; in nineteen their symptoms could be attributed to evacuation; and in thirty-one their symptoms were unchanged by evacuation. With regard to air-raids, out of a group of ninety-eight children, one child was improved; eighteen were worse; in seventy-three there was no change; and in six the symptom shown was linked with air-raids. Burbury concluded that 'the immediate effect of evacuation, which is separation from parents and a known and accepted environment, is worse than the immediate effect of raiding—that the fantasy, waking or dream of the raid is provocative of greater anxiety than the reality'. An American study agreed that it was evacuation rather than bombing that had caused the more severe and prolonged reactions. Children up to the age of 3 had adapted well to the raids, and indeed older children regarded them with excitement. Rosemary Pritchard and Saul Rosenzweig wrote that 'the youngster's more active curiosity and love of adventure could tend to make the experiences of war and especially of air-raids something of a thrill. Repetition of such experience would find him more adaptable than adults.' The most important psychological effects of war were the result of social separations.

Following the outbreak of the war, Anna Freud, the psychoanalyst and daughter of Sigmund, had been deeply concerned about the plight of children made homeless by bombing, and had established a residential war nursery in Hampstead, with a branch in the country for older children. Detailed reports of this work by Freud and Dorothy Burlingham were collected in *War and Children*, published in 1943. Freud again found that London children were in general much less upset by bombing than by evacuation. She was particularly concerned with the development of the relationship of the small child to its mother, and with the effects of separation. In a later study, published in May 1944, Frank Bodman, Acting Director of the Bristol Child Guidance Clinic, reported on a survey of 7,000 children after several air-raids. A boy called Peter had been referred to the clinic in June 1939 as a maladjusted boy who could not read or write: 'He attended for play therapy, and his play was aggressive, destructive; baby animals were shot, Indians chopped off cowboys' heads, cowboys cut off Indians' heads; boats were sunk; people drowned. Everything had to be completely destroyed.' When the bombing began his fantasies came true, and his aggressive tendencies became worse. But later he was evacuated to a farm, and was happy; he did not want to go home even when his mother visited. Bodman argued that what children feared most in the air-raids was not their own death but that of their parents, so that they would be left as orphans. Individual children illustrated the importance of the family circle, and the strength of the ties that bound members together. In general, children were adaptable and recovered well from air-raids, but the strain of separation from parents through evacuation was greater, and the effects more profound.

* * *

The work she did on evacuation was only one of Elizabeth Denby's many activities in wartime. She was a witness to some of the investigative committees set up by the Coalition Government as part of its plans for reconstruction, including the Scott Committee on Land Utilization in Rural Areas in early 1942, and the Dudley Committee, a sub-committee of the Central Housing Advisory Committee. In July 1942 she was recruited onto the Utility Furniture Advisory Committee, and curated an exhibition, called 'Homes to Live In', for the British Institute of Adult Education at St Martin's School of Art. She later served as a member of the Royal Institute of British Architects' Housing Group, whose report *Housing* was published in 1944, and was appointed as Director of Housing to Tarran Industries Ltd. Tarran was one of the Government's main suppliers of prefabricated buildings under the temporary housing programme begun in October 1944.

Although their survey was nearing completion, the members of the Women's Group on Public Welfare were experiencing difficulties with publishers owing to stringent regulations about paper quotas. Margaret Bondfield was in North America giving lectures for the British Information Service. In an address to the National Social Work Council, given in New York in early 1942, she referred to the report, hoping that it would be printed before too long. When Shelby M. Harrison, the General Director of the Russell Sage Foundation, heard this he sent $500 towards the printing costs, thinking that the report would also be useful outside England. Writing to thank him for this donation, Letty Harford noted that the work of the Sub-Committee had been spread over two years, that the report had already been circulated privately among the group members and other experts, and that it 'has already aroused the greatest interest'. However, Harford glossed over some problems. One had been the view taken by the Ministry of Health. Dr Alison Glover had written a 'tiresome letter', while Enid Russell-Smith, an Assistant Secretary, had telephoned, saying she was informing Glover that the Ministry was taking no responsibility for the report, and offering only informal comments.

The Women's Group discussed the publication of the report at a meeting on 7 April 1942. As soon as the revisions had been completed, publishers had been approached. It had been hoped that Penguin would accept the book, but it had exceeded its paper quota. Oxford University Press could publish the book at a cost of 5s. a copy, with a print-run of 5,000 copies. However, this was dependent upon paper being made available from some outside source. Spottiswoode, Ballantyne & Co. could supply the paper to OUP, but this was only just sufficient for a book of 50,000 words. There was no alternative but to cut the manuscript down. Celia St Loe Strachey accepted an invitation from Mrs Montagu Norman (the wife of the Governor of the Bank of England) to undertake this task. She was the wife of the political writer John St Loe Strachey, formerly Labour MP for Aston and a former friend of Oswald Mosley. Celia herself had worked as a journalist on the *Spectator*, but had been dismissed in 1931 for being too left-wing. More relevant was that she had written the survey *Borrowed Children: A Popular Account of Some Evacuation Problems and Their Remedies*, published in 1940. Oxford University Press might issue a thirty-two-page pamphlet in the Oxford Series on Home Affairs. In considering the offer by the Press, the Group regretted that a cheaper edition was not possible; this might be printed later on. Thus the women finally accepted the Oxford University Press offer, and the future possibility of a pamphlet.

Meanwhile the text was being checked by officials at the Board of Education and the Ministry of Health, and the Group hoped to hear soon from the Ministry of Information. The women agreed that the report should be published, as long as there was no objection from the ministries. The Women's Group on Public Welfare, in association with the NCSS would be responsible for it, but there should be no mention of evacuation in the title. Committee members were invited to send in suggestions to Amy Sayle. Letty Harford subsequently wrote to Elizabeth Denby in September on the wording of the subtitle. There remained a strong feeling that it was wiser to leave out any direct reference to evacuation on the cover. The final title was *Our Towns: A Close Up: A Study Made During the Years 1939–1942 Together with Certain Recommendations Submitted by the Hygiene Committee of the Women's Group on Public Welfare in Association with the National Council of Social Service*. It was felt that the date 1939 was associated with evacuation in any case, and this gave the impression that the whole thing was more up-to-date than it actually was. The final arrangements for publication were discussed at a meeting on 21 September 1942.

* * *

With Rab Butler at the helm, the debates about the health and welfare of children had rumbled on into the spring of 1942. Sir Maurice Holmes wrote the foreword to the so-called Green Book, *Education After the War*, and told Butler in 1942 that the duration of the war would determine the outcome of educational reforms, saying that 'the longer it lasts, the more clamant the demand for social equality is likely to be'. In April one of Holmes's colleagues wrote that experience had shown that it could not in fact be assumed, by the Treasury or any other Department, that any child being evacuated for the first time would be properly equipped by its parents and would not need Government help with clothing. It was as necessary to protect the householder against the new arrival who was badly equipped, as against the child who was evacuated with adequate clothing and wore it out.

In his Chadwick Trust Lecture, given in May 1942, Dr Alison Glover drew on the earlier discussions. He conceded that the School Medical Service was 'a *school* service paid for by educational funds in order to prevent waste of those funds in teaching children too defective or ill nourished to derive benefit from education, rather than to be a complete Child Health Service'. It was still hedged with artificial boundaries designed to prevent educational funds being diverted for health purposes. It was responsible for medical inspections and some forms of treatment, but not for medical treatment at home or in hospital, acute conditions, or infectious diseases. It could only offer advice on home conditions, and there were huge variations of staff and organization in the 315 LEAs. Nevertheless, if the child of 1939 was fitter than the child of 1914 to bear the strain of wartime, in Glover's view much of the credit for this should be given to the School Medical Service.

The main issue in the summer of 1942 was the debate about the growth rates of children evacuated to camp schools. While it had always been assumed that city children benefited from their stay in the countryside, the Bransby study was a serious statistical survey of the issue. It measured 4,626 children in camp schools; 4,337 children from thirteen Evacuation Areas from which the camp-school population was drawn; and 2,951 children from eight Neutral Areas. It had found that in the first year of residence in the camp schools, the height and weight rates of the boys were less than normal, and of the girls slightly less than normal. The explanation was thought to lie in the psychological shock of evacuation. The report noted that, 'it cannot be altogether unexpected that such a shock might be accompanied by a slightly reduced growth rate'. Civil servants at the Board of Education were surprised that the children in camp schools had not put on as much weight or grown as much as the children who remained in the Evacuation and Neutral Areas. One admitted that the conclusions were 'frankly rather disconcerting', another that they were 'rather different from what was expected'. Sir Edward Howarth, the Managing Director of the National Camps Corporation, admitted that the implication 'would appear to be that it is better for a child to stay in East London sleeping irregular hours in ill ventilated shelters and eating fish and chips than to have fresh air conditions in one of our camps with regular hours of sleep and plenty of well prepared wholesome food'.

A second study, for the period 1941–2, had produced similar results to the first one, with reductions in height- and weight-gain. The height and weight measurements of older boys in camp schools were less in 1942 than of boys of the same age in 1941. While the rates for girls were practically the same in both years, the growth of boys continued to be below pre-evacuation rates. Although some civil servants remained convinced that the children in the camp schools were living in better conditions than they would have had at home, with more sleep, a good diet, adequate milk, and plenty of exercise in the open air, one admitted that 'Bransby's findings are more surprising than ever, and I don't pretend to know what the explanation may be'. The Bransby report was published in October 1944, but its conclusions were toned down at the request of Sir Edward Howarth.

Despite the Bransby report, there was significant progress on school meals. Sir Maurice Holmes argued that a speech by Sir John Anderson, now Lord President of the Council and Chair of a Committee on Reconstruction Priorities, had made it clear that the school-meals service would have to be developed to supplement the family allowances that were planned to tackle the problem of poverty, and which had been boosted by the publication of the Beveridge report in December 1942. He wrote on 18 February 1943 that, as for the Government's readiness to consider a free service, Anderson 'could hardly have said less, since it is quite idle to pretend that the provision of school meals goes some way to filling the gap between 5s and 8s if the parents are to continue to pay any part of the cost of such meals'. The cost would have to be fully met from the Exchequer. But Holmes knew that the Treasury would not accept plans for free milk. He wrote to Rab Butler on 14 April: 'that free meals and milk will come one day as part of the Beveridge plan for children's allowances I do not doubt, but we clearly cannot anticipate the introduction of that scheme.' Nevertheless, provision of school meals and milk expanded further during the war, while the 1944 Education Act made provision for medical inspections and treatment, clothing, and for children with disabilities.

13
Going Home

Some of the social surveys had attempted to find out more about the return home of evacuees in the first wave. In the Cambridge Evacuation Survey, for example, interviews had been used, predominantly with parents in both Tottenham and Islington. Most of these visits were done by psychiatric social workers. An analysis of all the cases in the two boroughs (131 families) suggested that the main reasons why the children went home were family ties, reflected in the anxiety or loneliness of the parents, or homesickness or desire of the child to return; parents' dissatisfaction with the foster-home; and financial issues, either in terms of the costs of billeting, or the need to have a child of wage-earning age at home. But in practice it was difficult to separate the parents' anxiety and loneliness from the child's alleged homesickness. One report on a girl aged 13, for instance, said that: 'Kathleen is an only child. Her mother stated that she was not well (sores on her face), and was also unhappy. It was the visitor's strong impression that the mother was lonely and dependent upon Kathleen for company. She does not appear to have a very intimate relationship with her husband, and Kathleen is her main emotional outlet. The father was furious that the mother brought her home.' Another report on a girl aged 13 stated that:

Rose is the eldest child in a family of three girls. Her mother, described as 'a very pleasant and quiet woman', said that Rose 'fretted inwardly' whilst she was away. It had been reported to the mother by friends visiting Cambridge that she was looking ill because of homesickness, so she decided to bring her home. Subsequently she heard from a younger girl, that Rose cried herself to sleep every night 'for fear of what would happen to them if father and mother were killed in London'.

The second reason for children returning home was the parents' opinion of the foster-home. In the case of a boy aged 9, it was reported that:

The mother complained that in the billet the child was not kept clean; his ears were dirty, and his clothing was not properly washed. Every time the parents visited he was unhappy and cried to come home. (The School record confirmed the fact that the child had been homesick). The mother said that he was obviously not wanted, and both parents felt that this was bad for him. The billet, they said, consisted of an elderly couple of over 70, and one unmarried daughter.

The Cambridge survey argued there was no doubt that the expense of keeping the children away was one of the most important reasons for bringing them home. There were thought to be two main types of family. There was the 'conscientious' family of high standards and moderate earnings, who found they could not meet their obligations without falling below the level of home life they had set for themselves. The second was the 'feckless' family, living from hand to mouth, unable to save, and dependent upon the support of the children as soon as they reached wage-earning age. A report on a girl aged 14, for example, noted:

Parents unable to control any of the children. Both the two eldest brothers (who in 1940 had just joined the army) had Juvenile Court records, one for sexual misbehaviour with men, and one for assault with intent to rob. Ellen herself, at one time suspected of feeblemindedness, had been referred to a Child Guidance Clinic for 'dirty habits' and masturbation, and was said by the head teacher to be 'brow-beaten at home, frightened of her father'. The father, however, brought her regularly to the clinic and seemed to take a great interest in her. He actually paid three visits to this child in Cambridge, in spite of the poverty at home.

Apart from the three main reasons for bringing the children home, there were others ranging from illness, the desire of members of a family to be together for Christmas, or difficulties with younger or older brothers or sisters. But this aspect of the survey also served to indicate the variety of the experience. It was reported of a boy aged 11, for example, that the child's attitude towards war dangers was 'unconcerned. He is dying to use the new air-raid shelter, and is disappointed there has been no warning since his return.' Overall, what the survey demonstrated first and foremost was the strength of family ties. Susan Isaacs wrote that:

those who are constantly in touch with family life know that this often does not show itself in the simple expression of affection. It may be that bitter antagonisms exist within the family group but that even so the need for belonging may be stronger than the fear of neglect, anger or even cruelty. Scenes in the Juvenile Court constantly illustrate this truth. In time of danger and uncertainty individuals have even greater need for unity and for the reassurance provided by the familiar background of their lives.

* * *

The *Our Towns* report was finally published in March 1943. In the Introduction, the authors wrote that the plan had been to take the accusations levelled against the evacuees one by one, and to see what evidence existed to support them. It then sought to relate the accusations to urban conditions, and to suggest a means of remedying the defects complained of. Evacuation was 'a window through which English town life was suddenly and vividly seen from a new angle', and its effect was: 'To flood the dark places with light and bring home to the national consciousness that the "submerged tenth" described by Charles Booth still exists in our towns like a hidden sore, poor, dirty, and crude in its habits, an intolerable and degrading burden to decent people forced by poverty to neighbour with it.' Moreover, within this group were the 'problem families'. The task of improving social conditions was one of education as much as of environment. The campaign for better education must be waged side by side with the battle against poverty and bad material conditions.

The book was divided into two sections on 'Living Below Standard'. The first included 'wrong' spending, bad sleeping habits, bad feeding habits, juvenile delinquency and want of discipline, and dirty and inadequate clothing. Thus it covered heavy drinking and smoking, betting, and the football pools. The report argued that the statistics on malnutrition generated by school medical inspections were contradicted by other social surveys, such as those by Sir John Boyd Orr, and it was critical of the 'slum diet'. It looked at juvenile delinquency, and at the issue of clothing and footwear. The second section embraced lice, skin diseases such as scabies, impetigo, and ringworm, 'insanitary habits', and bodily dirtiness. Thus it explored the problems of infestation and skin infections, bedwetting, sanitation, and housing. In each section the report made various recommendations. The Conclusion noted that housing was poor, and there were striking regional variations in health. In addition it argued in support of nursery schools, which might be the only agency capable (in Elizabeth Denby's phrase) 'of cutting the slum mind off at the root'.

The book was widely and favourably reviewed. The *Times Educational Supplement*, for example, said the survey was: 'An honest and courageous book, which all those concerned with the shaping of post-war social and educational policy will neglect at their peril...their book should be read by every citizen who wishes to understand the background of the maladjustments in our society, which the Beveridge Report is designed to correct.' *The Times* claimed that it should be read by all social reformers. In the *Eugenics Review*, David Caradog Jones wrote that 'one of the most valuable parts of the book is the list of very practical and sensible recommendations following each separate section'. The social survey was mentioned in a leader article in the *Economist*, under the headline 'Spotlight on Poverty', and the reviewer for *Social Work* said it was a book 'full of wise and constructive suggestions'. The *Lancet*'s reviewer described it as a 'remarkable study', which was an 'eye-opener' and retained a 'human and almost racy style'. *Public Administration* asserted the book 'must be read to be fully appreciated', while the *New Statesman* said it was a 'first-class social document'. It was 'definitely not a bookshelf book, but a social document, which, being read, should be used for political action'. Margaret Bondfield was still on her lecture tour in North America. She wrote from New York of the book that 'it is much better than I had hoped. It has covered so much of the neglected ground, and the recommendations are so concise and practical.' Joanna C. Colcord, Director of the Charity Organization Department of the Russell Sage Foundation, wrote to Letty Harford that 'your Committee has done a brave and useful thing in presenting the facts about these sore spots'.

By 6 April 1943 the first edition of 5,000 copies was nearly sold out, and a reprint of 4,000 was ordered. *Our Towns* was mentioned by several of the speakers in a House of Lords debate on evacuation on 5 May. Lord Geddes said he had read it 'with extraordinary interest', while the Archbishop of York said it was a 'quite admirable report' and 'most valuable social document of the very first importance'. It was mentioned in the *Educational Reconstruction* White Paper in July. By October it had been reprinted three times, and the journal the *Medical Officer* again commended the book to its readers. Finally, in the House of Lords debate on neglected and homeless children on 29 March 1945, the Lord Bishop of Sheffield referred to 'that very competent report, *Our Towns*'.

* * *

Gradually the tide had turned in the war, from the battle of El Alamein in October 1942 to the D-Day landings on 6 June 1944. But with the first flying-bomb (V1) attack on London a few days later, on 12 June 1944, the final wave of evacuation began. The first mothers and children left London on 5 July. The flying-bomb attacks were on the South-East of England, particularly the capital, and so the geography of relative danger and safety had changed. The original categories of Evacuation, Neutral, and Reception Areas were now obsolete. Following the June 1944 evacuation, in September the authorities in London decided to operate 'evacuation in reverse' and bring the bulk of former evacuees home to the city. It was not an easy task. Mothers and children, infants, old people, the blind, and people with disabilities were scattered throughout England and Wales. The LCC had to arrange for children to be gathered from approximately 1,000 billeting areas, formed into parties, collected into train-loads, brought to London, sorted and sent to eighty evacuation districts in London, and then escorted to a particular house in a particular street. A count in March 1945 showed that during the previous six months 600,000 evacuees had left the Reception Areas. On 2 May the signal was given that all Londoners who had homes to return to could leave the Reception Areas, either in organized parties under escort travelling in special trains, or with the aid of free travel vouchers. The London movement was completed by 12 July 1945; 115 special trains had carried 29,701 unaccompanied schoolchildren, 21,127 mothers and accompanied children, and 3,489 other adults. Thus the evacuees returned in their thousands to a dilapidated London, to damaged and uncomfortable homes, and to the accompaniment of rockets. Housing remained a serious problem.

*   *   *

Lancaster had an opportunity in 1944 to test the plans that had been made for evacuation since the evacuations of September 1939 and June 1940. In Salford, the Director of Education conceded to head teachers that difficulties had arisen in Lancaster in September 1939 over the billeting of some children; if Billeting Officers knew more in advance of the possible arrival of such children who might be likely to cause problems they might be able to arrange more suitable homes. There continued to be debates about how many evacuees could be accommodated in particular areas; by June 1944 the boarding-houses in Grange-over-Sands, for example, were full of people from the South, many of whom had evacuated themselves privately. The number of evacuees in Lancaster fluctuated between 1,323 on 17 June, to 748 by 14 October. But there were other continuities. The Chief Constable wrote to G. M. Bland on 28 August about a boy called Ramon Drewitt, of 58 Wimbledon Road, Tooting; his sisters Joan and Valerie were also billeted in Lancaster. On Saturday, the father had come and taken the children home. The Chief Constable wrote that:

Apparently parents can register and evacuate at will and when convenient to themselves, while the country pays the piper. The irony of it all, is that if I refused to accept evacuees I am liable to prosecution. If I wish to object to receiving them I must appear before a Tribunal but parents, at the expense of the State, can take their children away without even the courtesy of informing the foster parents beforehand, and by so doing expose their children to the risk of bodily harm or even death. Truly, we are a wonderful nation.

Returning evacuees were particularly numerous in September; many had left Lancaster without consulting the Billeting Office. A lot of children had returned home because their parents had unsettled them; the parents were thought to be too weak in dealing with them. Many were from areas in South London or near the south coast, where they thought there was little danger from the flying bombs or from gunfire across the Channel. Poor weather in the North was another factor, while mothers claimed that husbands, sons, and daughters were living and working at home, and needed their children there. Only advice could be given, and there were no compulsory powers to prevent evacuees returning home. In some cases the advice to 'stay put' had been taken, but in others the evacuees had left Lancaster, and there had been no opportunity to use persuasion. The net effect was that while there were 748 evacuees in Lancaster on 15 October, the number had dropped to 566 by 11 November. On 31 March 1945, when Bland gave up his post as Chief Billeting Officer, there were 437 evacuees from London still billeted in Lancaster, along with another 13 in nearby areas. He had served since June 1939, and he signed off in typical fashion: 'I have relinquished my job without leaving a bad debt, an equipment query, or any outstanding matter for settlement.'

* * *

In 1942 Mary-Rose Benton had left Stafford temporarily, to live with her mother at her digs in Small Heath, in Birmingham. Her billet was at the end of Somerville Road, and Mary-Rose occupied herself there all day until the landlady's children came home from school, when they played together on the bank of the River Cole, little more than a stream at that point, but a rich playground for imaginative children. Mary-Rose longed to have a large family around her. She read stories of happy families, and idealized them.

In the autumn of 1942, because of the threat of aerial attacks, a colleague of her mother's, a fellow conductress at the Midland Red Bus Garage, took her in. Winnie Williams was 28, and lived with her 40-year-old sister Nellie and their mother, who was in her mid-sixties. Although they had two Scottish women billeted with them, Mary-Rose could be squeezed in, sharing a bed with Winnie. It was a small bed, and Winnie weighed some 12 to 13 stone. Mary-Rose spent a lot of time on her own while the four women were at work. She played in the garden, and bounced a ball against the wall in the yard. At first Winnie's mother was kind, until she realized that Mary-Rose was not quite the little slum child that she could impress with her gentility; from then on the girl could do nothing right. Abuse took the form of hitting her, while over Sunday lunch the three women would take turns listing her faults. Winnie planned her physical attacks. There was only one strike, usually a blow to the head, but meticulously set up, after Mary-Rose had been prompted to say the wrong thing. Nellie never hit the girl but joined in with the nagging. In its repetitions and rhythms, it was more damaging than the blows.

One day Mary-Rose's mother called round, and arranged to take her and Winnie for a holiday to London. They stayed at Mary-Rose's grandmother's house in Penge in Kent, and explored the city by day. But what greeted Mary-Rose's eyes was not what she had looked forward to. She had expected palaces, shops filled with toys, brightly lit theatres, huge parks, famous people. Instead, the parks had anti-aircraft batteries sited in them, everywhere there were bomb-damaged shops, bus windows had sheets of perforated yellow paper gummed to them to prevent flying glass, and office windows were also taped across with sticky paper.

When they went back to Birmingham they couldn't stay with Nellie, as her mother had gone into hospital with appendicitis.

Mary-Rose went back to her mother's lodgings in Golden Hillock Road. She had taken these digs in order to be closer to Digbeth Garage. It was only towards the end of 1942 that Mary-Rose's mother got the key to 3/27 Adelaide Street, in Balsall Heath. It was a back-to-back, part of a street-length terrace. Above the cellar the other three rooms were stacked on top of each other. There was no bathroom or garden, and the house was gas-lit. The rent at first was 5s. a week. Mary-Rose stayed at Adelaide Street with her mother, going with her on the buses except the very early or very late ones. But even though she slept with her mother, Mary-Rose began to have nightmares. She later remarked: 'It is said that the abused child spends the rest of her life paying for it. I now had the leisure for this process to begin.' In fact she stayed with her mother only for a matter of months, before she was moved to Penge, in Kent, to live with her grandmother. Mary-Rose was able to boast that she was the only child evacuated to London.

* * *

Eddy Rowley's cousin Ken had gone home in the summer of 1941, but she and her sister Jean were to stay in Drakes Broughton for nearly two years. It was only in October 1942 that her parents decided it was time for the children to come home. One day Eddy's foster-mother put the children on the single-decker Midland Red bus with their belongings and bus fare. They sat on the back seat and waved until they could no longer see the lady who had cared for them with great affection during a very difficult time of their young lives. Their mother met them at the bus station in the centre of Birmingham.

It was quite difficult for Eddy to fit in at school in Birmingham when she went home. Montgomery Street School was still closed, so they had to go to Golden Hillock Road Junior School. (Though they did not know it, this was close to Mary-Rose's mother's lodgings.)

The school in Birmingham assumed that the children's education had suffered while they were away. Schools in the city at that time were streamed, and Eddy was placed in the 'D' class. She was given a small blackboard and a piece of chalk to work with. Sums that Eddy found very easy were written on the large blackboard in the classroom, and the children had to copy them out and work out the answers. She copied them down and worked out the answers as quickly as the teacher wrote them up, but the rest of the class struggled. Eddy was used to writing in exercise books with pen and ink, could do much more advanced work than the other children in the class, and was miserably unhappy. Jean was luckier. She already knew some of the boys and girls in her class, so settled down quickly. It was the only time in Eddy's life when she didn't want to go to school, but she didn't say anything to her mother and father. Fortunately, at the end of term Eddy was moved to another class, but she didn't have a real friend for the rest of the three years and two terms that she was there. She just got her head down and worked as hard as she could.

*   *   *

In Rhymney, George Prager found that most of the older houses in the village were small, and many of the miners' cottages had front doors that were less than six feet high. Living in such a cottage in Morgan's Row was George's first serious girlfriend, Mary. By now George had grown so much he had to duck when he entered their front door. Mary and George were of the same height, and she had freckles and red hair. They spent many happy hours together, walking and talking, often in company with other couples of the same age. They visited the cinema, took part in the Sunday parades, and sat talking on warm evenings in the park. A few days before he left Rhymney, Mary's mother gave George a sizeable package. In it he found a grey suit in a fine check pattern that had belonged to her son. It no longer fitted him, but it would fit George well, and Mary's mother wished him to have it. But it was a platonic relationship; George and Mary only kissed when they said their farewells when he left for Gillingham.

Early in the autumn of 1942, George had realized that, in view of his grandfather's age, it would soon be necessary for him to become the family breadwinner, so he decided to follow in his grandfather's footsteps and enter the dockyard at Chatham as an apprentice. By then George was one of the last three evacuees from the County School for Boys left in Rhymney. He passed both the examinations, and after a medical at a doctor's surgery in Newport at the end of July 1943 he was requested to present himself at Chatham Dockyard on 23 August to select the trade he wished to pursue. On 20 August Mary, one of her friends, Mrs Pritchard, and a couple of neighbours accompanied George to Rhymney Station to kiss him and wave a tearful goodbye. He boarded the train bound for Gillingham, carrying the same suitcase that he had arrived with three years earlier. Three days later he started at the Chatham Dockyard as an engineering apprentice. At the end of that first week his pay-packet contained 17*s*. 3*d*.

* * *

While they were at Fortesque Road, Dave Pinchon and John Richman had been joined by a boy called Richards whose parents kept a pub in the Hampshire town of Romsey. He was a year older than Dave. But Dave didn't really know why he and John left Mrs Hawthorn in early 1944. She already had someone else staying with her, a young lady who worked in a local department store. Perhaps Mrs Hawthorn wanted a more permanent lodger. Instead, the boys moved to Fernheath Road in Wallisdown, to Mr and Mrs Sims. Although this was a brief stay, and a long way away from school, their sojourn there was pleasant. Mr Sims worked shifts, either in an engineering plant or on munitions. He worked long hours, and was seldom seen; the boys got into trouble for not washing up his dinner things. Mrs Sims was tall, auburn haired, and had been a model. The couple had a daughter of 7 or 8 who was learning to tap-dance. If any visitors came, a wooden mat would be unrolled and the routine performed. One incident stuck in Dave's mind. He and John were playing in the gorse-land at the back of the house. Their game involved making a small camp fire. The next thing the boys knew, a large gorse-bush was burning furiously. They could do nothing but watch it burn and make sure the fire didn't spread. They went back to the house in fear and trepidation, but the incident was greeted with something bordering on indifference.

One of Dave's clearest memories of Mrs Sims was on the morning of D-Day, 6 June 1944. She and the boys were having breakfast, accompanied by the continuous drone of aircraft overhead. Mrs Sims said, 'This has been going on all night. Something big is happening. Would you like a cigarette?' She offered Dave a Star cigarette, which he accepted. Round about the middle of June Dave finished at school and returned home. He had been away, apart from holidays, for nearly five years. He said goodbye to John, his room-mate of almost four years. Dave did not remember, but his guess was that they said, 'Cheerio—see you around'. The two did not meet again for over six decades.

When Dave returned home to Southampton there was plenty of military activity in and around the city; troops and stores were being shipped out and soon German prisoners of war and Allied wounded were being shipped in. Once at home, he quickly picked up the threads of normal family life. This was not difficult, as he had been at home for school holidays and the occasional weekend. He reflected that for the first two or three years of evacuation he did suffer from homesickness and had been fairly miserable.

It followed any holiday at home, but gradually lessened in length and intensity. At the time people seemed to be more emotionally restrained. For instance, Dave's cousin was killed in a raid on Hamburg. This news was broken to him in a very gentle and respectful manner, but in his presence was seldom referred to again.

* * *

In Leicestershire, where the forces were also being built up for the D-Day invasion, traffic through the village of Groby was greatly increased by convoys of soldiers, both British and American. The children waved and gave the 'thumbs up' sign to the British troops, and the 'victory' sign to the Americans. If the convoys came through the village at playtime, the children all ran to the school railings and cheered like mad. Sometimes, if they were lucky, the American soldiers threw sweets and chewing-gum. 'Got any gum, chum?', they chanted at every American vehicle.

It was during the holidays, in the summer of 1944, that Maggie Quinn finally returned home to Birmingham. She could remember the day vividly. Maggie later wrote: 'It marked the end of what had been for me a very happy period in my life.' Maggie had been happy in Groby, and it was hard to leave. In another way, though, she was excited about going home, because she had been in close contact with her own parents and had received regular visits and letters from her mother, father, and sister. But the reality of going home was a shock—not the return to her own loving family, but the change in her environment. For the previous five years she had lived in a small, sleepy village, with life proceeding at a slow pace and everything geared to the land and the weather. Going back to inner-city Birmingham was a culture-shock. Even the language was different. Maggie returned with a Leicestershire accent, and people looked at her quite strangely when she spoke.

When she went back, rationing and shortages took on a new perspective. Maggie's parents still ran their small corner shop, selling sweets, milk, sugar, tea, and various other packets and tins. With them, she saw rationing from the shopkeeper's point of view. The ration books had pages of points, 'A', 'B', and 'C', and many goods could only be purchased with these—dried fruit, biscuits, jam, custard powder, jellies, and nearly all tinned and packet goods. A tin of salmon could take a whole month's allocation of points. Personal points, 'D', and 'E', were for people's personal allowance of sweets. All these points had to be cut from the ration books at the time of purchase, and every month Maggie helped her mother and father count them. The form to be filled in with the totals had to be taken to the Food Office. Maggie and her parents needed to be very careful and accurate, as these were checked over by officials.

At first Maggie was desperately homesick—not only for the foster-family she had left, but also for the countryside. It was this that had the most impact on her. She soon got used to being with her mother and father, and brothers and sister, and made new friends, but it took her much longer to adjust to what seemed to her to be an alien environment. She had always had an instinctive love of animals and nature, and during her time in Groby she had learned to understand and love the country way of life. Sooty, industrial Birmingham, with factories and houses all jammed together, was not what she wanted, and she hated it. She missed the sky, the sunsets, and the space.

The granite house she had lived in at Groby was owned by her foster-family and was large and spacious, with a huge garden and numerous outhouses where she had played for hours in seemingly endless summer days. But Maggie felt she was again fortunate in many respects. Her mother and father owned their own house, and this was luxury compared with the back-to-back houses so many people were forced to live in. Maggie's parents were very understanding and allowed her to go back to Groby every school holiday, where she was welcomed with open arms. Gradually, everything settled into a pattern. She learned to take advantage of facilities that were not available at Groby, such as the library, which as an avid reader fascinated her, and the parks where she and her friends played tennis and putting. Her mother took Maggie to the local church and she joined the Sunday School and Girl Guides. But although she adjusted and lived in inner Birmingham for the next twelve years, she did not think, deep down, that she ever really came to terms with her city environment.

* * *

In the summer of 1944 Juliet Norden's life had also changed dramatically. With the rocket attacks on London, evacuees arrived in her village. Mrs Sage decided that she could squeeze in one small boy, who would share a room with Barry. Juliet was no longer the only evacuee, and had to share with a scruffy little cockney. Fortunately he didn't stay long. Juliet and Myriam had both taken the scholarship exam for the Southend High School, which was evacuated to the Queen Elizabeth Grammar School for Girls in Mansfield. By the time Juliet went there, most of the Southend pupils had gone home. Then, at last, came the end of the war in Europe. It was the food that Juliet remembered from the parties that were held to mark VE Day:

Now is the time for jubilation, down come the Blackout curtains and strips of brown paper criss-crossing the windows. Up go the banners and balloons, the flags and the bunting. Then the street parties begin. What a time we have, where has all this food come from? Tables the length of the street, laden with food I haven't seen since before the war. People must

have been hoarding it and keeping it for just this occasion. After eating we
dance the night away and I fall into bed thinking I can go home
tomorrow.

But when Juliet woke up in the morning, she realized that she
didn't have a home to go to. Her father had bought a small house
in Beeston, near Nottingham, hoping that one day they could all
go and live there and be a family again. However, Juliet's mother
had other ideas. She now had custody of the three children, and
having obtained a legal separation, had no intention of ever going
back to her husband. The war had enabled her to get out of an
unhappy marriage, and that was how she would remain. Of course,
she had no home, as she was expected to live in, where she worked.
So in the meantime the children had no choice but to stay in their
billets, with the agreement of their foster-parents. After three long
months the family did find a home. They went to live with a friend
of their mother, in a village called Sturton By Stow in Lincolnshire.
There was no running water, just a pump in the garden and a
chemical toilet; neither was there any electricity, just oil lamps and
candles; and all the cooking was done on the coal-fire range. The
children had to take their bath in a tub in front of the fire. But
apart from the toilet, they found it quite fun and certainly a challenge. They were back with their mother again, and Juliet had to
pinch herself to make sure it wasn't a dream.

* * *

Like Maggie Quinn in Leicestershire, Carl Coates found in
Lincolnshire that American soldiers had an impact on village life,
including providing plenty of chewing-gum for the local children.
Since many men were away fighting in the war, he often saw local
girls courting American soldiers. There was also a prisoner-of-war
camp in West Street in the village, which was guarded by American
soldiers. There was a serious incident one afternoon, when a flight

of Lancaster bombers had a mid-air collision over the Meadows. The American fire brigade left their camp at breakneck speed, followed by servicemen crowded into jeeps. Carl and other children were playing in the street at the time, and had no idea what was happening. They went down to the Meadows, where the first rescue vehicle had not even stopped to open the gates but drove straight through, wrecking the gate completely. Several of the aircrew had been able to bail out, but one parachute had not opened, and the word in the village was that, since it was marshland, they had to dig the dead airman out of the ground.

Carl and his sister June had only seen their mother and father once during their stay at Easton, before they returned home to London in September 1944. Their new home was a large Salvation Army establishment in Spa Road, Bermondsey, South London, where their parents were in charge. This was a men's hostel, complete with a paper-works, mattress-making section, laundry, salvage sales, transport section, and a base for Italian prisoners of war. Carl was now just 10 years old. The women in the paper-works made a fuss of him, while the men were helpful if he wanted to try the things they were working on. For instance, there was a large scrap section, and several of the men got together to build him a bicycle out of spare parts. Brindley Boon, the accountant and cashier there, recalled:

When I joined the staff the officers there were Major and Mrs Richard Coates. They were refined, sensitive people who gave themselves wholeheartedly to serving the men entrusted to their tender care. I never knew either of these gentle souls to raise their voices above a normal conversation level, yet they commanded the love and respect of all who lived or worked there... The Coates children, June and Carl, were very much part of the Spa Road family and were thoroughly spoiled by the staff and the men. It was never quite the same when the youngsters were at school

Although the war was now coming to an end, Carl did witness some doodlebug and V2 rocket attacks on London. When victory was finally declared he felt sure Tower Bridge would be raised when the announcement was made. He cycled a mile to get there, but the bridge didn't move. Apart from some bullying at his new school, Spa Road was a very happy place for Carl. However, within a year the family were on the move again, this time to Newcastle upon Tyne.

* * *

It was only in August 1945 that the time came for Judith Grunfeld to say goodbye to her hosts, to the countryside, to the White House, and to Shefford in general. On 31 July the staff and children had given a concert in the school hall in the presence of all the foster-parents, Billeting Officers, and village personalities. In songs, plays, recitals, and speeches, they put on a show to demonstrate their gratitude towards their hosts. Solomon Schonfeld, the principal, conceded that for most of the time he had been in London, dealing with administrative matters, but Abraham Levene, the head teacher, noted that during the years in Shefford over fifty pupils had been successful in the London matriculation exam. This was all the more remarkable because many of the children could speak little English on their arrival.

In her address, Judith said that the time had come to say goodbye, the familiar sights of Shefford would retreat, and London would once again become their home. But they would never forget the village. She remembered the day they had arrived, strangers lost in new surroundings. But the mothers had made them welcome, and the children had grown up and developed over the six long years. There were about 600 children who had passed through the school, and in their hearts Shefford would live on. Judith said:

Now we are going to say goodbye. A part of the road that is called life we have walked together. You were the hosts, we were the guests. The guests are leaving now and they are leaving with a blessing...Shefford may be small on the map, but we shall see to it that its fame will be spread far and wide. I hope you will remember us as we remember you, and when teachers at school want to drive home a lesson about how to live up to a great challenge, they will bring up the example of what happened during the Second World War in Shefford, the little village in Bedfordshire.

The school held its last prize-day in Shefford, and the proceedings ended with cheers for the village and its people. The *North Bedfordshire Courier* reported on 7 August that the Thursday morning 'saw Shefford streets full of children carrying cases of all sizes and conditions, making their way to the rendezvous in North Bridge Street where there were empty buses. Many townsfolk had come to wave goodbye.' The signal was given and the buses were quickly filled with pupils anxious to wave goodbye to friends on the pavement. Judith later recalled:

Once again we lined up on the village square—six years older. The streets were lined with our friends, there were hugs, moist eyes, farewell scenes. Some folks were really heartbroken and they showed it. The children who left Shefford now had grown in stature, in body as well as in mind, and were the richer for all the experiences they had gathered. The buses that had brought us in 1939 took us back home to London to pick up where we had left off.

* * *

On 31 March 1946, when the evacuation scheme came to an end, there were still 5,200 unaccompanied schoolchildren left in the Reception Areas of England and Wales; around 3,000 were living with foster-parents, 1,000 were in residential nurseries, and the rest were in hostels. Some had no homes to go to, others were orphans or had parents who had split up, and a few had been deserted by their parents. The closing down of the evacuation scheme was a slow business, and was still going on in 1948. Viewed against the upheavals of war, the problem of parental neglect was insignificant, and eventually the majority of the evacuees went home. Many children found it difficult to settle down after their return: their parents were strangers, they had acquired new accents, and their homes were unfamiliar. Many of these problems were psychological. The war had been exciting for some, anxious for others, boring for most. Fathers came back from the army with romantic ideas about home life and parenthood. Mothers wanted not a teenager, but a little girl again. And children accustomed to large middle-class homes were in some cases returning to crowded, noisy lives in small terraced houses.

14
Ordinary People in Extraordinary Circumstances

Along with Emanuel Miller and Donald Winnicott, the psychiatrist John Bowlby had argued as early as 1939 that the separation of small children from their mothers could lead to 'persistent delinquency' in later life. Bowlby subsequently concluded, from forty-four cases seen at the Child Guidance Unit of the Tavistock Clinic in London in the years 1936–9, that twelve were 'affectionless characters', and seventeen had suffered early and prolonged separation from their mothers. Bowlby wrote that:

The essential factor which all these separations have in common is that, during the early development of his object-relationships, the child is suddenly removed and placed with strangers. He is snatched away from the people and places which are familiar to him and whom he loves and placed with people and in surroundings which are unknown and alarming...it is the difficulty of developing new libidinal relationships where none have previously existed or in circumstances traumatic for those already in being which appear to be critical in the development of the Affectionless and Delinquent Character.

Of twenty-three persistent thieves, thirteen were affectionless, twelve out of fourteen cases of 'affectionless character' had suffered prolonged separation from their mothers during the first five years, fourteen of the twenty-three persistent thieves had suffered prolonged separation, and fourteen out of nineteen of those who suffered prolonged separation were persistent thieves. Bowlby concluded that a large proportion of children who stole persistently were of 'an affectionless character', a condition which resulted from 'their having suffered prolonged separations from their mothers or foster-mothers in their early childhood'.

What came to be called 'attachment theory' was further spread through Bowlby's World Health Organization (WHO) report *Maternal Care and Mental Health* (1951) and his popular book *Child Care and the Growth of Love* (1953). Bowlby wrote in 1951, for example, that: 'The proper care of children deprived of a normal home life can now be seen to be not merely an act of common humanity, but to be essential for the mental and social welfare of a community...deprived children, whether in their own homes or out of them, are a source of social infection as real and serious as are carriers of diphtheria and typhoid.' Thus, while Bowlby's theory was not formed through observations of the effects of evacuation, this popular book, which went through many editions, defined 'Bowlbyism' as 'keeping mothers in the home', and in the immediate post-war period made the question of the provision of childcare for working mothers almost unthinkable.

*   *   *

What, then, of the impact of the evacuation on the children themselves? David Hodge certainly found on his return to Edinburgh that there was an atmosphere around that said 'Live for the day, you may never see tomorrow'. It was this attitude that made people feel less guilty about committing crimes. One 'crime' which was popular was infidelity. Edinburgh was full of servicemen of other nationalities who were on leave, and the American presence was the largest. The Americans had a huge impact on the women of Edinburgh, and caused much anxiety to any serviceman who had left a young wife, fiancée, or girlfriend at home. Clothes, food, and sweets were rationed, and cigarettes were very hard to come by. In David's view, the ultimate luxury, from a girl's point of view, was silk stockings. The Americans had all these things in abundance through the stores on their bases. As well as having access to all these desirable goods, the Americans received more generous pay than their British counterparts. Another bonus was that their uniforms were very smart, and made of good-quality material. All in all, they had enormous advantages when it came to ingratiating themselves with the opposite sex. All this was common knowledge among British males, so they had good reason to worry. Infidelity was common, and so were terrible rows when servicemen came home on leave.

Very often, accusations were made that were unjustified, but in other cases they were. David's father was a jealous person, and his mother was an attractive woman. All his father's leaves were spoiled by his drinking, which was generally followed by accusations of infidelity. This was a scenario that was quite common. David never knew if his mother had had an affair or not. She certainly had plenty of opportunities. The irony is that David knew his father had a relationship with a WAAF while in the RAF. David's mother found some letters that the WAAF had written to him, which he had been foolish enough to keep. It certainly gave David's mother some ammunition to retaliate with when his father got going.

After he had joined up, in September 1939, David's father had loved life in the RAF, and had quickly risen to the rank of sergeant in the Motor Transport Section; he served most of this time with Coastal Command at Dyce Aerodrome close to Aberdeen. About October 1943 David's father had collapsed with a perforated duodenal ulcer. He recovered, but was discharged from the RAF, much to his disappointment, and returned to their house in the New Town. He started his own repair garage and was very busy most of the time, but the more money he made the more he drank, which usually left very little for David's mother to keep house with. His mother was a tailoress and sewed almost constantly to make up for her husband's shortcomings. She was a very resourceful, determined, strong woman, who kept a roof over the boys' heads and food on the table.

In retrospect, David never regretted being evacuated. Generally, his brother George's presence at Balmungo was reassuring; he missed his mother terribly, so having George around was some consolation. Although the brothers fought frequently, they were very close, and loyal to one another in other ways. Had George not been there too, David would not have enjoyed his time at Balmungo so much. Jim Ridley had given David and George the shooting bug, and they continued to shoot all their lives. David had seen, at first hand, people living very simple and hard-working lives. It was really a feudal system, but in spite of being treated as inferiors and with contempt, Hendry Ballantyne, Jim Ridley, and most of the others who worked for the Nish family were quite happy and loyal to their employer.

* * *

Eddy Rowley often reflected on the experiences of children who, like her, were evacuated. Some, she knew, had terrible times and were not treated well. Others, like herself, Jean, and their older sister, kept in touch with their foster-parents for the rest of their lives, exchanging birthday and Christmas cards every year. When Eddy's own children were born, many years later, her foster-mother sent them a little present. Eddy had read other accounts of the lives of evacuees, and there always seem to be far more unhappy stories than positive ones. She wondered if this was an accurate summing-up of the time, or whether horror stories were more often passed on than happy ones.

*   *   *

Mary-Rose Benton has distinguished between the effects of her experiences on her as an individual, and those of evacuation on British society more generally. In part of her poem 'Vackies', she wrote:

> Hard landlady dealt the blows
> Something deep within me froze
> The thaw that came in future years
> Would compensate the hate and jeers
>
> But first the present, harsh and crude
> The scavenging for bits of food
> The coarsened life—childhood's thief
> The ever overwhelming grief.

Mary-Rose remembered that during her life as an evacuee she looked back on her first seven years of home life, regulated though it was by a normal range of discipline and almost Spartan living, as a period of indulgence, licence, and affectionate cosseting. Her story is therefore an important corrective to the stereotype of the child evacuated to a middle-class home, whose mental horizons were widened as a consequence and whose experiences were broadly positive.

*   *   *

His experiences at Easton remained highly significant for Carl Coates. Tom Browett had died in 1963 at the age of 76, and Carl was present at the funeral; he walked with Minnie on his arm behind the coffin, once it was taken from the hearse up the church path and into the church. Minnie continued to run the shop for twelve years after Tom's death. She died on 1 May 1975, at the age of 86. Carl had been named as next of kin, and once his sister and he knew Minnie was in hospital they arranged to meet to go and see her. Minnie was very poorly and considerably frail, something Carl had never before seen in her. Within days of returning home he received a telephone-call one evening to say that Minnie was near to death and was asking for her little evacuee, 'who we believe is you'. He left Sheffield straight after the call and drove to the hospital. He spent some time into the night with Minnie, just standing by the bed with nobody talking until he felt that he should leave and head back home. Next day the hospital telephoned to say that Minnie had died.

Carl attended the funeral in Easton Parish Church with his wife and sister. A few weeks later the solicitor's clerk who lived in Easton and who had always handled Minnie and Tom's legal affairs wrote to Carl and his sister to say that Minnie had left each of them £300 in her will. Carl and the family attended the auction when the contents of the house and shop were to be sold. The oil lamps, brass articles, and metal advertising boards for Bovril, Player's Capstans, and Woodbine all went quickly, at high prices. Carl only managed to buy Tom's easy-chair, in which he used to sit smoking in front of the fire, and a chest of drawers. He loaded his car with the chest of drawers on the roof-rack and the two chairs inside, his daughters having to sit cross-legged for the drive back to Sheffield. Overall, it had been a tiring and disappointing day.

Towards the end of the 1970s Carl was struggling with various issues that may have been associated with his childhood experience. His strict Salvation Army upbringing and loyal sense of duty meant he was living a lifestyle with a very clear sense of right and wrong, and it was causing him difficulties in a variety of ways. He enrolled for personal one-to-one discussions with the Christian School of Psychotherapy. He met a man called George Gale once a fortnight to begin with, and then once a month for a period of about two years. It was George who coined the phrase 'Thank God for Auntie Minnie', and as Carl and he got into the therapy they used it many times. Carl felt that, overall, his evacuation experience had been for the good. He was very much loved, and secure in the knowledge that Minnie and Tom were there for him. He felt that their love and affection never waned.

* * *

Juliet Norden realized that it was only much later that she stopped to think about the effect that the evacuation had had on both children and adults. She felt that she would have been unable to let her own children go, and fortunately never had to make that decision. The foster-parents must have found the evacuation a massive disruption to their lives, especially those who hadn't really wanted evacuees billeted with them. Juliet later apologized to Valerie Sage for all the trouble that she had caused, and thanked her for all she had done and for teaching her so much. Looking back, Juliet felt grateful to her foster-mother, but remarked: 'I think what I missed more than anything, during all the war years, was being cuddled by my parents.' Having read how badly some evacuees were treated by their foster-parents, Juliet thought that on the whole she and her brother and sister had got off lightly. However, there was no doubt that they were all quite traumatized by the episode, and that it had had a profound effect on all their lives.

* * *

Maggie Quinn reflected that she had been a submissive child, and that in those days whatever happened in life, people just got on with it. So much time and energy had to be used up in the practicalities of everyday living. The huge bonus for Maggie was that evacuation had literally been a lifesaver. As a delicate 5-year-old, deemed not strong enough to undergo a tonsilectomy, she had been given less than a year to live if she remained in Birmingham. When she looked back on her two families, whom she loved and was loved by, she felt that they shared a lot of the same beliefs. They could both be described as upper working-class. Their beliefs included good manners, kindness, thrift and self-respect, consideration for others, respect for learning and education generally, and hard work, morals, and a belief in God (albeit from different traditions). So there was never any conflict. The downside was the trauma of twice being taken from a safe, secure family to have to adjust to an entirely new environment and way of life. Even later in life Maggie had a feeling of never quite belonging.

Maggie continued to have a strong parent–daughter relationship with her foster-parents. Amy Sedgley always called her the daughter she never had, and Ernest gave her away at her wedding; they were godparents to Maggie's children, whom they regarded more as grandchildren. Maggie and her husband continued to visit them once a month until Amy's death in August 2002. Overall, Maggie considered herself to be very fortunate in that she had been the cherished daughter of two families, both of whom she loved dearly, and it said much for the generosity of spirit that both 'mothers' understood her dilemma. For whatever their private thoughts, Maggie never once heard a word of criticism from either of them about the other, as she shared her life between them. She knew her biological mother was always grateful that Maggie had survived her childhood ill-health, so for her sharing a child rather than losing it completely was preferable. With two 'mothers', Maggie had a double measure of pleasure for helping to care for them in their old age, but also a double measure of grief when she finally had to say goodbye to them.

* * *

Probably the most persistently detrimental effect of the evacuation for Dave Pinchon was the absence of parental day-to-day interest in his school work and activities. By nature Dave was quiet and reserved. This resulted in his attitude to school being one of, 'Keep your head down and do no more than necessary to keep out of trouble'. Most of the time he managed to follow this principle fairly successfully. However, he was sure a much closer interest in his schoolwork by his father would have resulted in better academic results. On the other hand, Dave judged that the evacuation experience stood him in good stead for his future life. He was an only child from a comfortable background, and up until then had had only a limited appreciation of other people's lives and problems. Evacuation gave him some insight into other people's lifestyles. Overall, it made him both more independent and better able to get on with other people, and he learned to cope with day-to-day problems without recourse to parental guidance or immediate help. Dave later reflected that the evacuation had been one of the most influential periods of his life; it had a part in shaping his character and in establishing his views on many topics. In many ways it made his later call-up to the RAF much easier than it would otherwise have been.

* * *

When she gave an address to the school at the end of the war, Judith Grunfeld said that the staff and children should carry away from Shefford the educational principle that character-training was more important than the imparting of knowledge, and people were in the world to serve a greater purpose than they themselves realized. She hoped that the staff and pupils would keep in front of them a vision that had the power to take life out of its small frame and make them see a wider horizon. Judith recalled that the ties of friendship between the people of Shefford and those who had been evacuees there and who were now men and women in the prime of life remained strong over many years. Many former pupils coming from Australia or Israel to visit England went to Shefford to visit their wartime foster-families and to have a look around. They were received warmly, and parcels and cards with seasonal greetings still arrived in Shefford from all over the globe. At weddings in London after the war, old landlords and landladies from the village were among the honoured guests.

While Shefford pupils had become settled members of society, had responsible jobs and their own children and grandchildren, the magic of those years had not entirely evaporated, and the spark that had lit up their world there was still alive. Judith wrote:

There are men and women, doctors, lawyers, scientists, Rabbis and teachers in almost every part of the world who, when the occasion stirs their memory, will tell their children or their friends what their world offered them when they were youngsters in Shefford. They will remember many small events that I may never have known, fun that warmed them, laughter that cheered them, hopes that were dashed and revived, humour of those days that becomes more poignant as the years roll by, as all the hardship is forgotten and only the memory of the sweet heroic time remains.

Shefford was especially important to those children who could not go back to their parental homes after the war. Years later, Judith was visited by one pupil, now a mother of four, happily married in Israel to another former pupil. She had come to the village aged 12, when her sister, two years older, took her away from a non-Jewish foster-family so that she could receive a Jewish education. It was only thirty years later that she went to Berlin to visit the grave of her father, who had died in a concentration camp. She found a neglected and overgrown cemetery, but had felt the need to say prayers at the grave. Returning to Israel and her own family, she believed that she had redeemed her father. This experience of one of the Shefford children seemed to Judith to have a symbolic importance. She wrote:

Like the seeds of the dandelion—a humble flower of the field—which, blown into the wind, fly away and find their soil elsewhere, so the human kindness of the people of Shefford, as well as of Campton, Clifton, Meppershall and Stotfold, is remembered all over the world by those who were the children in this story, and are now men and women rearing their families into the third generation.

Epilogue

One of the ironies of the *Our Towns* report was that, despite its recommendations on tackling poverty and improving the social environment, in the mid-1940s it was best-known for having coined the phrase 'problem family'. Apart from her work on the survey, Elizabeth Denby continued to run a small architectural practice from her home during the war. It organized her 'All Europe House' as a prototype which could be tailored to all purposes, built alongside flats as necessary, and scaled up or down according to need and purpose. She also planned prefabricated housing. Elizabeth designed her own work, making the plans, elevations, and sections, and collaborated with qualified architects who checked the drawings and supervised construction. Nevertheless, while now seen as an originator of tenants' participation and interdisciplinary collaboration, and in spite of good connections with the Labour Party, Elizabeth had difficulty in finding outlets for her work.

Although she designed a room for the important 'Britain Can Make It' exhibition of 1946, and intervened in the 'overspill' debates of the 1950s, her ideas were generally dismissed as unfeasible. Thereafter her output was confined to writing, and she never again received a commission as significant as Kensal House. Her advocacy of high-density housing and urban centralization was lost in the post-war fervour for the New Town. One problem was that she suffered serious ill-health both before and after the war; in any case, she was 51 when the war ended. In the 1930s she had flourished when welfare had not been institutionalized, but she could not have the same influence in the more professional and bureaucratic world of the welfare state. After 1945 people were required to be more specialized and to possess professional qualifications. Elizabeth's colleague on the Women's Group on Public Welfare, Margaret Bondfield, had died on 16 June 1953. Elizabeth herself moved from her home in Wilmington Square in Clerkenwell to Hythe in Kent in the 1960s, and died, unmarried, at Hythe Nursing Home, on 3 November 1965.

* * *

Apart from his involvement in the debates about the health and welfare of evacuees, Sir Maurice Holmes was largely responsible for managing the major educational debates which culminated in the 1944 Education Act. He worked with the key figures, and developed the potential role of committees, such as the Norwood Committee on the secondary school curriculum in 1943, and the Fleming Committee on public schools in 1944. Holmes' authority and his experience as an administrator were key factors in the success of the Board in negotiating a safe passage for the 1944 Education Act, and it has been seen as his major contribution to the development of education and social policy in twentieth-century Britain. He helped to ensure not only broad social and political support, but also lasting agreement, around measures that were potentially divisive. After the war, in semi-retirement, Holmes remained influential as an adviser to Ellen Wilkinson, the Education Minister in the Labour Government. He retired in 1945, served on the East African Salaries Commission in 1947, chaired the Caribbean Public Services Commission in 1948–9, and also undertook a number of local inquiries for the Ministry of Transport, as well as finding the time to write biographies of George Bernard

Shaw and Captain James Cook. He died at his London home on 4 April 1964.

* * *

The Branksome Dene Hotel in Bournemouth had subsequently been taken over by the Ministry of Defence, and airmen of the Canadian Air Force had been billeted there until the end of hostilities. In 1947 it was de-requisitioned and turned into luxury flats, which were never occupied, then in 1951 the building was again sold and converted for use as a convalescent home. Later, having been renamed Zetland Court in May 1980, it became a residential home managed by the Royal Masonic Benevolent Institution.

* * *

Of Sir Maurice's colleagues at the Board of Education and Ministry of Health, Sir Arthur MacNalty had retired early in 1940, at the age of 60. In 1941 he was commissioned by the Nuffield College Reconstruction Survey to contribute to its investigations into the reform of local government. His *Reform of the Public Health Services* was published in 1943. He then turned to his work as editor-in-chief of the official medical history of the war, which he completed shortly before his death in 1969. He died at his home in Epsom on 17 April. Dr Alison Glover had died in 1963, and Cecil Maudslay in 1969.

Edgar Wilkins, Assistant SMO in Birmingham, died in 1946, leaving the manuscript of a proposed book on medical inspections incomplete. A group of the Society of Medical Officers of Health decided to make itself responsible for the completion of the work. In the book, Wilkins again argued that diagnosis and therapy could do little without a policy of 'social betterment'. On head lice, little progress could be expected until the problem was dealt with as part of the standard of living of those affected; punitive measures were of limited value, and it was futile to try to educate people while they were living under the impossible conditions of a 'slum environment'. Wilkins was a progressive figure who represented those more in tune with the mood of wartime reconstruction, and for whom evacuation had been a formative experience. However, in part because of the impact of the *Our Towns* report, other public-health doctors continued to criticize what were now called 'problem families'.

* * *

Rab Butler became, successively, Chancellor of the Exchequer in 1951, Home Secretary, and Foreign Secretary, but failed to win the Conservative Party leadership in 1963; he subsequently became Master of Trinity College, Cambridge. Although it has been said that he was 'more a public servant than a politician', Butler was largely responsible for the 'one nation' Toryism of the post-war period. He died in 1982.

In his autobiography, *The Art of the Possible*, published in 1971, Butler reflected on how the war had brought the building of schools and education itself to a halt in many areas, as evacuation threw the educational system into disorder and thoughts of reform were put aside. By January 1940 half-a-million children had been getting no education at all. Gradually, energetic action by the Board restored the position. He wrote that he was fortunate to be served by an outstanding group of civil servants, including 'the brilliant Sir Maurice Holmes, Permanent Secretary, derisive of many of the persons and fatuities that came our way, yet acute in ideals and practice'. Moreover, Butler argued that: 'The revelations of evacuation administered a severe shock to the national conscience; for they brought to light the conditions of those unfortunate children of the "submerged tenth" who would also rank among the citizens of the future. It was realised with deepening awareness that the "two nations" still existed in England a century after Disraeli had used the phrase.' It was this realization that led to plans for reconstruction, in which education formed an integral part. Educational problems were seen as an essential part of the social system, and the need for reform was increasingly acknowledged. The achievement was due both to Butler and to the civil servants who had started planning in their Bournemouth hotel even before he arrived at the Board.

* * *

Apart from his work on head lice, Kenneth Mellanby had set up a research unit in December 1940 to study the effects of scabies infestation, gathering together a group of conscientious objectors to serve as human guinea-pigs. This led to extensive observation and treatment of military personnel in a special hospital for infested soldiers. He conducted experiments on water deprivation in 1942, and on vitamins, and also suggested infecting his volunteers with malaria and typhus. The Medical Research Council prohibited these experiments, but Mellanby wrote up his experiences in *Human Guinea Pigs*, published in 1945. In the same year he turned to typhus research, which was relevant for the war in the Far East, and travelled to Burma and New Guinea. In December 1946 he went to Germany to hunt for medical documents, and attended the trials of Nazi doctors at Nuremberg and Dachau. He was the *British Medical Journal*'s observer at the Nuremberg medical trial, and drew attention to the scientific quality of some of the experiments, particularly those on malaria and typhus. In the 1950s he headed the Department of Entomology at the Rothamsted Experimental Station and from 1961 to 1974 was Director of the Nature Conservancy's new experimental station at Monks Wood in Hertfordshire. At first he advocated environmentalist views, but later defended the use of chemicals in farming, along with other modern techniques. In retirement he continued as a scientific consultant and author. He died in 1993.

* * *

Judith Grunfeld retired in 1955 to look after her husband Isidor, who had fallen seriously ill. He was to die of a heart attack in 1975. Judith maintained a public profile, giving lectures and classes to Jewish audiences and former pupils in Britain, North America, and Israel, until succumbing to ill-health herself. Her book *Shefford: The Story of a Jewish School Community in Evacuation 1939–1945* was published in 1980 by the Soncino Press. She died on 14 May 1998 in the Homerton Hospital, Hackney, London, and was buried next to her husband in the Har Menuhot cemetery in Jerusalem.

* * *

What of the evacuees themselves, in the period between the end of the war and when they came to record their memories some fifty or sixty years later? If there is any 'finally' in Mary-Rose Benton's narrative we might place it in 1953, when, aged 20, she got away from the Williamses in Birmingham and went to stay with the remnants of her family in Birmingham, in Balsall Heath. She had gone back to live with them in 1944 because of the danger of the V1 and V2 rocket attacks on London. Then, in 1962, they were moved to Hall Green, also in Birmingham. Mary-Rose later became a professional actress. In 1996 she began working on a book about her experiences, joined a writer's circle for feedback, and found she was able to write fiction and verse. The verse was light-hearted, and the stories mostly imaginative or science fiction. She also wrote journalistic pieces, for instance on the Poll Tax march of 1991. Her book, with the ironic title *Family Values: Pillar to Post—Early Stages for a Touring Actor*, was published privately in 1998.

David Hodge worked as an engineer and subsequently set up his own business, living in Edinburgh and retiring finally in 2005. He sometimes returned to Balmungo with his brother George for a few days' holiday, but let this lapse after a while, until

Mrs Ballantyne died in an accident when her nightdress caught fire. The shock of this loss was too much for her husband, who also died a short time afterwards. David drove up to Balmungo years later, in 1998. The farm had gone, and the original farmhouse and all the barns and stables had been converted into modern houses. The Ballantynes' house looked very much the same, but the Ridleys' had been abandoned. The big house was still there, and so was the walled garden. The whole time that David was there he did not meet a living soul who he could ask for any information. He would have loved to knock at the door at Hendry Ballantyne's and ask to look round, but did not dare.

Juliet Norden's parents didn't live together after the war, but were never divorced. Many of her father's friends and relatives had died in the Holocaust; he died in 1964, aged 80. Juliet later found he had been born in Hamburg. Her mother died in 2000, aged 94. Juliet married Clive Blick, and had two children. Her book, *Pass the Parcel: Evacuee 1940–1945*, was published by Norden Books in 2005. Carl Coates was unusual in that he went back to stay at Easton-on-the-Hill for an extended period after his father's death and mother's illness, in March 1948. The family had continued to keep in touch with Minnie and Tom, after his parents had been sent by the Salvation Army to Newcastle upon Tyne in January 1946 and to Sheffield in February 1947. This last move coincided with one of the worst winters ever recorded. Carl's father died the following year, and it was decided that Carl would go back and live with Minnie and Tom. He was then 12 years old. Some sixty years later, living in Sheffield, Carl began to write a memoir with the title 'Thank God for Auntie Minnie', for his daughters and grandchildren, including a chapter on his evacuation to Easton.

Dave Pinchon was called up for the RAF immediately after the war, and subsequently worked in industrial relations. Dave only met his friend and billet-mate John Richman again sixty years later, at a reunion of evacuees in 2004. Dave wrote the memoir '"The Day War Broke Out" and the Subsequent Five Years: A Personal Recollection of the Years 1939–1944' for his grandchildren. Before the end of the war, as we have seen, George Prager became an apprentice at Chatham Dockyard. He and his stepbrother Ronald did not meet again until after George's grandfather died in 1950. George's book *With Schoolcap, Label and Cardboard Box (Recollections of a World War Two Evacuee)* was published in 1999 by the Pentland Press, with a foreword by Countess Mountbatten of Burma. Again, as with many of the evacuees, he continued to live where he had been born, in Gillingham.

Shortly after Maggie Quinn returned home she passed the scholarship exam for Kings Norton Grammar School on the edge of Bournville, in Birmingham. Even when the war was over she felt the effects of continued rationing and shortages. When Maggie did cookery at school in 1946, for example, the recipes were still very Spartan. Eggs and milk for scones were often reconstituted from dried egg and milk powder. When Maggie and her friends were lucky enough to be able to go to Switzerland with the Girl Guides in 1951, the presents they brought back for their families were mainly foodstuffs. She could remember bringing back tea, coffee, and chocolate for her mother, and even tinned pineapple, which was a rare treat. Maggie got married when she was 20, lived on the outskirts of Birmingham, and had two daughters. She returned to work part-time in 1970, when her youngest child started school, and did a variety of office jobs to bring in some extra money. Maggie has published various pieces about her experiences, including in Carl Chinn, Malcolm Stree, and Laurie Hornsby's *The Brummagem Air: Recollections of Good Old Brum*, in 1998, and 'An Evacuee in Groby' at the request of the Groby History Society.

In her garden she still has a single white peony bush grown from a cutting taken from Markfield Road when she and her husband moved to their house in Great Barr, Birmingham, in 1957; she regards it as a little bit of Groby with her forever.

Eddy Rowley went back to live in West Heath, near Birmingham, and kept in touch with her foster-parents for the rest of their lives. She gives talks about her experiences as an evacuee in local schools. Frank Walsh became a keen cyclist, riding to Nice, racing on the Fallowfield track, as well as participating in time trials and massed start events on the Cheshire roads. He also rode in the three-lap international Isle of Man cycling road race. Frank worked as an apprentice compositor in the printing industry, and later as a civil servant, before becoming a full-time Branch and Regional Officer with the NGA Print Union. He was involved in the Warrington and Wapping disputes with Eddie Shah and Rupert Murdoch. Aged 73, Frank returned to the farm in Catforth in August 1999, with his wife and his grandson, who, at 12, was nearly the same age as Frank when he went there in 1939. They were also accompanied by a reporter and photographer from the *Manchester Evening News*. Frank's autobiography, *From Hulme to Eternity*, was published in 2007.

* * *

I opened the book with my recollections of 'Crosshill', my mother's childhood home—memories similar in some respects to those of Carl Coates about Aunt Minnie's in Lincolnshire. My grandmother and great aunt are now dead, of course, while the house has been sold, its rooms modernized, and its contents dispersed to other people's homes, including my own. Like my own parents, the children evacuated in September 1939 are now in their seventies and eighties, and like my own memories, memory is problematic. However, it is clear that the feelings of love and separation experienced by the evacuees had a significant influence on them at the time and in their subsequent lives. The evacuation offered new experiences across geographical and class divides, which were positive for children such as George and Maggie, but which led to misery and abuse for others, like Juliet and Mary-Rose. Moreover, the physical condition and behaviour of the children were reflected upon by those who were adults in wartime: teachers, Billeting Officers, civil servants, and politicians. As demonstrated by the lives of Elizabeth Denby, G. M. Bland, and Sir Maurice Holmes, evacuation created both tensions and unity, but gradually had a major impact on ideas about poverty and state intervention, and on British society as a whole. The evacuees, therefore, and the debates about them, together did much to shape post-war Britain. Evacuation would not happen today. Changes in military technology, in the nature of war itself, and in the way that child abuse has been exposed mean that children would never be sent away to live with strangers. The aim in this book has been to capture the experiences of Churchill's children as they grew up in wartime Britain, to give them an opportunity to tell their stories, and to record their voices for future generations.

Notes

Introduction

Of the huge literature on evacuation, see for example, R. M. Titmuss, *Problems of Social Policy* (1950); Angus Calder, *The People's War: Britain 1939–1945* (1969); P. H. J. H. Gosden, *Education in the Second World War: A Study in Policy and Administration* (1976); Carlton Jackson, *Who Will Take Our Children? The Story of Evacuation in Britain 1939–1945* (1985); Travis L. Crosby, *The Impact of Civilian Evacuation in the Second World War* (1986); Ruth Inglis, *The Children's War: Evacuation 1939–1945* (1989); Edward Stokes, *Innocents Abroad: The Story of British Child Evacuees in Australia, 1940–45* (1994); Bob Holman, *The Evacuation: A Very British Revolution* (1995); Mike Brown, *Evacuees: Evacuation in Wartime Britain 1939–1945* (2000); Sonya O. Rose, *Which People's War? National Identity and Citizenship in Britain 1939–1945* (2003); and Jessica Mann, *Out of Harm's Way: The Wartime Evacuation from Britain* (2005).

For individual accounts, see B. S. Johnson, *The Evacuees* (1968); Audrey Jones, *Farewell Manchester: The Story of the 1939 Evacuation* (1989); and Sue Ashworth, *The Evacuees Story* (1999). For literary accounts see John Rae, *The Custard Boys* (1960); Nina Bawden, *Carrie's War* (1973); and Jack Rosenthal, *By Jack Rosenthal: An Autobiography in Six Acts* (2005).

For more academic accounts see, John Welshman, 'Evacuation and Social Policy During the Second World War: Myth and Reality', *Twentieth Century British History*, 9: 1 (1998), 28–53; id., 'Evacuation, Hygiene, and Social Policy: The *Our Towns* Report of 1943', *Historical Journal*, 42: 3 (1999), 781–807; John Stewart and John Welshman, 'The Evacuation of Children in Wartime Scotland: Culture, Behaviour, and Poverty', *Journal of Scottish Historical Studies*, 26: 1 and 2 (2006), 100–20. On memory, see Mark Connelly, *We Can Take It: Britain and the Memory of the Second World War* (2004), and on abuse, see James Marten (ed.), *Children and War: A Historical Anthology* (2002). On the experiences of children with disabilities, see Sue

Wheatcroft, 'Children's Experiences of War: Handicapped Children in England During the Second World War', *Twentieth Century British History*, 19: 4 (2008), 480–501.

The use of autobiographies as a source for historians is discussed in David Vincent, *Bread, Knowledge and Freedom: A Study of Nineteenth-Century Working Class Autobiography* (1981; Methuen 2nd edn.), and in John Burnett, *Destiny Obscure: Autobiographies of Childhood, Education and Family from the 1820s to the 1920s* (1982; Penguin edn. 1984). On children in war, see also Nicholas Stargardt, *Witnesses of War: Children's Lives Under the Nazis* (2005; Pimlico edn. 2006).

Chapter 1

Judith Grunfeld's story is contained in her book *Shefford: The Story of a Jewish School Community in Evacuation 1939–1945* (1980). Biographical information for Solomon Schonfeld, Judith Grunfeld, and Isidor Grunfeld is taken from the *Oxford Dictionary of National Biography* [*ODNB*] (2004). Fears of the potential impact of aerial bombing are well conveyed in L. E. O. Charlton's *War Over England* (1936), and in George Orwell's *Homage to Catalonia and Looking Back on the Spanish Civil War* (1938) and *Coming Up for Air* (1939). The Baldwin comment is in House of Commons debates [H. of C. deb.], 1931–32, vol. 270, col. 632, and the Churchill comment in H. of C. deb., 1934–35, vol. 295, col. 859. The Report of the Anderson Committee can be found in Parliamentary Papers [PP] 1937–38, X, *Report of Committee on Evacuation*. Hoare's presentation of the Report to the House of Commons is in H. of C. deb., 1937–38, vol. 338, cols. 3283–6, while details of the conference and the early meetings of the Advisory Committee on Evacuation are at the National Archives, Kew, London (hereafter NA) files ED 136/110 and ED 136/111–113.

Details of Elizabeth Denby's life can be found in her entry in the *ODNB*; in Elizabeth Darling, ' "The Star in the Profession she Invented for Herself ": A Brief Biography of Elizabeth Denby, Housing Consultant', *Planning Perspectives*, 20: 3 (2005), 271–300; and in Elizabeth Darling, ' "The House that is a Woman's Book Come True": The All-Europe House and Four Women's Spatial Practices in Inter-War England', in Elizabeth Darling and Lesley Whitworth (eds.), *Women and the Making of Built Space in England 1870–1950* (2007), 123–40.

The best account of planning is still Titmuss, *Problems of Social Policy*, 23–44. The comment about London hop-pickers is in NA HLG 7/60. David Hodge's story is in his unpublished account sent to the author, and details of planning in Scotland are in Stewart and Welshman, 'The Evacuation of Children in Wartime Scotland'. Comments by civil servants about footwear are in NA ED 50/204, and the drafting of the memorandum on clothing and footwear is in NA HLG 7/321 and NA ED 10/245. The memo was published by the Ministry of Health as *Memo EV. 4. Government Evacuation Scheme* (1939). Comments on evacuation rehearsals in Chelsea, Hull, Leeds, Bradford, and the North East are in NA HLG 7/321, NA HLG 7/74, and NA HLG 7/75. The rehearsals of 28 August are described in NA ED 136/111.

Details of the work of G. M. Bland are in the Bland Papers, Lancaster Central Library, Old Town Square, Lancaster, files F4, Red 1 and Red 2.

Chapter 2

The eyewitness accounts of the early hours of 1 September 1939 are in William Boyd (ed.), *Evacuation in Scotland: A Record of Events and Experiments* (1944). Dave Pinchon's story is in David G. Pinchon, ' "The Day War Broke Out…" And the Subsequent Five Years: A Personal Recollection of the Years 1939–1944' (unpublished, Southampton, 2006), 4–5, 17, 23–39. Frank Walsh's story is in his *From Hulme to Eternity* (2007), 93–113, and George Prager's in his *With Schoolcap, Label and Cardboard Box (Recollections of a World War Two Evacuee)* (1999). Maggie Quinn, as Maggie Cade, has written various accounts of her experiences, including 'Sixty Years On'.

The accounts of evacuees at Ealing Broadway Station and at Manchester are by H. E. B. Green and H. W. Brand respectively, and are in NA ED 138/51. The Newcastle report is in NA HLG 7/73. Details of the life of Sir Maurice Holmes can be found in his entry in the *ODNB*. The most reliable calculations of numbers of evacuees are in NA CAB 102/698, and in Titmuss, *Problems of Social Policy*, 101–8, Appendices 3, 4, and 9.

Mary-Rose Benton's story is in her *Family Values: Pillar to Post Evacuee: Early Stages for a Touring Actor* (1998), and Juliet Norden's in Juliet Blick, *Pass the Parcel: Evacuee 1940–1945* (2005). Eddy Rowley's story is (as Eddy Ackrill) in a letter to the author, 10 February 2008, and Carl Coates's in his 'Thank God for Auntie Minnie' (unpublished).

Chapter 3

Details of the journey are in Titmuss, *Problems of Social Policy*, 108–9, and the eyewitness account (by Alexander Belford) is in Boyd (ed.), *Evacuation in Scotland*, 38–43. The arrival of evacuees in Lancaster is described in the Bland Papers, and individual experiences of evacuees in Sue Ashworth, *The Evacuees Story* (1999). The text of the Elliot broadcast is in Boyd (ed.), *Evacuation in Scotland*. Maggie Quinn's journey is described in 'An Evacuee in Groby'.

Details of the arrival of evacuees in Sussex on 2 September 1939, by J. E. Underwood, and in Surrey, by 'R. H.', are in NA ED 138/51, as are the cuttings from the *Portsmouth Evening News* and the *Folkestone, Hythe and District Herald*. The stories from Hemsworth, by J. H. Goldsmith, and from Kirk Sandall are in the same file. Details of the arrival of children from Southampton in Poole and Wimborne are also in NA ED 138/51, while the Reading and Abingdon stories, by W. Green, are in NA ED 138/50.

Details of the numbers of children received in the Reception Areas are from Titmuss, *Problems of Social Policy*, 106, Appendix 5.

Chapter 4

Evelyn Waugh's biography is taken from the *ODNB*, and his letter of 24 December 1939 from Mark Amory (ed.), *The Letters of Evelyn Waugh* (1980; Penguin edn. 1982), 131.

The letters in *The Times* were published on 12 September 1939, p. 4, and on 22 September 1939, p. 6. The Adjournment Debate is in H. of C. deb., 1938–39, vol. 351, cols. 802–86. Harold Nicolson's biography is taken from the *ODNB*, and his diary entry for 14 September 1939 from Nigel Nicolson (ed.), *Harold Nicolson: Diaries and Letters 1939–1945* (1967), 33. Neville Chamberlain's biography is taken from the *ODNB*, and his letter to his sister Hilda on 17 September 1939 is in the Neville Chamberlain papers, University of Birmingham Library, NC 18/1/1121. Oliver Lyttelton's biography is taken from the *ODNB*, and his story from Viscount Chandos, *The Memoirs of Lord Chandos* (1962), 152.

Chapter 5

The letter from Dr Kerr and others are in the *British Medical Journal* (1939), ii, 745, 831, 896. The *Lancet* editorials are in (1939), ii, 794, 940, and comments on the *Scotsman* articles in ibid. 1177. The *Medical Officer* editorials are in 62 (1939), 123, 144. The article by J. E. Haine is 'The Medical Side of Evacuation', ibid. 147–8, and the Dunstan letter is in ibid. 149. Details of the evacuation to Spalding are in C. W. Dixon, 'Some Experiments in the Cleansing of Children', ibid. 181–2, and the comments by W. G. Booth in ibid. 149. The *Public Health* editorial is in 53 (1939), 24, and the article by R. C. Webster is 'Some Public Health Aspects of the Evacuation Scheme', ibid. 33–4.

Cecil Maudslay's memo of 11 September is in NA ED 136/175, and his biography is taken from *Who Was Who*. The letter from May Collins is in NA ED 138/50, as is the correspondence between Earl De La Warr and Sir Richard Maconachie. Arthur Hinsley's letter of 9 October is also in NA ED 138/50, while details of Catholic evacuees are in NA HLG 7/81 and NA HLG 7/322. Lord Portal's letter of 25 October to Earl De La Warr is in NA ED 10/246, and G. Ridley's letter of 3 November to Walter Elliot in NA ED 50/206. Lily Boys's letter of 9 November is in NA ED 50/212, as is the reply of Earl De La Warr, on 14 November. Earl De La Warr's biography is taken from the *ODNB*, and his letter of 24 November is in NA ED 50/207. Sir Arthur MacNalty's letter of 20 November to Walter Elliot, Maudslay's memo of 5 December, and Sir Maurice Holmes's memo of 29 November are all in the same file.

Kenneth Mellanby's biography is taken from the *ODNB*, and one of his earliest articles was C. G. Johnson and K. Mellanby, 'Bed-Bugs and Cockroaches', *Proceedings of the Royal Entomological Society*, 14 (1939), 50. The Mellanby investigation is described in Gosden, *Education in the Second World War*, 173–4. The correspondence between Alison Glover and Maudslay is in NA ED 50/196.

The memo from A. M. Hargreaves, County Inspector of Schools in Northumberland, is in NA ED 136/122, and the memo on women from Leeds in NA HLG 7/76. Sir John Rowland's letter of 8 September is in NA HLG 7/321. Walter Elliot's biography is taken from the *ODNB*, and the Ministry's circular of 12 September, 'Government Evacuation Scheme', is in NA ED 136/112. Sir George Chrystal's memo of 12 September is in NA HLG 7/321. The letter by Lily Boys, of 13 September, is in NA HLG 7/74, and the report from Wales is in NA HLG 7/81. Lord Derby's letter of 3 October is in NA HLG 7/321, as is that by Elsie Corbett, on behalf of the WVS, and by E. Sandford Carter, on behalf of the NCSS. The Ministry's circular of 7 November is in NA MH 101/15.

The survey by the Association of Architects, Surveyors and Technical Assistants (Evacuation Committee), *Report on the Accommodation of Evacuees in the Reception Areas* (1939), is in the Bland Papers. Its other report was *Evacuation in Practice: A Study of a Rural Reception Area.* See also P. Coe and M. Reading, *Lubetkin and Tecton: Architecture and Social Commitment: A Critical Study* (1981), 44–66, 89–93.

Elizabeth Denby's work in wartime is described in Elizabeth Darling's PhD thesis 'Elizabeth Denby, Housing Consultant: Social Reform and Cultural Politics in the Inter-War Period', University of London (2000). The letter by Margaret Bondfield was published in *The Times*, 6 November 1939, p. 7, and Bondfield's biography is taken from the *ODNB*. Elizabeth Denby's response and subsequent activities are in the Denby Papers, 116674. These were previously at the Building Research Establishment, Garston, Hertfordshire, but are now in the Harry Simpson Memorial Library, University of Westminster, London. The letter from the Billeting Officer in Reading is in the Fawcett Library, London, Women's Forum (hereafter WF)/D5, as is the text for the radio broadcast of 12 December, in WF/A40.

Chapter 6

Diana Cooper's biography is taken from the *ODNB*, while her letter of March 1940 is in Diana Cooper, *Trumpets From the Steep* (1960), 37. The bad winter of 1940 is referred to in school logbooks, and in numerous other sources, including Richard Broad and Suzie Fleming (eds.), *Nella Last's War: A Mother's Diary 1939–45* (1981), 29; Peter Donnelly (ed.), *Mrs Milburn's Diaries: An Englishwoman's Day-to-Day Reflections 1939–45* (1979), 19; and A. J. P. Taylor, *A Personal History* (1983), 191.

Details of the return of the evacuees are given in Titmuss, *Problems of Social Policy*, 431–41, while the statistics for 1939 and 1940 are in NA MH 101/17. The Scottish survey is Boyd (ed.), *Evacuation in Scotland*, 77–123.

The article by A. D. K. Owen is 'The Great Evacuation', *Political Quarterly*, 11: 1 (1940), 30–44, and that by William Robson is 'Evacuation, Town Planning, and the War', ibid. 45–58; their biographies are taken from the *ODNB*. The article by Cyril Burt was 'The Incidence of Neurotic Symptoms Among Evacuated School Children', *British Journal of Educational Psychology*, 10: 1 (1940), 8–15; Burt's biography is taken from the *ODNB*. John Bowlby's biography is taken from the *ODNB*, and his letter appeared in the *Lancet* (1939), ii, 1203. His article of March 1940 was 'The Problem of the Young Child', *The New Era in Home and School*, 21: 3 (1940), 59–63.

Hugh Paul's comment is in the *Medical Officer* (1940), 114, while the article by W. C. V. Brothwood is 'Experience of Evacuation in a County Reception Area', *Public Health*, 53 (1940), 125–9. The report on evacuees in Essex is in the *Lancet*, (1940), i, 763, and on Kent in the *Lancet*, (1940), ii, 575. The report on Bootle is in the *Lancet*, (1940), i, 854, while the comment by the Leicestershire doctor is in the *Lancet*, (1940), ii, 602. The comment by the MOH is in the *Medical Officer* (1940), 185, and those by the *Lancet* on London statistics for 1938 in the *Lancet*, (1940), ii, 387, 427.

The Board of Education's circular of 14 December was Circular 1490, 'The School Health Services in War-Time' (1939), while the comments on school milk are in NA MH 56/526, as are the Milk Marketing Board's proposals of 8 January 1940. The letter from the Director of Education in Grimsby is in NA ED 50/212, and the letter from Margaret Bondfield in NA ED 10/247. The Ministry's memos were *Memorandum on the Louse and How to Deal with It* (1940) and *Memorandum on Scabies* (1940). The comment by Lord Addison is in House of Lords debates [H. of L. deb.], 1939–40, vol. 115, 7 February 1940, p. 482, and correspondence between Kenneth Mellanby and Alison Glover about investigations into head lice in Leicestershire is in NA ED 50/196. Correspondence between Sir Arthur MacNalty and Sir Maurice Holmes, and between Sir Maurice Holmes and Earl De La Warr, about an inquiry into the School Medical Service, is also in NA ED 50/196, and Sir Arthur MacNalty's biography is taken from the *ODNB*.

Chapter 7

The biographies of Tom Harrisson and Charles Madge are taken from the *ODNB*, while the teacher quoted is in Tom Harrisson and Charles

Madge (eds.), *War Begins at Home* (1940), 327–8. The report on Bermondsey is in the National Federation of Women's Institutes, *Town Children Through Country Eyes: A Survey on Evacuation 1940* (1940), 22. The Lancaster evidence is from the Bland Papers, apart from the stories of Albert Shaw and Enid Lindsay, which are in Ashworth, *The Evacuees Story*.

The debate about head lice is in F. Pygott, 'Condition of Evacuated School Children', *British Medical Journal*, (1940), ii, 587–8, and in M. E. Lampard, 'Verminous Evacuees', ibid. 756. The editorial was in the *Medical Officer*, 64 (1940), 57. The letter from the doctor in Derbyshire was in the *Lancet*, (1940), ii, 1166.

Irene Barclay's recollections are in her *People Need Roots: The Story of the St Pancras Housing Association* (1976), 85–6. Herwald Ramsbotham's biography is taken from the *ODNB*. The Mellanby report was published as Kenneth Mellanby, 'The Incidence of Head Lice in England', *Medical Officer*, 66 (1941), 39–43, and Glover's comments on the draft report are in NA ED 50/196; his biography is taken from *Who Was Who*. Clement Attlee's biography is taken from the *ODNB*, and the memo from Ramsbotham is in NA ED 50/215. Attlee's paper to the Food Policy Committee of the War Cabinet is also in NA ED 50/215, while Maudslay's memo on the plans is in NA ED 50/231. A copy of the Ministry of Health's circular 'Supply of Milk to Mothers and Children', is in NA MH 56/527.

Chapter 8

Details of the evacuation of 1940 are in Titmuss, *Problems of Social Policy*, 355–69. The debate about whether the Mellanby report should be published is in NA ED 50/196, including the comment by Sir Maurice Holmes on 15 August; it is summarized in Gosden, *Education in the Second World War*, 174. The comments by the Earl of Malmesbury and the Earl of Radnor are in H. of L. deb., 1939–40, vol. 116, 9 July 1940, cols. 830, 834. The letter from the Association of Municipal Corporations is in NA ED 50/178, and comments by civil servants in NA ED 50/212. Correspondence from LCC officials is in NA HLG 7/223.

The Vernon study was 'A Study of Some Effects of Evacuation on Adolescent Girls', *British Journal of Educational Psychology*, 10: 2 (1940), 114–34. The article on bedwetting was Samuel E. Gill, 'Nocturnal Enuresis:

Experiences with Evacuated Children', *British Medical Journal*, (1940), ii, 199–200.

Chapter 9

The article on the psychological effects of evacuation was Evelyn Fox, 'Emergency Hostels for Difficult Children', *Mental Health*, 1: 4 (1940), 97–102, while the article on hostels was I. M. Leslie, 'Some Problems of a Hostel in a Reception Area', *Social Work*, 1: 5 (1939–41), 307–12. The article by Burt's colleagues was M. A. Davidson and I. M. Slade, 'Results of a Survey of Senior School Evacuees', *British Journal of Educational Psychology*, 10: 3 (1940), 179–95, while the Liverpool study was the University Press of Liverpool, *Our Wartime Guests—Opportunity or Menace? A Psychological Approach to Evacuation* (1940). The Fabian Society survey was Richard Padley and Margaret Cole (eds.), *Evacuation Survey: A Report to the Fabian Society* (1940).

Popular books generally dealing with evacuation were Mrs St Loe Strachey, *Borrowed Children: A Popular Account of Some Evacuation Problems and Their Remedies* (1940); Richmal Crompton, *William and the Evacuees* (1940); and Joyce Cary, *Charley is My Darling* (1940).

The account by Carl Coates is in 'Thank God for Auntie Minnie', but there is an account of the arrival of evacuees in Easton-on-the-Hill in the *Lincoln, Rutland, and Stamford Mercury*, 11 October 1940, p. 1. The account by Jimmy Benton is taken from his letter to the author, 21 December 2007, while his water-tank story was published in the journal *The Evacuee*. The story about the comment by Leslie Hughes came from Mary-Rose Benton in a letter to the author, May 2009.

Details of the evacuation of the Board of Education are in Gosden, *Education in the Second World War*, 238. The Ministry's circular of 2 October 1940, 'Boots and Clothing for Evacuated Children', is in NA HLG 7/324, and details of the London Clothing Scheme are in NA ED 138/49. The letter from the Mayor of Barnstaple is in NA HLG 7/223, and the admissions by the Board's civil servants in NA ED 50/212. Glover's comments on nutrition and school medical inspections are in NA ED 50/204, as are Maudslay's comments on Glover's report. Plans for school meals are in NA ED 50/235, and the report on heights and weights of evacuees is in NA ED 50/211. The debate about whether to publish the Mellanby report is in NA

ED 50/196. The role of the Board in plans for reconstruction is covered in Gosden, *Education During the Second World War*, 238, and the memo by Sir Maurice Holmes of 2 November 1940 is in NA ED 136/212. His memo on the WEA deputation, written on 29 January 1941, is in NA ED 136/260.

Chapter 10

Moya Woodside's reports for Mass Observation are summarized in Brian Barton, *The Blitz: Belfast in the War Years* (1989). The Huntingdonshire report was A. T. Alcock, 'War Strain in Children', *British Medical Journal*, (1941), i, 124. Susan Isaacs's biography is taken from the *ODNB*, and from Adrian Wooldridge, *Measuring the Mind: Education and Psychology in England, c.1860–1990* (1994), 111–35. The preliminary report on the Cambridge survey was Aymeric Straker and Robert H. Thouless, 'Preliminary Results of Cambridge Survey of Evacuated Children', *British Journal of Educational Psychology*, 10: 2 (1940), 97–113, while the survey itself was published as Susan Isaacs (ed.), *The Cambridge Evacuation Survey: A Wartime Study in Social Welfare and Education* (1941).

The letter to Malcolm MacDonald is in NA HLG 7/267, while his radio broadcast of 15 December 1940 is in NA MH 101/16. The Shakespeare report was published as Ministry of Health, *Report on Conditions in Reception Areas: By a Committee Under the Chairmanship of Mr Geoffrey Shakespeare, MP* (1941), while Shakespeare's biography is taken from the *ODNB*, and his recollections of the survey from Geoffrey Shakespeare, *Let Candles be Brought In* (1949).

The report on mothers in Leicestershire and County Durham are in NA ED 10/248. The comment by Sir Maurice Holmes on 21 April 1941, on footwear and clothing, is cited by Gosden, *Education in the Second World War*, 205–6. Comments by civil servants on footwear and clothing are in NA HLG 7/325, NA HLG 7/223, and NA HLG 7/218. Comments on school meals are in NA ED 50/215 and NA ED 50/204. The comment by Sir Maurice Holmes on 24 May 1941, on cuts in the meat supply, is cited by Gosden, *Education in the Second World War*, 198.

Chapter 11

Moya Woodside's reports for Mass Observation are summarized in Barton, *The Blitz*. The study by Cyril Burt of billeting was 'The Billeting of Evacuated

Children', *British Journal of Educational Psychology*, 10: 2 (1941), 85–98, while the articles by Edgar Wilkins were 'The Environmental Background of the School Child', *Medical Officer*, 65 (1941), 145–7, 153–4; 'Feet: With Particular Reference to School Children', *Medical Officer*, 66 (1941), 5–6, 13–15, 21–2, 29–30, 37–9, and 'The Future of the School Medical Service: Some Suggested Reforms', ibid. 109–12. A biography of G. D. H. Cole is in the *ODNB*.

The Committee of Senior Officials on Postwar Educational Reconstruction is covered in Gosden, *Education in the Second World War*, 238–63; R. G. Wallace, 'The Origins and Authorship of the 1944 Education Act', *History of Education*, 10: 4 (1981), 283–90; Kevin Jeffreys, 'R. A. Butler, The Board of Education and the 1944 Education Act', *History*, NS 69 (1984), 415–31; Peter Gosden, 'From Board to Ministry: The Impact of the War on the Education Department', *History of Education*, 18 (1989), 183–93; and id., 'Putting the Act Together', *History of Education*, 24: 3 (1995), 195–207. The memo by Sir Maurice Holmes of 13 May 1941, and the response by Herwald Ramsbotham, are in NA ED 136/212. The biography of Butler is taken from the *ODNB*, while his account of his interview with Churchill and reflections on Holmes and other civil servants are in Baron Butler of Saffron Walden, *The Art of the Possible: The Memoirs of Lord Butler* (1971), 90–1, 93.

Chapter 12

The Child Guidance Council report was *The Future of Child Guidance in Relation to War Experience* (1941). Hermann Mannheim's earlier work on juvenile delinquency was reported in *Social Aspects of Crime in England Between the Wars* (1940), while his 1940 lectures were published as *War and Crime* (1941). The Bristol report was F. H. Bodman and M. Dunsdon, 'Juvenile Delinquency in War-Time: Report from the Bristol Child Guidance Clinic', *Lancet*, (1941), ii, 572–4.

The Bangor study was Enid M. John, 'A Study of the Effects of Evacuation and Air Raids on Children of Pre-School Age', *British Journal of Educational Psychology*, 11: 2 (1941), 173–82, while the Manchester study was W. Mary Burbury, 'Effects of Evacuation and of Air Raids on City Children', *British Medical Journal*, (1941), ii, 660–2. The American study was

Rosemary Pritchard and Saul Rosenzweig, 'The Effects of War Stress Upon Childhood and Youth', *Journal of Abnormal and Social Psychology*, 37: 3 (1942), 329–44, while Anna Freud's work was reported in Anna Freud and Dorothy T. Burlingham, *War and Children* (1943), and in Anna Freud, *Infants Without Families and Reports on the Hampstead Nurseries 1939–1945* (1974). Frank Bodman's study was 'Child Psychiatry in War-Time Britain', *Journal of Educational Psychology*, 35: 5 (1944), 293–301.

The activities of Elizabeth Denby in wartime are covered in Elizabeth Darling's PhD thesis, chapter 9 and Appendix 2. The minutes of the Women's Group on Public Welfare for this period are in the Fawcett Library, WF/D4, and the biography of Celia St Loe Strachey is taken from her husband's entry in the *ODNB*.

The comment by the civil servant on clothing is in NA HLG 7/325, while Alison Glover's Chadwick Lecture of May 1942 is in NA ED 136/664. Details of the Bransby survey on heights and weights are in NA ED 23/983 and NA ED 50/211. The comments by Sir Maurice Holmes on 18 February and 14 April 1943, on school meals, are cited in Gosden, *Education in the Second World War*, 207–8.

Chapter 13

The *Our Towns* report was published as Women's Group on Public Welfare, *Our Towns: A Close Up: A Study Made in 1939–1942 with Certain Recommendations by the Hygiene Committee of the Women's Group on Public Welfare* (1943). The reviews that are cited were in *Times Educational Supplement*, 3 April 1943, p. 158; *The Times*, 29 March 1943, p. 5; *Eugenics Review*, 25 (1943), 12–13; *Economist*, 144 (1943), 545–6; *Social Work*, 2: 8 (1943), 326–7; *Lancet* (1943), i, 631; *Public Administration*, 21 (1943), 102–3; and *New Statesman and Nation*, 25 (1943), 292–3. The House of Lords debate mention is in H. of L. deb., 1942–43, vol. 127, 5 May 1943, cols. 365–95. The White Paper mention is in PP 1942–43, xi, *Educational Reconstruction*, para. 25. The *Medical Officer* mention is in 70 (1943), 115–16.

Details of the evacuation of 1944 are in Titmuss, *Problems of Social Policy*, 426–30. The Cambridge survey is Isaacs (ed.), *The Cambridge Evacuation Survey*, 123–55. The recollections of Brindley Boon are in *The Musician*, 16 October 1982, p. 663.

Chapter 14

John Bowlby's report was *Forty-Four Juvenile Thieves: Their Characters and Home-Life* (1946). His later books were *Maternal Care and Mental Health* (1951) and *Child Care and the Growth of Love* (1953). Carl Coates's reflections are in his correspondence with the author, 6 July 2008. Dave Pinchon provided additional information in correspondence with the author (June 2008), as did Maggie Cade.

Epilogue

Elizabeth Darling offers some conclusions on the post-war period in her '"The Star in the Profession she Invented for Herself"', 293–5, and in '"The House that is a Woman's Book Come True"', 137–40. Later reports which seized on the mention of problem families in *Our Towns* include Tom Stephens (ed.), *Problem Families* (1945). The book by Wilkins was *The Medical Inspection of School Children* (1952). Butler's reflections on evacuation are from his *The Art of the Possible*, 92–3. Mary-Rose Benton provided some further information in correspondence to the author (5 July 2008), as did David Hodge, in February 2009. Frank Walsh's later life is taken from his *From Hulme to Eternity* and from correspondence with the author, 11 December 2007.

Index

[Note on locations: most smaller towns and villages are listed by modern county; larger cities by name of city. Locations in Northern Ireland, the Republic of Ireland, Scotland, and Wales are listed separately.]